Fallen
Angels

Fallen Angels

Six Noir Tales Told for Television

With a Preface by
James Ellroy

Grove Press
New York

"I'll Be Waiting" by Raymond Chandler was first published in the *Saturday Evening Post,* copyright © 1939 by Curtis Publishing Company. Copyright renewed by the Estate of Raymond Chandler. Reprinted by permission of the Estate of Raymond Chandler.

"The Frightening Frammis" by Jim Thompson was first published in Alfred Hitchcock's *Mystery Magazine,* copyright © 1957 by H.S.D. Publications Inc. Copyright renewed in 1985 by Davis Publications Inc. Reprinted by permission of the author's estate.

"Dead-End for Delia" copyright © 1950 by William Campbell Gault. Reprinted by permission of the author.

"Murder, Obliquely" copyright © Cornell Woolrich. Copyright renewed in 1986 by The Chase Manhattan Bank, NA, as the executor of the estate.

"The Quiet Room" copyright © 1953 by Jonathan Craig. Reprinted by permission of the author and Scott Meredith Literary Agency, Inc.

"Since I Don't Have You" copyright © 1988 by James Ellroy. Reprinted by permission of the author.

Library of Congress Cataloging-in-Publication Data

Fallen angels: six noir tales told for television.
    Contents: I'll be waiting / Raymond Chandler, adapted by C. Gaby
Mitchell — The frightening Frammis / Jim Thompson, adapted by Jon
Robin Baitz — Dead-end for Delia / William Campbell Gault, adapted
by Scott Frank — Murder, obliquely / Cornell Woolrich, adapted by
Amanda Silver — The quiet room / Jonathan Craig, adapted by Howard
Rodman — Since I don't have you / James Ellroy, adapted by Steven
Katz.
    ISBN 0-8021-3383-5
    1. Television plays, American.   2. Detective and mystery stories,
American—Film and video adaptations.
PN6120.T4F35   1993   812'.02508—dc20   93-22888

Published simultaneously in Canada
Printed in the United States of America

Design by Laura Hough

Grove Press
841 Broadway
New York, NY 10003

FIRST PRINTING

For Miro,

a treasury of bedtime stories.

Contents

Preface

Inside of seventy years ago some writers hatched a revisionist notion that, contrary to commonly held gospel, America was the wrong place at the wrong time, led by the wrong leaders, feeding a wronged population a line of jive that sounded good but had to go wrong because the entire American venture was a freak curve ball arcing the wrong way; gathering power and veering out of control, held temporarily aloft by a pervasive corruption intrinsic to its momentum, but bound to hit the gutter anyway.

Venal politicians selling the poor down the river with a smile.

Sex-starved millions singed by the guilt-coals of organized religion.

Draculean industrialists sucking working men's blood.

The police as hired guns for a nation momentarily thriving via epic systemic dysfunction.

Gangsters ascendent: persecuted immigrants forming a new power elite. The implicit American sanction pushed to the limit: Get it any way you can.

Booze, dope, and illicit sex as the antidote to reigning madness. When "Get it any way you can" rules as ethos, "Take it back any way you can" plays well as counterpoint.

America seventy years ago.

America now.

The intervening years produced the hard-boiled school of literature. Cause and effect, easy to trace: social conditions create a popular fictional response.

And a powerfully melodramatic one. Mobsters, whores, crooked cops, perverts, sex killers, gunmen, and demonic entrepreneurs are more entertaining than the malaise-mangled housewives and intellectual wimps that so-called mainstream writers posit as the net result of two-hundred-plus years of American insanity. Hard-boiled fiction, spawned in the violent and flush 1920s, began as a prophecy: This country will most likely crash and burn. If it doesn't, the price of the political accommodations and human sacrifices made in order to retain a corrupt system will be very, very high.

Hard-boiled fiction is about that price.

It is the colloquial language of America's Fallen Angels.

The Fallen Angel patriarch was Dashiell Hammett. He was a tall, handsome man who served as an operative for the Pinkerton Detective Agency before and after World War I. His duties included stints as a strikebreaker and strong-arm goon. He observed the Anaconda Copper war up close, from a management perspective. His sympathies were with the workers—guilt dogged him for years. His first novel, *Red Harvest*, hits the dark tonal chord for the entire hard-boiled canon.

Anaconda becomes a fictional copper combine located in Personville, aka "Poisonville"—read as Butte, Montana. Gangsters are at war with striking workers and copper-company goon squads. The milieu is hyperbolic violence, greed, and the pursuit of empire compressed into a week's time and contained within the boundaries of a western boomtown. The Continental Op is sent in to restore "order"; in the process he plays warring factions off against each other and wakes up with a dead woman, uncertain of whether or not he murdered her. In the end, order *is* restored—via wholesale slaughter. Countless gangsters, goons, and workers are dead; the copper company and its inhuman policies have triumphed. The Continental Op goes on to his next assignment—and hard-boiled fiction notches its first masterpiece.

Red Harvest was published in 1929. Dashiell Hammett went on to write four more novels, many short stories, and some film scripts. He was a drunk, a womanizing misogynist, a committed Marxist, and for many years the lover of Lillian Hellman. His last novel was published in 1935; he lived until 1961. Lung disease plagued him—years of booze and cigarettes exacerbated it. He bopped off into the pantheon spitting blood-streaked loogies, aware that he had produced literary offspring: good, bad, most derivative, a few inspired.

Little Fallen Angels: scribbling, imitating, co-opting American history to assuage personal demons, make money, and advance ideologies of all stripes. Three generations of writers reaping the harvest of *Red Harvest*—whether they had read it or not making no difference, the work simply out there in the spiritus mundi, hard-boiled profundity to feed from in ways the writers themselves could probably never assess.

From 1929 to 1993—close to seventy years. America's still here, arguably no better or worse off than it was then. Daily life has become more convenient—at the expense of the environment. Criminology has greatly advanced, but DNA testing threatens civil liberties. America's cops are now less corrupt and more media-scrutinized than they have ever been, but are impinged on by a statistically staggering criminal horde zorched to the gills on sophisticated drugs and armed to the teeth with space-age weapons. Dashiell Hammett's Fallen Angel offspring dig it all to one degree or another—we're nothing if not ghouls hot to exploit the apocalypse. It's here, it's now; it was there, it was then. It is ONGOING and, frankly, America should not stake a sole claim to apocalyptic exploitation—we just *do it better* than anyone else. It's like jazz: *we* got there first; *we* feel it more precisely and BIGGER.

America has been the world's number-one pop culture supplier for *more* than three decades: books and movies top our export list.

Pop culture is synonymous with *Melodrama*.

Melodrama is synonymous with *Crime Drama*.

Crime Drama equals *Crime Fiction* and *Crime Films*. The former crossbreeds into the latter with consistent success; this hybrid has proven itself to be a significant art form and a fount of bravura entertainment that both perpetuates and debunks American myths.

Hammett's children: your perpetuators and debunkers. Fallen Angels soon to zap you with a cross-fertilized media extravaganza that will blow your mind, suck your soul, and scorch your sexuality!

We named it after ourselves.

And now you can have us two ways: in print via this book, and on your cable TV screen via half-hour adaptations of the stories collected herein.

These tales were carefully culled: they are quick, punchy, darkly evocative. Showtime will be bringing you the filmed versions—you will have the opportunity to inhabit complementary and contradictory visions and see where they take you. It's a roll call of tormented souls confronting their monsters within; it's a picaresque look at Los Angeles back in the forties. It's the world of pulp on celluloid, pure translations that augment the stark power of great short fiction.

Fallen Angels: an ambiguous title applicable to the characters who rage in these stories, their creators, and you, the audience—especially you, who share a bond with all of Hammett's children.

You sense the darkness around you and want to know *why*. *We* have been haunted by that curiosity and wish to explore it with you for unfathomable personal motives and the near-paradoxical need to hold hands with a friend when night falls. *You* sense that the deepest human truths boil forth in fiction; *we* seek to render newscast body counts powerless through the alchemy of our horrific perceptions. *We* want to touch fire with you, to ensure both of us a tenuous safety from the flames.

Because angels, fallen and otherwise, have wings. Today we use them to traverse seventy years of an American cultural tradition; tomorrow we may need them for more precarious extrications. Angels are often frail—their creative lifespan burns almost less than ephemeral. Thus we scald ourselves to carry report to you.

William Campbell Gault, Jonathan Craig, Jim Thompson, Cornell Woolrich, Raymond Chandler, and myself, James Ellroy. Read these stories we've written; see them dramatized. Think of all of us—dead and living—in flight for secrets to share with you.

JAMES ELLROY

I'll Be Waiting

Raymond Chandler

At one o'clock in the morning, Carl, the night porter, turned down the last of three table lamps in the main lobby of the Windermere Hotel. The blue carpet darkened a shade or two and the walls drew back into remoteness. The chairs filled with shadowy loungers. In the corners were memories like cobwebs.

Tony Reseck yawned. He put his head on one side and listened to the frail, twittery music from the radio room beyond a dim arch at the far side of the lobby. He frowned. That should be his radio room after one A.M. Nobody should be in it. That red-haired girl was spoiling his nights.

The frown passed and a miniature of a smile quirked at the corners of his lips. He sat relaxed, a short, pale, paunchy, middle-aged man with long, delicate fingers clasped on the elk's tooth on his watch chain; the long delicate fingers of a sleight-of-hand artist, fingers with shiny, molded nails and tapering first joints, fingers a little spatulate at the ends. Handsome fingers. Tony Reseck rubbed them gently together and there was peace in his quiet sea-gray eyes.

The frown came back on his face. The music annoyed him. He got up with a curious litheness, all in one piece, without moving his clasped hands from the watch chain. At one moment he was leaning back relaxed, and the next he was standing balanced on his feet, per-

3

fectly still, so that the movement of rising seemed to be a thing perfectly perceived, an error of vision. . . .

He walked with small, polished shoes delicately across the blue carpet and under the arch. The music was louder. It contained the hot, acid blare, the frenetic, jittering runs of a jam session. It was too loud. The red-haired girl sat there and stared silently at the fretted part of the big radio cabinet as though she could see the band with its fixed professional grin and the sweat running down its back. She was curled up with her feet under her on a davenport which seemed to contain most of the cushions in the room. She was tucked among them carefully, like a corsage in the florist's tissue paper.

She didn't turn her head. She leaned there, one hand in a small fist on her peach-colored knee. She was wearing lounging pajamas of heavy ribbed silk embroidered with black lotus buds.

"You like Goodman, Miss Cressy?" Tony Reseck asked.

The girl moved her eyes slowly. The light in there was dim, but the violet of her eyes almost hurt. They were large, deep eyes without a trace of thought in them. Her face was classical and without expression.

She said nothing.

Tony smiled and moved his fingers at his sides, one by one, feeling them move. "You like Goodman, Miss Cressy?" he repeated gently.

"Not to cry over," the girl said tonelessly.

Tony rocked back on his heels and looked at her eyes. Large, deep, empty eyes. Or were they? He reached down and muted the radio.

"Don't get me wrong," the girl said. "Goodman makes money, and a lad that makes legitimate money these days is a lad you have to respect. But this jitterbug music gives me the backdrop of a beer flat. I like something with roses in it."

"Maybe you like Mozart," Tony said.

"Go on, kid me," the girl said.

"I wasn't kidding you, Miss Cressy. I think Mozart was the greatest man that ever lived—and Toscanini is his prophet."

"I thought you were the house dick." She put her head back on a pillow and stared at him through her lashes.

"Make me some of that Mozart," she added.

"It's too late," Tony sighed. "You can't get it now."

She gave him another long lucid glance. "Got the eye on me,

haven't you, flatfoot?" She laughed a little, almost under her breath. "What did I do wrong?"

Tony smiled his toy smile. "Nothing, Miss Cressy. Nothing at all. But you need some fresh air. You've been five days in this hotel and you haven't been outdoors. And you have a tower room."

She laughed again. "Make me a story about it. I'm bored."

"There was a girl here once had your suite. She stayed in the hotel a whole week, like you. Without going out at all, I mean. She didn't speak to anybody hardly. What do you think she did then?"

The girl eyed him gravely. "She jumped her bill."

He put his long delicate hand out and turned it slowly, fluttering the fingers, with an effect almost like a lazy wave breaking. "Unh-uh. She sent down for her bill and paid it. Then she told the hop to be back in half an hour for her suitcases. Then she went out on her balcony."

The girl leaned forward a little, her eyes still grave, one hand capping her peach-colored knee. "What did you say your name was?"

"Tony Reseck."

"Sounds like a hunky."

"Yeah," Tony said. "Polish."

"Go on, Tony."

"All the tower suits have private balconies, Miss Cressy. The walls of them are too low for fourteen stories above the street. It was a dark night, that night, high clouds." He dropped his hand with a final gesture, a farewell gesture. "Nobody saw her jump. But when she hit, it was like a big gun going off."

"You're making it up, Tony." Her voice was a clean dry whisper of sound.

He smiled his toy smile. His quiet sea-gray eyes seemed almost to be smoothing the long waves of her hair. "Eve Cressy," he said musingly. "A name waiting for lights to be in."

"Waiting for a tall dark guy that's no good, Tony. You wouldn't care why. I was married to him once. I might be married to him again. You can make a lot of mistakes in just one lifetime." The hand on her knee opened slowly until the fingers were strained back as far as they would go. Then they closed quickly and tightly, and even in that dim light the knuckles shone like little polished bones. "I played him a low trick once. I put him in a bad place—without meaning to. You wouldn't care about that either. It's just that I owe him something."

He leaned over softly and turned the knob on the radio. A waltz formed itself dimly on the warm air. A tinsel waltz, but a waltz.

He turned the volume up. The music gushed from the loudspeaker in a swirl of shadowed melody. Since Vienna died, all waltzes are shadowed.

The girl put her hand on one side and hummed three or four bars and stopped with a sudden tightening of her mouth.

"Eve Cressy," she said. "It was in lights once. At a bum night club. A dive. They raided it and the lights went out."

He smiled at her almost mockingly. "It was no dive while you were there, Miss Cressy . . . That's the waltz the orchestra always played when the old porter walked up and down in front of the hotel entrance, all swelled up with his medals on his chest. *The Last Laugh.* Emil Jannings. You wouldn't remember that one, Miss Cressy."

" 'Spring, Beautiful Spring,' " she said. "No, I never saw it."

He walked three steps away from her and turned. "I have to go upstairs and palm doorknobs. I hope I didn't bother you. You ought to go to bed now. It's pretty late."

The tinsel waltz stopped and a voice began to talk. The girl spoke through the voice. "You really thought something like that—about the balcony?"

He nodded. "I might have," he said softly. "I don't any more."

"No chance, Tony." Her smile was a dim lost leaf. "Come and talk to me some more. Redheads don't jump, Tony. They hang on—and wither."

He looked at her gravely for a moment and then moved away over the carpet. The porter was standing in the archway that led to the main lobby. Tony hadn't looked that way yet, but he knew somebody was there. He always knew if anybody was close to him. He could hear the grass grow, like the donkey in *The Blue Bird*.

The porter jerked his chin at him urgently. His broad face above the uniform collar looked sweaty and excited. Tony stepped up close to him and they went together through the arch and out to the middle of the dim lobby.

"Trouble?" Tony asked wearily.

"There's a guy outside to see you, Tony. He won't come in. I'm doing a wipe-off on the plate glass of the doors and he comes up beside me, a tall guy. 'Get Tony,' he says, out of the side of his mouth."

Tony said: "Uh-huh," and looked at the porter's pale blue eyes. "Who was it?"

"Al, he said to say he was."

Tony's face became as expressionless as dough. "Okey." He started to move off.

The porter caught his sleeve. "Listen, Tony. You got any enemies?"

Tony laughed politely, his face still like dough.

"Listen, Tony." The porter held his sleeve tightly. "There's a big black car down the block, the other way from the hacks. There's a guy standing beside it with his foot on the running board. This guy that spoke to me, he wears a dark-colored, wrap-around overcoat with a high collar turned up against his ears. His hat's way low. You can't hardly see his face. He says, 'Get Tony,' out of the side of his mouth. You ain't got any enemies, have you, Tony?"

"Only the finance company," Tony said. "Beat it."

He walked slowly and a little stiffly across the blue carpet, up the three shallow steps to the entrance lobby with the three elevators on one side and the desk on the other. Only one elevator was working. Beside the open doors, his arms folded, the night operator stood silent in a neat blue uniform with silver facings. A lean, dark Mexican named Gomez. A new boy, breaking in on the night shift.

The other side was the desk, rose marble, with the night clerk leaning on it delicately. A small neat man with a wispy reddish mustache and cheeks so rosy they looked roughed. He stared at Tony and poked a nail at his mustache.

Tony pointed a stiff index finger at him, folded the other three fingers tight to his palm, and flicked his thumb up and down on the stiff finger. The clerk touched the other side of his mustache and looked bored.

Tony went on past the closed and darkened newsstand and the side entrance to the drugstore, out to the brassbound plate-glass doors. He stopped just inside them and took a deep, hard breath. He squared his shoulders, pushed the doors open, and stepped out into the cold damp night air.

The street was dark, silent. The rumble of traffic on Wilshire, two blocks away, had no body, no meaning. To the left were two taxis. Their drivers leaned against a fender, side by side, smoking. Tony walked the other way. The big dark car was a third of a block from the hotel entrance. Its lights were dimmed and it was only when he was almost up to it that he heard the gentle sound of its engine turning over.

A tall figure detached itself from the body of the car and strolled toward him, both hands in the pockets of the dark overcoat with the high collar. From the man's mouth a cigarette tip glowed faintly, a rusty pearl.

They stopped two feet from each other.

The tall man said, "Hi, Tony. Long time no see."

"Hello, Al. How's it going?"

"Can't complain." The tall man started to take his right hand out of his overcoat pocket, then stopped and laughed quietly. "I forgot. Guess you don't want to shake hands."

"That don't mean anything," Tony said. "Shaking hands. Monkeys can shake hands. What's on your mind, Al?"

"Still the funny little fat guy, eh, Tony?"

"I guess." Tony winked his eyes tight. His throat felt tight.

"You like your job back there?"

"It's a job."

Al laughed his quiet laugh again. "You take it slow, Tony. I'll take it fast. So it's a job and you want to hold it. Okey. There's a girl named Eve Cressy flopping in your quiet hotel. Get her out. Fast and right now."

"What's the trouble?"

The tall man looked up and down the street. A man behind in the car coughed lightly. "She's hooked with a wrong number. Nothing against her personal, but she'll lead trouble to you. Get her out, Tony. You got maybe an hour."

"Sure," Tony said aimlessly, without meaning.

Al took his hand out of his pocket and stretched it against Tony's chest. He gave him a light lazy push. "I wouldn't be telling you just for the hell of it, little fat brother. Get her out of there."

"Okey," Tony said, without any tone in his voice.

The tall man took back his hand and reached for the car door. He opened it and started to slip in like a lean black shadow.

Then he stopped and said something to the men in the car and got out again. He came back to where Tony stood silent, his pale eyes catching a little dim light from the street.

"Listen, Tony. You always kept your nose clean. You're a good brother, Tony."

Tony didn't speak.

Al leaned toward him, a long urgent shadow, the high collar almost touching his ears. "It's trouble business, Tony. The boys won't like it, but I'm telling you just the same. This Cressy was married to a lad named Johnny Ralls. Ralls is out of Quentin two, three days, or a week. He did a three-spot for manslaughter. The girl put him there. He ran down an old man one night when he was drunk, and she was with him. He wouldn't stop. She told him to go in and tell it, or else. He didn't go in. So the Johns come for him."

Tony said, "That's too bad."

"It's kosher, kid. It's my business to know. This Ralls flapped his mouth in stir about how the girl would be waiting for him when he got out, all set to forgive and forget, and he was going straight to her."

Tony said, "What's he to you?" His voice had a dry, stiff crackle, like thick paper.

Al laughed. "The trouble boys want to see him. He ran a table at a spot on the Strip and figured out a scheme. He and another guy took the house for fifty grand. The other lad coughed up, but we still need Johnny's twenty-five. The trouble boys don't get paid to forget."

Tony looked up and down the dark street. One of the taxi drivers flicked a cigarette stub in a long arc over the top of one of the cabs. Tony watched it fall and spark on the pavement. He listened to the quiet sound of the big car's motor.

"I don't want any part of it," he said. "I'll get her out."

Al backed away from him, nodding. "Wise kid. How's Mom these days?"

"Okey," Tony said.

"Tell her I was asking for her."

"Asking for her isn't anything," Tony said.

Al turned quickly and got into the car. The car curved lazily in the middle of the block and drifted back toward the corner. Its lights went up and sprayed on a wall. It turned a corner and was gone. The lingering smell of its exhaust drifted past Tony's nose. He turned and walked back to the hotel and into it. He went along to the radio room.

The radio still muttered, but the girl was gone from the davenport in front of it. The pressed cushions were hollowed out by her body. Tony reached down and touched them. He thought they were still warm. He turned the radio off and stood there, turning a thumb slowly in front of his body, his hand flat against his stomach. Then he went back through the lobby toward the elevator bank and stood beside a majolica jar of white sand. The clerk fussed behind a pebbled-glass screen at one end of the desk. The air was dead.

The elevator bank was dark. Tony looked at the indicator of the middle car and saw that it was at 14.

"Gone to bed," he said under his breath.

The door of the porter's room beside the elevators opened and the little Mexican night operator came out in street clothes. He looked

at Tony with a quiet sidewise look out of eyes the color of dried-out
chestnuts.

"Good night, boss."

"Yeah," Tony said absently.

He took a thin dappled cigar out of his vest pocket and smelled it.
He examined it slowly, turning it around in his neat fingers. There was
a small tear along the side. He frowned at that and put the cigar away.

There was a distant sound and the hand on the indicator began to
steal around the bronze dial. Light glittered up in the shaft and the
straight line of the car floor dissolved the darkness below. The car
stopped and the doors opened, and Carl came out of it.

His eyes caught Tony's with a kind of jump and he walked over to
him, his head on one side, a thin shine along his pink upper lip.

"Listen, Tony."

Tony took his arm in a hard swift hand and turned him. He
pushed him quickly, yet somehow casually, down the steps to the dim
main lobby and steered him into a corner. He let go of the arm. His
throat tightened again, for no reason he could think of.

"Well?" he said darkly. "Listen to what?"

The porter reached into a pocket and hauled out a dollar bill.
"He gimme this," he said loosely. His glittering eyes looked past
Tony's shoulder at nothing. They winked rapidly. "Ice and ginger
ale."

"Don't stall," Tony growled.

"Guy in Fourteen B," the porter said.

"Lemme smell your breath."

The porter leaned toward him obediently.

"Liquor," Tony said harshly.

"He gimme a drink."

Tony looked down at the dollar bill. "Nobody's in Fourteen B.
Not on my list," he said.

"Yeah. There is." The porter licked his lips and his eyes opened
and shut several times. "Tall dark guy."

"All right," Tony said crossly. "All right. There's a tall dark guy
in Fourteen B and he gave you a buck and a drink. Then what?"

"Gat under his arm," Carl said, and blinked.

Tony smiled, but his eyes had taken on the lifeless glitter of thick
ice. "You take Miss Cressy up to her room?"

Carl shook his head. "Gomez. I saw her go up."

"Get away from me," Tony said between his teeth. "And don't
accept any more drinks from the guests."

He didn't move until Carl had gone back into his cubbyhole by
the elevators and shut the door. Then he moved silently up the three
steps and stood in front of the desk, looking at the veined rose marble,
the onyx pen set, the fresh registration card in its leather frame. He
lifted a hand and smacked it down hard on the marble. The clerk
popped out from behind the glass screen like a chipmunk coming out
of its hole.

Tony took a flimsy out of his breast pocket and spread it on the
desk. "No Fourteen B on this," he said in a bitter voice.

The clerk wisped politely at his mustache. "So sorry. You must
have been out to supper when he checked in."

"Who?"

"Registered as James Watterson, San Diego." The clerk yawned.
"Ask for anybody?"

The clerk stopped in the middle of the yawn and looked at the top
of Tony's head. "Why yes. He asked for a swing band. Why?"

"Smart, fast, and funny," Tony said. "If you like 'em that way."
He wrote on his flimsy and stuffed it back into his pocket. "I'm going
upstairs and palm doorknobs. There's four tower rooms you ain't
rented yet. Get up on your toes, son. You're slipping."

"I made out," the clerk drawled, and completed his yawn.
"Hurry back, pop. I don't know how I'll get through the time."

"You could shave that pink fuzz off your lip," Tony said, and
went across to the elevators.

He opened up a dark one and lit the dome light and shot the car
up to 14. He darkened it again, stepped out, and closed the doors.
This lobby was smaller than any other, except the one immediately
below it. It had a single blue-paneled door in each of the walls other
than the elevator wall. On each door was a gold number and letter with
a gold wreath around it. Tony walked over to 14A and put his ear to
the panel. He heard nothing. Eve Cressy might be in bed asleep, or in
the bathroom, or out on the balcony. Or she might be sitting there in
the room, a few feet from the door, looking at the wall. Well, he
wouldn't expect to be able to hear her sit and look at the wall. He went
over to 14B and put his ear to that panel. This was different. There was
a sound in there. A man coughed. It sounded somehow like a solitary
cough. There were no voices. Tony pressed the small nacre button
beside the door.

Steps came without hurry. A thickened voice spoke through the
panel. Tony made no answer, no sound. The thickened voice repeated
the question. Lightly, maliciously, Tony pressed the bell again.

Mr. James Watterson, of San Diego, should now open the door and give forth noise. He didn't. A silence fell beyond that door that was like the silence of a glacier. Once more Tony put his ear to the wood. Silence utterly.

He got out a master key on a chain and pushed it delicately into the lock of the door. He turned it, pushed the door inward three inches and withdrew the key. Then he waited.

"All right," the voice said harshly. "Come in and get it."

Tony pushed the door wide and stood there, framed against the light from the lobby. The man was tall, black-haired, angular, and white-faced. He held a gun. He held it as though he knew about guns.

"Step right in," he drawled.

Tony went in through the door and pushed it shut with his shoulder. He kept his hands a little out from his sides, the clever fingers curled and slack. He smiled his quiet little smile.

"Mr. Watterson?"

"And after that what?"

"I'm the house detective here."

"It slays me."

The tall, white-faced, somehow handsome and somehow not handsome man backed slowly into the room. It was a large room with a low balcony around two sides of it. French doors opened out on the little private open-air balcony that each of the tower rooms had. There was a grate set for a log fire behind a paneled screen in front of a cheerful davenport. A tall misted glass stood on a hotel tray beside a deep, cozy chair. The man backed toward this and stood in front of it. The large, glistening gun drooped and pointed at the floor.

"It slays me," he said. "I'm in the dump an hour and the house copper gives me the bus. Okey, sweetheart, look in the closet and bathroom. But she just left."

"You didn't see her yet," Tony said.

The man's bleached face filled with unexpected lines. His thickened voice edged toward a snarl. "Yeah? Who didn't I see yet?"

"A girl named Eve Cressy."

The man swallowed. He put his gun down on the table beside the tray. He let himself down into the chair backwards, stiffly, like a man with a touch of lumbago. Then he leaned forward and put his hands on his kneecaps and smiled brightly between his teeth. "So she got here, huh? I didn't ask about her yet. I'm a careful guy. I didn't ask yet."

"She's been here five days," Tony said. "Waiting for you. She hasn't left the hotel a minute."

The man's mouth worked a little. His smile had a knowing tilt to it. "I got delayed a little up north," he said smoothly. "You know how it is. Visiting old friends. You seem to know a lot about my business, copper."

"That's right, Mr. Ralls."

The man lunged to his feet and his hand snapped at the gun. He stood leaning over, holding it on the table, staring. "Dames talk too much," he said with a muffled sound in his voice as though he held something soft between his teeth and talked through it.

"Not dames, Mr. Ralls."

"Huh?" The gun slithered on the hard wood of the table. "Talk it up, copper. My mind reader just quit."

"Not dames, guys. Guys with guns."

The glacier silence fell between them again. The man straightened his body out slowly. His face was washed clean of expression, but his eyes were haunted. Tony leaned in front of him, a shortish plump man with a quiet, pale, friendly face and eyes as simple as forest water.

"They never run out of gas—those boys," Johnny Ralls said, and licked at his lip. "Early and late, they work. The old firm never sleeps."

"You know who they are?" Tony said softly.

"I could maybe give nine guesses. And twelve of them would be right."

"The trouble boys," Tony said, and smiled a brittle smile.

"Where is she?" Johnny Ralls asked harshly.

"Right next door to you."

The man walked to the wall and left his gun lying on the table. He stood in front of the wall, studying it. He reached up and gripped the grillwork of the balcony railing. When he dropped his hand and turned, his face had lost some of its lines. His eyes had a quieter glint. He moved back to Tony and stood over him.

"I've got a stake," he said. "Eve sent me some dough and I built it up with a touch I made up north. Case dough, what I mean. The trouble boys talk about twenty-five grand." He smiled crookedly. "Five *C*s I can count. I'd have a lot of fun making them believe that, I would."

"What did you do with it?" Tony asked indifferently.

"I never had it, copper. Leave that lay. I'm the only guy in the world that believes it. It was a little deal that I got suckered on."

"I'll believe it," Tony said.

"They don't kill often. But they can be awful tough."

"Mugs," Tony said with a sudden bitter contempt. "Guys with guns. Just mugs."

Johnny Ralls reached for his glass and drained it empty. The ice cubes tinkled softly as he put it down. He picked his gun up, danced it on his palm, then tucked it, nose down, into an inner breast pocket. He stared at the carpet.

"How come you're telling me this, copper?"

"I thought maybe you'd give her a break."

"And if I wouldn't?"

"I kind of think you will," Tony said.

Johnny Ralls nodded quietly. "Can I get out of here?"

"You could take the service elevator to the garage. You could rent a car. I can give you a card to the garage man."

"You're a funny little guy," Johnny Ralls said.

Tony took out a worn ostrich-skin billfold and scribbled on a printed card. Johnny Ralls read it, and stood holding it, tapping it against a thumbnail.

"I could take her with me," he said, his eyes narrow.

"You could take a ride in a basket too," Tony said. "She's been here five days, I told you. She's been spotted. A guy I know called me up and told me to get her out of here. Told me what it was all about. So I'm getting you out instead."

"They'll love that," Johnny Ralls said. "They'll send you violets."

"I'll weep about it on my day off."

Johnny Ralls turned his hand over and stared at the palm. "I could see her, anyway. Before I blow. Next door to here, you said?"

Tony turned on his heel and started for the door. He said over his shoulder, "Don't waste a lot of time, handsome. I might change my mind."

The man said, almost gently: "You might be spotting me right now, for all I know."

Tony didn't turn his head. "That's a chance you have to take."

He went on to the door and passed out of the room. He shut it carefully, silently, looked once at the door of 14A and got into his dark elevator. He rode it down to the linen-room floor and got out to remove the basket that held the service elevator open at that floor. The door slid quietly shut. He held it so that it made no noise. Down the corridor, light came from the open door of the housekeeper's office. Tony got back into his elevator and went on down to the lobby.

The little clerk was out of sight behind his pebbled-glass screen, auditing accounts. Tony went through the main lobby and turned into the radio room. The radio was on again, soft. She was there, curled on the davenport again. The speaker hummed to her, a vague sound so low that what it said was as wordless as the murmur of trees. She turned her head slowly and smiled at him.

"Finished palming doorknobs? I couldn't sleep worth a nickel. So I came down again. Okey?"

He smiled and nodded. He sat down in a green chair and patted the plump brocade arms of it. "Sure, Miss Cressy."

"Waiting is the hardest kind of work, isn't it? I wish you'd talk to that radio. It sounds like a pretzel being bent."

Tony fiddled with it, got nothing he liked, set it back where it had been.

"Beer-parlor drunks are all the customers now."

She smiled at him again.

"I don't bother you being here, Miss Cressy?"

"I like it. You're a sweet little guy, Tony."

He looked stiffly at the floor and a ripple touched his spine. He waited for it to go away. It went slowly. Then he sat back, relaxed again, his neat fingers clasped on his elk's tooth. He listened. Not to the radio—to far-off, uncertain things, menacing things. And perhaps to just the safe whir of wheels going away into a strange night.

"Nobody's all bad," he said out loud.

The girl looked at him lazily. "I've met two or three I was wrong on, then."

He nodded. "Yeah," he admitted judiciously. "I guess there's some that are."

The girl yawned and her deep violet eyes half closed. She nestled back into the cushions. "Sit there for a while, Tony. Maybe I could nap."

"Sure. Not a thing for me to do. Don't know why they pay me."

She slept quickly and with complete stillness, like a child. Tony hardly breathed for ten minutes. He just watched her, his mouth a little open. There was a quiet fascination in his limpid eyes, as if he was looking at an altar.

Then he stood up with infinite care and padded away under the arch to the entrance lobby and the desk. He stood at the desk listening for a little while. He heard a pen rustling out of sight. He went around the corner to the row of house phones in little glass cubbyholes. He lifted one and asked the night operator for the garage.

It rang three or four times and then a boyish voice answered: "Windermere Hotel. Garage speaking."

"This is Tony Reseck. That guy Watterson I gave a card to. He leave?"

"Sure, Tony. Half an hour almost. Is it your charge?"

"Yeah," Tony said. "My party. Thanks. Be seein' you."

He hung up and scratched his neck. He went back to the desk and slapped a hand on it. The clerk wafted himself around the screen with his greeter's smile in place. It dropped when he saw Tony.

"Can't a guy catch up on his work?" he grumbled.

"What's the professional rate on Fourteen B?"

The clerk stared morosely. "There's no professional rate in the tower."

"Make one. The fellow left already. Was there only an hour."

"Well, well," the clerk said airily. "So the personality didn't click tonight. We get a skip-out."

"Will five bucks satisfy you?"

"Friend of yours?"

"No. Just a drunk with delusions of grandeur and no dough."

"Guess we'll have to let it ride, Tony. How did he get out?"

"I took him down the service elevator. You was asleep. Will five bucks satisfy you?"

"Why?"

The worn ostrich-skin wallet came out and a weedy five slipped across the marble. "All I could shake him for," Tony said loosely.

The clerk took the five and looked puzzled. "You're the boss," he said, and shrugged. The phone shrilled on the desk and he reached for it. He listened and then pushed it toward Tony. "For you."

Tony took the phone and cuddled it close to his chest. He put his mouth close to the transmitter. The voice was strange to him. It had a metallic sound. Its syllables were meticulously anonymous.

"Tony? Tony Reseck?"

"Talking."

"A message from Al. Shoot?"

Tony looked at the clerk. "Be a pal," he said over the mouthpiece. The clerk flicked a narrow smile at him and went away. "Shoot," Tony said into the phone.

"We had a little business with a guy in your place. Picked him up scramming. Al had a hunch you'd run him out. Tailed him and took him to the curb. Not so good. Backfire."

Tony held the phone very tight and his temples chilled with the evaporation of moisture. "Go on," he said. "I guess there's more."

"A little. The guy stopped the big one. Cold. Al—Al said to tell you good-bye."

Tony leaned hard against the desk. His mouth made a sound that was not speech.

"Get it?" The metallic voice sounded impatient, a little bored. "This guy had him a rod. He used it. Al won't be phoning anybody any more."

Tony lurched at the phone, and the base of it shook on the rose marble. His mouth was a hard dry knot.

The voice said: "That's as far as we go, bub. G'night." The phone clicked dryly, like a pebble hitting a wall.

Tony put the phone down in its cradle very carefully, so as not to make any sound. He looked at the clenched palm of his left hand. He took a handkerchief out and rubbed the palm softly and straightened the fingers out with his other hand. Then he wiped his forehead. The clerk came around the screen again and looked at him with glinting eyes.

"I'm off Friday. How about lending me that phone number?"

Tony nodded at the clerk and smiled a minute frail smile. He put his handkerchief away and patted the pocket he had put it in. He turned and walked away from the desk, across the entrance lobby, down the three shallow steps, along the shadowy reaches of the main lobby, and so in through the arch to the radio room once more. He walked softly, like a man moving in a room where somebody is very sick. He reached the chair he had sat in before and lowered himself into it inch by inch. The girl slept on, motionless, in that curled-up looseness achieved by some women and all cats. Her breath made no slightest sound against the vague murmur of the radio.

Tony Reseck leaned back in the chair and clasped his hands on his elk's tooth and quietly closed his eyes.

I'll Be Waiting

Teleplay by

C. Gaby Mitchell

Cast

Bruno Kirby	Tony Reseck
Marg Helgenberger	Eve Cressy
Jon Polito	Al
Dan Hedaya	Johnny Ralls
Dick Miller	Carl
Peter Scolari	Clerk
Tom Hanks	Trouble Boy

Executive Producer: Sydney Pollack
Producers: William Horberg, Lindsay Doran, Steve Golin
Co-Producer: David Wisnievitz
Directed by: Tom Hanks
Director of Photography: Peter Suschitzky
Production designed by: Armin Ganz
Costumes designed by: Shay Cunliffe
Casting by: Owens Hill and Rachel Abroms
Fallen Angels theme by: Elmer Bernstein
Music by: Peter Bernstein
Edited by: David Siegel
Story Editor: Geoffrey Stier

INTERIOR: WINDEMERE HOTEL LOBBY. NIGHT.

CARL, *the night porter, turns down the table lamps in the lobby.*
TONY RESECK, *sitting in a chair behind a palm, yawns, winds the stem of
his pocket watch, which is showing one o'clock, eyes the elevator doors, fingers the elk's tooth on his chain, checks the watch again, the elevator doors,
then slips the watch back in his pocket as the doors open. A red-haired
woman in silk pajamas steps off the elevator.* TONY *stiffens, averts his eyes
until she is past, then studies her through the palm fronds until she disappears into the radio room. Pricking his ears to the indistinct music, he
frowns, smiles vaguely, then frowns again, and moves toward the radio
room with a surprising suppleness.*

Floor: *Tony's small polished shoes move delicately across the blue carpet. The music becomes louder as he walks.*

Radio: *A large radio cabinet of deep mahogany with a fretted front
and a professional dial that smiles and glows in the dim light. The music
is blaring louder still.*

INTERIOR: HOTEL. RADIO ROOM.

*The red-haired lady in ribbed silk pajamas sits tucked into a sofa
staring at the radio that is jamming the room with music that is too*

much for the night. TONY *walks in, smooths his cheap suit over his paunch, and takes advantage of his momentary invisibility to savor the black lotus buds embroidered in her nightclothes.*

TONY: You like Goodman, Miss Cressy?

   (She moves her violet eyes slowly, dream-like, around the room and then to him.)

EVE: Not to cry over.

   (He reaches down and mutes the radio.)

EVE: Jitterbug gives me the jitters.

TONY: Maybe you like Mozart?

EVE: A house cop who plays Mozart? Next you'll be telling me you read books.

   *(*TONY *pulls at the hem of his coat and looks away.)*

EVE: Well, make me some of that Mozart, then.

TONY *(shrugs, shy now)*: It's too late. You can't get it now.

EVE *(smiling lightly)*: Got the eye on me, haven't you? What'd I do?

TONY: Nothing, Miss Cressy. But maybe you need some fresh air. Been here five days and haven't stepped out once that I know of.

EVE: And you know everything, don't you?

   (She is teasing him but TONY *glances at her seriously, thinking.)*

TONY: I know you got a tower room.

EVE: So? Why do you say it like that?

TONY *(seeing her interest, plays it up with a secretive tone)*: There was a girl here once with a tower room, stayed a week, like you, hardly talked to anybody, never went out, and then what do you think she did?

   *(*EVE *smiles, thinking perhaps he is joking with her, but still not certain.)*

EVE: Jumped her bill.

TONY *(almost whispering now, as if telling a ghost story)*: No, paid it, even told the hop to come up for suitcases in half an hour. *(*EVE *is hooked. She leans forward, listening.)* Then she went out on her balcony in the rain.

EVE: What's your name?

TONY: Tony Reseck.

EVE: What happened in the rain, Tony?

TONY: It was dark that night, the balconies are low. *(He drops his hands with a final, farewell gesture and stares at the radio.)* When she hit the sidewalk, it was so loud, I thought it was a gun shot on the radio.

(She searches his face, then leans back into the cushions.)

EVE: You're making it up.

TONY *(giving her a half smile and looking over the waves of her hair)*: Am I?

(She feels the look across her hair and decides something about it that lets her continue.)

EVE: It's the waiting, isn't it, Tony? That's why they jump. Nobody can do it for long.

TONY: Is that what you're doing, Miss Cressy, waiting?

(She thinks about it.)

EVE: The clock stops after a while and there's no tomorrow or yesterday, only now.

TONY: Maybe it's what you're waiting for.

EVE: It's always a guy. What else does any girl wait for? And I was even married to this one once. Might be again. You can make a lot of mistakes in just one lifetime, Tony—some of 'em twice. *(Her hand on her knee opens slowly until it is strained as far back as it will go.)* But I put him in a bad place and now I have to put him back where he was. It's only right.

(The knuckles in her hand are as white as polished bones, and TONY *would like to ease them back into their normally beautiful shape. Instead he turns the radio up and lets a waltz do the job for him. She moves the hand numbly to her side and looks up at him.)*

EVE: They played that almost every night in the dive I sang in.

TONY: It was no dive when you were in it, Miss Cressy. *(She is surprised that he knows. He turns away.)* I have to go palm doorknobs. I hope I didn't bother you.

EVE: You didn't.

TONY: It's late.

EVE: It's Now.

(TONY nods and turns but the radio is suddenly quiet and he turns back.)

EVE: You really thought that, about the balcony?

TONY: It was just a story.

EVE: Redheads don't jump, Tony. They hang on . . . and wither.

INTERIOR: LOBBY.

CARL, *the night porter, is waiting for* TONY *when he steps back into the lobby and they walk together, talking in near whispers.*

TONY: Trouble?

CARL: There's a guy outside, I'm wiping the glass, he comes up, says, "Get Tony."

TONY: Uh-huh, who was it?

CARL: Al, he said to say he was.

TONY: Okay.

(They pull up in the center of the lobby. TONY thinks a moment, then moves toward the door.)

CARL: Listen Tony, you got enemies? *(TONY just smiles.)* There's a black car down the block. Guy asking for Tony, he don't show his face and I'm thinking maybe you got enemies.

TONY: Black car, ashamed of his face. Probably a lawyer.

(TONY steps up into the entrance lobby, past the elevator night operator and the night clerk at the front desk. He points a finger gun at the clerk and fires, which makes the clerk yawn. TONY continues on past the

newsstand and the entrance to the drugstore. He stops at the doors, thinks, then steps out into the night.)

EXTERIOR: STREET.

TONY *nods to the hacks huddled against their cabs, then turns left and walks down toward the black car. The light puff of exhaust from the tailpipe drifts across the coat of the tall man who is walking toward him. They pull up, two feet apart.*

AL: Tony, long time no see.

TONY: How's it goin', Al?

*(*AL *takes his hand out of his pocket, then stops and smirks.)*

AL: Almost started to shake hands.

TONY: Shaking hands don't mean anything, Al. They teach monkeys to do it. What's on your mind?

AL: Still the funny little guy, eh?

TONY: Don't let the little fool you, I'm not that funny.

(They stare at each other as if they have had this conversation before.)

AL: So, you liking your job or what?

TONY: It's a job.

*(*AL *snorts and shakes his head.)*

AL: Yeah, your own little world. Run the bad guys out, tuck the old ladies in. Everything neat and clean, huh?

TONY: It's a job.

AL: You want to keep it? *(*TONY *lets the threat die out in the dark.)* You got a girl named Eve Cressy flopping in your place. Get her out. Now.

TONY: Why?

AL: She's hooked with a wrong number, little brother, just do it.

TONY: Anything you say.

*(*AL *pushes* TONY *lightly on the chest.)*

AL: It's no joke, Tony. *(TONY stares at him until AL turns for the car. And then AL is back, even closer, up to Tony's face.)* You don't get it, do you?

(TONY just stands there, waiting to get it. AL sighs, looks around the street, then leans in.)

AL: Look, this Cressy was married to Johnny Ralls. He just pulled a three-spot in Quentin for manslaughter. Get this. He runs down an old guy one night with her in the car and didn't stop. She told him to turn himself in or she would. He thought she was joking him. Had three long years to laugh it off.

TONY: So she has a conscience.

AL: What she's got is Ralls coming back for her. The word is they made up, but the Johnny boy I know don't forgive so easy.

TONY: What's it to you?

AL: Nothing. But the trouble boys got business with him. Before he went up, he was runnin' a spot on the Strip for 'em and figured out a scheme. He and another guy took the house for fifty grand. The other lad coughed up, but they're still looking for Johnny's twenty-five, and you know how they are about that.

TONY: I don't want any part of it.

AL: So we leave your part out. Just put her on the sidewalk and go back to sleep.

TONY: And you'll treat her nice, right?

(AL studies TONY a minute, then shrugs.)

AL: Only thing she's got that they want is him.

TONY: Okay.

(AL takes a step back and smiles.)

AL: How's Mom?

TONY: Why don't you go see her and find out?

AL: Tell her I was asking for her.

TONY: Asking for her isn't anything, Al.

(But AL *is already turning away and crawling into the car.* TONY *watches for a moment, then turns back as the car's headlights splash against a wall.)*

INTERIOR: RADIO ROOM.

The radio is still muttering but EVE *is gone.* TONY *reaches down and touches the cushions, which are still hollowed out by her body. Then, turning off the radio, he walks out.*

INTERIOR: LOBBY.

TONY *stares up at the elevator's floor indicator, which is resting all the way over to 14. Then it slowly steals back down around the bronze dial.* TONY *takes out a cigar and fingers the elk's tooth on his chain while he waits.* CARL *steps off the elevator and is immediately next to* TONY.

CARL: Listen, Tony.

*(*TONY *takes him by the arm and pushes him into a corner.)*

TONY: Listen to what?

CARL *(taking a crumpled dollar bill out of his pocket and holding it up):*
　　He gimme this.

TONY: Who?

CARL: Guy in 14B.

*(*TONY *leans in and sniffs Carl's breath.)*

CARL: Okay, half a shot too.

TONY: Nobody in 14B, Carl.

CARL: There is now. Kinda big guy with dark hair.

TONY: A big guy. So what?

CARL: Got a gun under his arm.

TONY: You take Miss Cressy up to her room?

CARL: No, but I saw her go.

TONY: You want to drink in a room, Carl, you rent one.

CARL: Sorry, Tony.

INTERIOR: FRONT DESK.

TONY *stands at the front desk thinking, then slaps the veined rose marble. The* CLERK *pops up from behind the glass screen like a chipmunk out of its hole.* TONY *takes a flimsy out his pocket and spreads it on the desk.*

TONY: No 14B on this.

    (The CLERK *preens his fuzzy new mustache proudly.)*

CLERK: So sorry. You must of been out to supper when he checked in.

TONY: Who?

CLERK *(looking over the register):* Registered as James Watterson, of San Diego.

TONY: Ask for anybody?

CLERK: Yeah, a Kabuki with geisha girls. I told him we were a little short on girls but you might slip on a kimono and bring him a sake.

    *(*TONY *pencils something in on his flimsy and stuffs it back in his pocket.)*

TONY: Always the razoo, aren't you?

CLERK: What else have I got to do?

TONY: I know a guy in radio could maybe use you.

CLERK: What's he do, comedy?

TONY: Repair.

    (The CLERK *drops back down out of sight.)*

CLERK *(offscreen):* A little silk number in red to go with your eyes, Tony. He might not even miss the sake.

    (But TONY *is off, his eyes already leading him to the elevator.)*

INTERIOR: FOURTEENTH FLOOR.

TONY *steps off the elevator and onto the fourteenth floor. A corridor of single blue-panelled doors with gold-wreathed numbers and letters stretch out before him. He stops at 14A, puts his ear to the door, and listens.*

INTERIOR: 14A, EVE CRESSY'S ROOM.

Lightning impressions tangle in imagination as:

EVE, *sitting at her dressing table, brushes sparks through her red hair.* FLASH.

EVE, *sleeping soundly in a halo of light.* FLASH.

EVE, *standing at her balcony window, a sheer drape undulating like a wraith around her, her rain-soaked silk pajamas clinging to her in the cold wet wind.* FLASH.

INTERIOR: HALL.

TONY *jerks away from the possibilities behind the door. He presses his hand gently against the blue paint and moves over to 14B. Listening again, he hears a man cough. He touches the nacre button beside the door and listens to the footsteps.*

VOICE *(offscreen):* Yeah?

(TONY *just stands there.*)

VOICE *(offscreen):* Who is it?

(TONY *again pushes the button and the voice stops. There is no sound. He takes a master key out of his pocket and inserts it delicately into the lock. He turns it, pushes the door open a few inches, withdraws the key, and waits.*)

VOICE *(offscreen):* Don't stop now.

(TONY *pushes the door open wide and stands framed in the light from the lobby. A tall, black-haired man with an angular white face is standing just inside the door looking comfortable with the gun in his hand.*)

MAN: That's it, fat boy, in you come.

(TONY *smiles, walks in as though it were his room and there is no gun pointed at his heart.*)

INTERIOR: ROOM 14B.

TONY *closes the door with his shoulder, leaving his hands at his side.*

TONY: Mr. Watterson?

MAN: He talks.

TONY: House detective.

MAN: Try it on the other side of the door next time.

(The MAN *backs slowly past the grate set for a log fire to a cozy chair set up near French windows that lead out to the balcony. He stands in front of the chair with the gun drooping in his hand.)*

MAN: In the dump an hour and I got a keyhole peeper shaking the room. Go ahead, peeper, look under the bed, but she just left.

TONY: I don't think she's been here yet.

(The man's face blanks.)

MAN: Who?

TONY: A lady named Eve.

(The MAN *thinks about that, then puts his gun down on the table beside the tray. He lets himself down stiffly into the chair, then leans forward and puts his hands on his kneecaps and smiles.)*

MAN: So she got here.

TONY: Never left for a minute in five days.

(The MAN *bends his hands back till the knuckles whiten.* TONY *watches them, transfixed.)*

MAN: You know a lot about my business, peeper.

*(*TONY *glances up from the hands to the man's face.)*

TONY: More than I want to, Mr. Ralls.

*(*RALLS *lunges to his feet, and snaps at the gun. He stands, leaning over, holding it on the table.)*

RALLS: Women got a condition where they talk about what they don't know about.

TONY: Not just women, and it wasn't her.

*(*RALLS *stares at* TONY, *then straightens up.* TONY *moves over so he is in front of him and stands there quietly, with his pale friendly face.* RALLS *doesn't know how to take it.)*

TONY: What I hear comes from guys who say they know something for sure.

RALLS *(wearily):* What's for sure is, they never sleep, these guys. *(Trouble rolls across Ralls's face.* TONY *stands there reading it.)* Where is she?

TONY: Other side of the wall.

(RALLS walks over to the wall and stares at it a moment, thinking. Then he looks out over the balcony before coming back and staring at Tony's ears.)

RALLS: Big ears, like garbage cans. What else you got in there, Mr. Detective?

TONY: They said you took what wasn't yours.

RALLS: Like what?

TONY: Like twenty-five large.

RALLS: Bullshit. Only money I've seen is what the sweetheart sent me for cigarettes once a month.

TONY: Nobody's ever done wrong, have they, Mr. Ralls? Quentin's more like a church with all the saints they got in there.

(TONY has a certain edge in his voice that makes RALLS take another look at him—a look a little less certain than it was a moment ago.)

RALLS: I got suckered. My partner took a fifty, gave twenty-five back, kept twenty-five and now I'm supposed to come up with what I ain't ever had.

TONY: And you told 'em?

RALLS: They don't listen too good. *(He stares across the room at the opposite wall, her wall.)* All they got's a way of asking till you ain't got a mouth to answer with no more. *(RALLS picks up his glass from the table and drains it. The ice cubes tinkle softly as he puts it down. He picks up his gun, palms it, then tucks it into an inner breast pocket.)* So if you're lookin' for a payoff, keep lookin'. I ain't got it.

TONY: I thought maybe you'd give her a break.

RALLS *(studying* TONY *carefully):* What's it to you what I give her?

TONY: Nothing at all.

(RALLS *nods and glances back at the wall.*)

RALLS: Goddamn right, nothing.

TONY: But she's been spotted. Guy that called me about you said to get her out. So you go ahead and show with her if you think it's a good idea.

(RALLS *has another look at* TONY, *trying to figure his angle.*)

RALLS: You're the idea man, you gonna keep 'em comin' now or you done?

(TONY *takes out a worn ostrich-skin billfold and scribbles on a printed card. He hands the card to* RALLS, *who reads it, then taps it against his thumbnail.*)

TONY: Give it to the attendant in the basement. When you get where you're going, call, and I'll pick the car up.

RALLS: I could take her with me.

TONY: They said to send her out, Mr. Ralls. She's the last place you want to be. (*He turns and starts for the door.*)

RALLS: Maybe I'll see her 'fore I go.

TONY: I got one good idea left.

RALLS: Yeah?

TONY: Don't.

(*The way* TONY *says it puzzles* RALLS *again.* TONY *opens the door and starts through.*)

RALLS: You're a funny little guy, you know that? You wouldn't be settin' me up, would you?

TONY: Don't let the little fool you, Mr. Ralls. I'm not that funny. Take the service elevator.

INTERIOR: FOURTEENTH FLOOR. HALL.

TONY *stops at 14A and listens briefly.*

INTERIOR: FOURTEENTH FLOOR. STAIRWELL.

TONY *cracks the stairwell door and watches as* JOHNNY RALLS *comes out of his room with a small bag.* RALLS *walks to the service elevator, thinks, then walks back to 14A and thinks some more. Finally he goes back to the elevator and pushes the call button.*

INTERIOR: LOBBY. FRONT DESK.

TONY *stands at the lobby desk, looking at the* CLERK, *who is staring at him.*

TONY: What's the professional rate on 14B?

CLERK: No professional rate on the towers, you know that.

TONY: There is tonight. Call it an hour.

CLERK: What's the matter, he didn't like the kimono?

TONY: Five bucks? *(He thinks about the figure and nods to himself.)*

CLERK: What'd you, show up naked and scare him out?

*(*TONY *pulls out the ostrich-skin billfold, takes out a five-dollar bill, and presses it out on the marble.)*

TONY: The trouble with honest money is that there's never enough of it.

CLERK: If Watterson skipped, we'll just let it ride, Tony.

*(*TONY *pushes the bill to him, waits for him to pick it up, then looks over at the radio room, which is suddenly alive again with music.)*

INTERIOR: RADIO ROOM.

EVE *is there, curled up again on the davenport. The radio is on, soft, the speaker humming like the murmur of trees. She turns her head and smiles when* TONY *comes in.*

EVE: I couldn't sleep. Finish palming your doorknobs?

(He returns her smile, nods, sits down in a green chair, and plumps the arms.)

TONY: Yes, Miss Cressy.

EVE: I decided to stay away from the balcony tonight.

*(*TONY *thinks, staring at the radio.)*

INTERIOR: FAST FORD.

JOHNNY RALLS *pulls out of the underground garage into an alley.*
He spins the dial on the radio.

Close on Radio Dial: the dial moves slowly across static and silence.

INTERIOR: RADIO ROOM.

EVE *leans back from the radio where she has been looking for music*
and sighs.

EVE: I wish you'd talk to the radio, Tony, it won't sing for me.

(TONY *gets up and fiddles with the dial, not finding much either.*)

TONY: Mostly sings for drunks this time of night.

EVE: I know the feeling.

(*Finally* TONY *locates something not more than half bad and moves*
back to his chair. She lays her head down on the cushion. The hum in the
radio grows louder, nearly covering the music. She doesn't seem to notice,
but TONY *frowns, listening, as the hum becomes an engine, racing into*
the room, then screaming brakes.

INTERIOR: FAST FORD.

RALLS *is standing on his brakes. A big black car is sitting crossways*
at the end of the alley. The fast Ford fishtails and slides on the wet bricks.
The music on the radio makes it seem unreal.

INTERIOR: RADIO ROOM.

The screaming brakes are gone from the radio. TONY *thoughtfully*
fingers his elk's tooth.

TONY *(as much to himself as to* EVE*):* Nobody's all bad.

(EVE *looks up lazily.*)

EVE: I've met a few I was wrong about then.

(*He glances over at her, replaying her words, and nods.*)

INTERIOR: FAST FORD.

RALLS *sits dazed behind the wheel. The Ford is inches from the black*
car and at first, the soft music from the radio doesn't fit with the look on
the face of AL, *who is walking toward him, pulling back his wet coat,*
reaching for something inside. But then, as Johnny's hand snakes down

inside his own jacket and two men, angling toward him from another car across the street, fall in behind AL, *all their movements slow to a kind of synchronized ballet of death.*

INTERIOR: RADIO ROOM.

TONY *clinches the elk's tooth in his fist as shots cut through the music and slam around the room. Eve's eyes are closed and she is breathing deeply.*

TONY: The trouble with all bad is like all good, you know? Neither one holds up if you look at 'em too hard.

(EVE *sighs, sinking further into the cushion.*)

EVE: Stay with me a while, Tony. I could maybe sleep if you were here.

TONY *(whispering):* Sure. Nothing for me to do, anyway. I don't know why they pay me.

(*And she is gone. And at last he can look at her openly, tenderly, now that she won't look back.*)

INTERIOR: DOORWAY.

The CLERK *stands quietly in the doorway, hesitant to break the spell that Tony seems to be under. Finally he backs away from the intimacy, hums the tune from the radio loudly, and steps back into the doorway again.* TONY *is staring at him.*

CLERK: Guy to see you, Tony.

(TONY *nods as if he was expecting this but is in no hurry to get to it.*)

TONY: Tell him to wait.

(*The* CLERK *nods and steps away.*)

INTERIOR: LOBBY.

A man in a long wet coat is waiting near the top of the lobby entrance stairs. He looks as if he could wait forever. As TONY *walks up, he pushes away from the wall and smiles.*

TROUBLE BOY: You got to be Tony.

TONY: We all got to be somebody. (TROUBLE BOY *smiles again.*) Who do you have to be?

(TROUBLE BOY *nods toward a car puffing quietly at the curb.* TONY *looks, then looks back at* TROUBLE BOY.*)*

TONY: No parking in front of the doors.

TROUBLE BOY: We're not parking, trust me.

*(*TONY *glances back at the front desk, at the clerk who is watching from the top of a newspaper, and finally over to the door of the radio room. Turning, he nods to* TROUBLE BOY *to go ahead.* TROUBLE BOY *shrugs as if he couldn't think of such a discourtesy.* TONY *walks out into the cold.)*

EXTERIOR: SIDEWALK.

TROUBLE BOY *holds open the back door of the car for* TONY, *then walks around and crawls in the passenger door in front. The car pulls out from the curb and does a* U-*turn in the street.*

INTERIOR: FRONT SEAT OF CAR.

TROUBLE BOY *twists around, looking into the back seat.*

TROUBLE BOY: He knew you wouldn't send the girl out, Tony. He used to say you were so straight you couldn't drive a crooked road.

Close on TONY *in the Back Seat: Headlights and streetlamps flicker in the glass next to* TONY. *He is pale, scrunched in next to the door, thinking.*

Front Seat: TROUBLE BOY *shakes his head.*

TROUBLE BOY: I bet Charlie here that you'd shake Ralls out in less than an hour. Fifty-eight minutes, Tony. Here's your cut.

(TROUBLE BOY *dangles some bills over the seat. When* TONY *doesn't take them, he leans over into the back seat.)*

Back Seat: TROUBLE BOY *stuffs the bills into Al's jacket.* AL *is slumped next to the window opposite* TONY, *his wide shoulders scrunched up so close to his neck that he looks small and childlike. He has three holes in his chest and neck that are draining into his damp clothes. His eyes, having looked into another world, will never see this one the same way again.* TONY *turns away and stares out the window.*

EXTERIOR: STREET.

The car pulls up in front of the hotel and stops. TONY *stares out at the Windemere as if he can't believe it is there or that he is.*

Close on Back Seat: TONY *looks over at his brother and gives him the only help he can—he closes his eyes. Then he reaches past* AL *toward the floor.*

Floor: Wedged in between the two seats, propped up against the door is JOHNNY RALLS. *Tony's fingers brush briefly over those eyes of absent wonder and close them as well.*

TROUBLE BOY *(offscreen):* You want to hear funny, Tony? When Al gave back the first twenty-five grand, we figured he still had the other twenty-five. We just wanted to get him and Johnny together to see who blinked first.

Back Seat: TONY *stares into the front seat and thinks.*

TROUBLE BOY: Now nobody's blinkin', and we still ain't got our money. Al maybe hand you a bag of something to hold for him, Tony? We come by later to talk, you'll wait up, right?

(He smiles. TONY *stares hard at him, thinking, then reaches for Al's arm to pull him out.)*

TROUBLE BOY: Leave him.

*(*TONY *thinks it over, then drapes Al's arm over his own shoulder to pull him out.)*

TROUBLE BOY: I said leave him.

*(*TONY *pulls* AL *away from the window and slides across the seat with his burden.* TROUBLE BOY *sets a revolver on top of the seat, pointing it lazily at Tony's head.)*

TROUBLE BOY: It's a big place where he's going, Tony, plenty of room.

*(*TONY *looks at the gun and eases* AL *back into his corner, staring at him mournfully. Suddenly there is a flash and roar from the back seat.* TROUBLE BOY *forms a tight round O with his lips and cracks the window glass with his head, twice, like a puppet gone mad. The driver is just turning around when the speedometer explodes in front of him. He frowns down at the hole in his shirt, watches another bullet spit from it and into the dash, then loses interest in everything. Smoke floats in the empty air as*

TONY, *still staring at his brother, stuffs the hot gun in his hand down in Rall's belt.)*

Close on Floor. Tony's wet, scuffed shoes tread heavily across the blue carpet.

INTERIOR: RADIO ROOM

TONY *is sunk into an armchair, waiting. He looks over at* EVE, *who is still curled up in the cushions. Her breathing is distant, peaceful, full of sleep. She tucks her head closer to her chest.* TONY *leans back in his chair, fingers the elk's tooth on his chain, and stares at his brother on the other sofa, waiting forever for morning.*

The Frightening Frammis

Jim Thompson

For perhaps the hundredth time that day, Mitch Allison squared his shoulders, wreathed his face with an engaging grin, and swung his thumb in a gesture as old as hitchhiking. And for perhaps the hundredth time his appeal was rudely ignored. The oncoming car roared down on him and past him, wiping the forced grin from his face with the nauseous blast of its exhausts.

Mitch cursed it hideously as he continued walking, damning the car's manufacturer, its owner, and finally, and most fulsomely, himself.

"Just couldn't be satisfied, could you?" he grumbled bitterly. "Sitting right up on top of the world, and it wasn't good enough for you. Well, how do you like this, you stupid dull-witted moronic blankety-blank-blank!"

Mitch Allison was not the crying kind. He had grown up in a world where tears were more apt to inspire annoyance than sympathy, and a sob was likely to get you a punch in the throat. Still, he was very close to weeping now. If there had been any tears in him, he would have bawled with sheer shame and self-exasperation.

Less than a day ago, he had possessed almost twenty thousand dollars, the proceeds from robbing his wife, swindling the madam of a parlor house, and pulling an intricate double double-cross on several "business" associates. Moreover, since it had been imperative for him to clear out of Los Angeles, his home town, he had had a deluxe state-room on the eastbound Super Chief. Then . . .

Well, there was this elderly couple. Retired farmers, ostensibly, who had just sold their orange grove for a five-figure sum. So Mitch had tied into them, as the con man's saying is, suggesting a friendly little card game. What happened then was figuratively murder.

The nice old couple had taken him like Grant took Richmond. Their apparently palsied hands had made the cards perform in a manner which even Mitch, with all his years of suckering chumps, would have declared impossible. He couldn't believe his own eyes, his own senses. His twenty grand was gone and the supposed suckers were giving him the merry ha-ha in a matter of two hours.

Mitch had threatened to beat them into hamburger if they didn't return his dough. And that, of course, was a mistake, the compounding of one serious error with another. For the elderly couple—far more practiced in the con than he—had impeccable references and identification, while Mitch's were both scanty and lousy.

He couldn't establish legitimate ownership to twenty cents, let alone twenty grand. Certainly, he was in no position to explain how he had come by that twenty grand. His attempts to do so, when the old couple summoned the conductor, had led him into one palpable lie after another. In the end, he had had to jump the train, sans baggage and ceremony, to avoid arrest.

So now, here he was. Broke, disgusted, footsore, hungry, hitch-hiking his way back to Los Angeles, where he probably would get killed as soon as he was spotted. Even if no one else cared to murder him, his wife Bette would be itching to do so. Still, a guy had to go some place, didn't he? And having softened up Bette before, perhaps he could do it again. It was a chance—his only chance.

A hustling man needs a good front. Right now, Mitch looked like the king of the tramps.

Brushing the sweat from his eyes, he paused to stare at a sign attached to a roadside tree: Los Angeles—125 Miles. He looked past the sign into the inviting shade of the trees beyond it . . . the ocean would be over there somewhere, not too far from the highway. If he could wash up a little, rinse out his shirt and underwear . . .

He sighed, shook his head and walked on. It wasn't safe. The way his luck was running, he'd probably wade into a school of sharks.

In the distance, he heard another car approaching. Wearily, knowing he had to try, Mitch turned and swung his thumb.

It was a Cadillac, a big black convertible. As it began to slow down, Mitch had a feeling that no woman had ever given him such a going over and seemed to like so well what she saw as the one sitting next to the Cad's driver.

The car came on, slower and slower. It came even with him, and the woman asked, "How far to El Ciudad?"

"El Ciudad?"—the car was creeping past him; Mitch had to trot along at its side to answer the question. "You mean, the resort? About fifty miles, I think."

"I see." The woman stared at him searchingly. "Would you like a ride?" she asked.

"Would I!"

She winked at Mitch, spoke to the man behind the wheel. "All right, stupid. Stop. We're giving this guy a ride."

The man grunted a dispirited curse. The car stopped, then spurted forward savagely as Mitch clambered into the back seat.

"What a jerk!" The woman stared disgustedly at her companion. "Can't even give a guy a ride without trying to break his neck!"

"Dry up," the man said wearily. "Drop dead."

"So damned tight you squeak! If I'd only known what you were like before I married you!"

"Ditto. Double you in spades."

The woman took a pint of whiskey from the compartment, drank from it, and casually handed it back to Mitch. He took a long thirsty drink and started to pass the bottle back. But she had turned away again, become engrossed in nagging at her husband.

Mitch was just a little embarrassed by the quarrel, but only a little. Mitch Allison was not a guy to be easily or seriously embarrassed. He took another drink, then another. Gratefully, he settled down into the deeply upholstered seat, listening disinterestedly to the woman's brittle voice and her husband's retorts.

"Jerk! Stingy! Selfish . . . ," she was saying.

"Aw, Babe, lay off, will you? It's our honeymoon, and I'm taking you to one of the nicest places in the country."

"Oh sure! Taking me there during the off-season! Because you're just too cheap and jealous to live it up a little. Because you don't want anyone to see me!"

"Now that isn't so, Babe. I just want to be alone with you, that's all."

"Well, I don't want to be alone with you! One week in a lifetime is enough for me . . ."

Mitch wondered what kind of chump he could be to take that

sort of guff from a dame. In his own case, if Bette had ever talked that way to him—*pow!* She'd be spitting out teeth for the next year.

The woman's voice grew louder, sharper. The slump to her husband's shoulders became more pronounced. Incuriously, Mitch tried to determine what he looked like without those out-size sunglasses and the pulled-low motoring cap. But he didn't figure long. The guy straightened suddenly, swerved the car off into a grass-grown trail, and slammed on the brakes.

Mitch was almost thrown from the seat. The husband leapt from the car and went stomping off into the trees. She called after him angrily—profanely. Without turning, he disappeared from view.

The woman shrugged and looked humorously at Mitch. "Some fun, huh, mister? Guess I rode hubby a little too hard."

"Yeah," said Mitch. "Seems that you did."

"Well, he'll be back in a few minutes. Just has to sulk a little first."

She was red-haired, beautiful in a somewhat hard-faced way. But there was nothing hard-looking about her figure. She had the kind of shape a guy dreams about, but seldom sees.

Mitch's eyes lingered on her. She noticed his gaze.

"Like me, mister?" she said softly. "Like to stay with me?"

"Huh?" Mitch licked his lips. "Now, look, lady—"

"Like to have this car? Like to have half of fifty thousand dollars?"

Mitch always had been a fast guy on the uptake, but this babe was pitching right past him.

"Now look," he repeated shakily. "I-I-"

"You look," she said. "Take a good look."

There was a briefcase on the front seat. She opened it and handed it back to Mitch. And Mitch looked. He reached inside, took out a handful of its contents.

The briefcase was filled, or at least half-filled, with traveler's checks of one-hundred-dollar bills. They would have to be countersigned, of course, but that was—

"—a cinch," the woman said intently. "Look at the signature. No curly-cues, no fancy stuff. All you have to do is sign it plain and simple—and we're in."

"But—" Mitch shook his head. "But I'm not—"

"But you could be Martin Lonsdale—you could be my husband. If you were dressed up, if you had his identification." Her voice faded at the look Mitch gave her, then resumed again, sulkily.

"Why not, anyway? I've got a few rights, haven't I? He promised me the world with a ring around it if I'd marry him, and now I can't get a nickel out of him. I can't even tap his wallet because he keeps all of his dough out of my hands with tricks like this."

"Tough," said Mitch. "That's really tough, that is."

He returned the checks to the briefcase, snapped the lock on it and tossed it back into the front seat. "How could I use his identification unless he was dead? Think he'd just go to sleep somewhere until I cashed the checks and made a getaway?"

The girl flounced around in the seat. Then she shrugged and got out. "Well," she said, "as long as that's the way you feel . . ."

"We'll get hubby, right?" Mitch also got out of the car. "Sure, we will—you and me together. We'll see that he gets back safe and sound, won't we?"

She whirled angrily, and stomped off ahead of him. Grinning, Mitch followed her through the trees and underbrush. There was an enticing roll to her hips—a deliberately exaggerated roll. She drew her skirt up a little, on the pretext of quickening her stride, and her long, perfectly shaped legs gleamed alluringly in the shade-dappled sunlight. Mitch admired the display dispassionately. Admired it, without being in the least tempted by it.

She was throwing everything she had at him, and what she had was plenty. And he, Mitch Allison, would be the first guy to admit that she had it. Still, she was a bum, a hundred and ten pounds of pure poison. Mitch grimaced distastefully. He wished she would back-talk him a little, give him some reason to put the slug on her, and he knew she was too smart to do it.

They emerged from the trees, came out on the face of a cliff overlooking the ocean. The man's trail clearly led here, but he was nowhere in sight. Mitch shot an inquiring glance at the girl. She shrugged, but her face had paled. Mitch stepped cautiously to the edge of the cliff and looked down.

Far below—a good 100 feet at least—was the ocean: roiled, oily-looking, surging thunderously with the great foam-flecked waves of the incoming tide. It was an almost straight up-and-down drop to the water. About halfway down, snagged on a bush which sprouted from the cliff face, was a man's motoring cap.

Mitch's stomach turned sickishly. Then he jumped and whirled as a wild scream rent the air.

It was the girl. She was kneeling, sobbing hysterically, at the base of a tree. Her husband's coat was there, suspended from a broken-off branch, and she was holding a slip of paper in her hands.

"I didn't mean it!" she wept. "I wouldn't have done it! I was just sore, and—"

Mitch told her curtly to shut up. He took the note from her and read it, his lips pursed with a mixture of disdain and regret.

It was too bad, certainly. Death was always regrettable, whether brought on by one's own hand or another's. Still, a guy who would end his life over a dame like this one—well, the world hadn't lost much by the action and neither had he.

Mitch wadded the note and tossed it over the cliff. He frisked the coat and tossed it after the note. Then, briskly, he examined the wallet and personal papers of the late Martin Lonsdale.

There was a telegram, confirming reservations at El Ciudad Hotel and Country Club. There was a driver's license, and a photostat of Martin Lonsdale's discharge from the army. Mitch examined the last two items with particular care.

Brown hair, gray eyes—yep, that was all right; that matched the description of his own eyes and hair. Weight one hundred and eighty—right on the nose again. Complexion fair—okay, also. Height six feet one inch . . .

Mitch frowned slightly. Lonsdale hadn't looked to be over five eight or nine, so—So? So nothing. Lonsdale's shoulders had been slumped; he, Mitch, had only seen the man on his feet for a few seconds. At any rate, the height on these papers matched his own and that was all that mattered.

The girl was still on her knees, weeping. Mitch told her to knock it off, for God's sake, and when she persisted he kicked her lightly in the stomach. That stopped the tears, but it pulled the stopper on some of the dirtiest language he had ever heard.

Mitch listened to it for a moment, then gave her a stinging slap on the jaw. "You've just passed the first plateau," he advised her pleasantly. "From now on, you won't get less than a handful of knuckles. Like to try for it, or will you settle for what you have?"

"You dirty, lousy, two-bit tinhorn." She glared at him. "I just lost my husband, and—"

"Which was just what you wanted," Mitch nodded, "so cut out the fake sob stuff. You wanted him dead. Okay, you got your wish, and with no help from me. So now let's see if we can't do a little business together."

"Why the hell should I do business with you? I'm his widow. I've got a legal claim on the car and dough."

"Uh-huh," Mitch nodded judiciously. "And maybe you can collect, too, if you care to wait long enough—and if there aren't any other claims against the estate. And if, of course, you're still alive."

"Alive? What do you—"

"I mean you might be executed. For murder, you know. A certain tall and handsome young man might tell the cops you pushed Martin off of that cliff."

He grinned at her. The girl's eyes blazed, then dulled in surrender.

"All right," she mumbled. "All right. But do you have to be so—so nasty, so cold-blooded? Can't you act like—uh—"

Mitch hesitated. He had less than no use for her, and it was difficult to conceal the fact. Still, when you had to do business with a person, it was best to maintain the appearance of friendliness.

"We'll get along all right, Babe." He smiled boyishly, giving her a wink. "This El Ciudad place. Is Martin known there?"

"He was never even in California before."

"Swell. That strengthens my identification. Gives us a high-class base of operations while we're cashing the checks. There's one more thing, though—" Mitch looked down at the telegram. "This only confirms a reservation for Martin Lonsdale."

"Well? It wouldn't necessarily have to mention his wife, would it? They have plenty of room at this time of year."

Mitch nodded. "Now, about the clothes. Maybe I'm wrong, but Marty looked quite a bit smaller than—"

"They'll fit you," the girl said firmly. "Marty bought his clothes a little large. Thought they wore longer that way, you know."

She proved to be right. Except for his shoes, the dead man's clothes fitted Mitch perfectly.

Mitch retained only his own shoes and socks, and threw his other clothes into the ocean. Redressed in clean underwear, an expensive white shirt and tie and a conservative-looking blue serge suit, he climbed behind the wheel of his car. The girl, Babe, snuggled close to him. He backed out onto the highway and headed for El Ciudad.

"Mmmm . . ." Babe laid her head against his shoulder. "This is nice, isn't it, honey? And it's going to be a lot nicer, isn't it, when we get to the hotel?"

She shivered deliciously. Mitch suppressed a shudder.

"We'll cash the checks," she murmured, "and split on that. We'll divide everything, even-stephen, won't we, honey? . . . Well, won't we?"

"Oh, sure. Naturally," Mitch said hastily. "You just bet we will!" And he added silently: *Like hell!*

2

El Ciudad is just a few miles beyond the outer outskirts of Los Angeles. A truly magnificent establishment during the tourist season, it was now, in midsummer, anything but. The great lawns were brown, tin-der-dry. The long rows of palm trees were as unappetizing as banana stalks. The tennis courts were half-hidden by weeds. Emptied of water and drifted almost full of dried leaves and rubble, the swimming pool looked like some mammoth compost pit. The only spots of brightness were the red-and-white mailbox at the head of the driveway and a green telephone booth at the first tee of the golf course.

Briefly, the exterior of the place was a depressing mess; and inside it was even less prepossessing. The furniture was draped with dust covers. Painter's dropcloths, lumber, and sacks of plaster were strewn about the marble floor. Scaffolds reared toward the ceiling, and ladders were propped along the walls.

There was only a skeleton staff on duty; they were as dejected-looking as the establishment itself. The manager, also doubling as clerk, was unshaven and obviously suffering from a hangover. He apologized curtly for the disarray, explaining that the workmen who were refurbishing the place had gone on strike.

"Not that it makes much difference," he added. "Of course, we regret the inconvenience to you"—he didn't appear to regret it—"but you're our only guests."

He cashed one of the hundred-dollar checks for Mitch, his fingers lingering hungrily over the money. A bellboy in a baggy uniform showed "Mr. and Mrs. Lonsdale" to their suite. It consisted of two rooms and a connecting bath. Mitch looked it over, dismissed the bell-boy with a dollar tip, and dropped into a chair in front of the air-conditioning vent.

"You know," he told Babe, "I'm beginning to understand your irritation with Marty. If this is a sample of his behavior, going to a winter resort in the middle of summer—"

"A double-distilled jerk," Babe agreed. "Scared to death that someone might make a play for me."

"Mmm-hmmm," Mitch frowned thoughtfully. "You're sure that was his only reason? No matter how scared he was of competition, this deal just doesn't seem to make sense."

"Well—" the girl hesitated. "Of course, he probably didn't know it would be this bad."

The kitchens and dining room of El Ciudad were not in operation, but the bellboy made and served them soggy sandwiches and muddy coffee. He also supplied them with a bottle of whiskey at double the retail price. They had a few drinks and ate. Then, with another drink before him, Mitch sat down at the desk and began practicing the signature of Martin Lonsdale.

For the one check—the one cashed by the manager—he had done all right. There was only a hundred dollars involved, and the manager had no reason to suspect the signature. But it would be a different story tomorrow when he began hitting the banks. Then, he would be cashing them with people whose business it was to be suspicious. His forgeries would have to be perfect, or else.

So he practiced and continued to practice, pausing occasionally to massage his hand or to exchange a word with the girl. When, finally, he achieved perfection, he started to work on the checks. Babe stopped him, immediately wary and alarmed.

"Why are you doing that? Aren't they supposed to be counter-signed where they're cashed?"

Mitch shrugged. "Not necessarily. I can write my name in front of the person who does the cashing. Just establish, you know, that my signature is the same as the one on the checks."

"Yes, but why—"

"To save time, dammit! This is a forgery job, remember? We hold all the cards, but it is forgery. Which means we have to hit and get—cash in and disappear. Because sooner or later, there's going to be a rumble. Now, if you're afraid I'm going to lam out with these things—"

"Oh, now, of course I'm not, honey." But she stuck right with him until he had finished countersigning the checks. She was quite prepared, in fact, to spend the rest of the night. Mitch didn't want that. He shoved the checks back into the briefcase, locked it and thrust it into her hands.

"Keep it," he said. "Put it under your pillow. And now get out of here so I can get some sleep."

He began to undress. The girl looked at him, poutingly.

"But, honey. I thought we were going to—uh—"

"We're both worn out," Mitch pointed out, "and there's another night coming."

He climbed into bed and turned on his side. Babe left, reluctantly. She took the briefcase with her, and she locked the connecting door on her side of the bathroom.

Mitch rolled over on his back. Wide-eyed, staring into the darkness, he pondered the problem of giving Babe a well-deserved rooking. It was simple enough. After—and *if* he successfully cashed the checks tomorrow, he had only to catch her off guard and put her on ice for the night. Bind and gag her, and lock her up in one of the clothes closets. From that point on, however, he wasn't sure what to do. Or, rather, he knew what to do, but he didn't know how the hell he was going to do it.

He couldn't scram in the Cad. A wagon like that would leave a trail a blind man could follow. For similar reasons, he couldn't zoom away in a taxi—if, that is, it was possible to get taxi service this far from the city.

How was he going to do it, then? Equally important, where would he hide out if he was able to do it? For he would sure as hell have to hide out fast after this caper. Babe would squawk bloody murder. It wouldn't make her anything, but she'd sure squawk. Her body was soft and lush but one look at that cast-iron mug of hers, and you knew she would.

So . . . ?

Mitch scowled in the darkness. Now Bette, his wife, had a nondescript car. She could get him away from here, and she could—but it was preposterous to think that she would. Not after that last stunt he'd pulled on her.

Yes, he'd planned on pleading for forgiveness before his meeting with Martin and Babe Lonsdale. But the situation had been different then. There wasn't any fifty grand at stake. There wasn't the risk of a long prison stretch. If he appealed to Bette, he'd have to give her the full pitch on this deal. Which meant, naturally, that he'd be completely at her mercy. And if she wasn't feeling merciful, if he couldn't fast-talk her into giving him a break, well, that would be the end of the sleigh ride.

Enter the cops. Exit Mitch Allison and fifty grand.

I'm going to have to stop crooking everyone, Mitch thought. From now on I'm going to be honest, with at least one person.

He fell asleep on this pious thought. Almost immediately, it seemed, it was morning and Babe was shaking him awake.

They headed into Los Angeles, stopping at a roadside diner for breakfast. As they ate, Mitch consulted the classified telephone directory, organizing an itinerary for the day's operations. Because of the time factor, his targets—the banks—had to be separated by a discreet distance, lest he be spotted in going from one to another. Needless to say, it was also essential that he tackle only independent banks. The branch banks, with their central refer system, would nail a paper-pusher on his second try.

Babe watched Mitch work, admiration in her eyes—and increasing caution. Here was one sharp cookie, she thought. As sharp as she was tough. A lot sharper than she'd ever be. Being the kind of dame she was, she'd contemplated throwing a curve to win. Now she knew that wouldn't do it: she'd have to put the blocks to him before he could do it to her.

She was lingering in the background when he approached the teller's cage at the first bank. She was never more than a few feet away from him throughout the day, one of the most nerve-wracking in Mitch Allison's career.

He began by pushing ten of the traveler's checks, a thousand bucks at a time. A lead-pipe cinch with his appearance and identification. Usually a teller would do it on his own, or, if not, an executive's okay was a mere formality. Unfortunately, as Mitch soon realized, these thousand-dollar strikes couldn't get the job done. He was too short on time. He'd run out of banks before he ran out of checks. So he upped the ante to two grand, and finally to three, and things really tightened up.

Tellers automatically referred him to executives. The executives passed him up the line to their superiors. He was questioned, quizzed, studied narrowly. Again and again, his credentials were examined—the description on them checked off, item by item, with his own appearance. By ten minutes of three, when he disposed of the last check, his nerves were in knots.

He and Babe drove to a nearby bar where he tossed down a few quick ones. Considerably calmer, then, he headed the car toward El Ciudad.

"Look, honey," Babe turned suddenly in the seat and faced him. "Why are we going to that joint, anyway? We've got the dough. Why not just dump this car for a price and beat it?"

"Just go off and leave our baggage? Start a lot of inquiries?" Mitch shook his head firmly.

"Well, no, I guess that wouldn't be so good, would it? But you said we ought to disappear fast. When are we going to do it?"

Mitch slanted a glance at her, deliberating over his reply. "I can get a guy here in L.A. to shoot me a come-quick telegram. It'll give us a legitimate excuse for pulling out tomorrow morning."

Babe nodded dubiously. She suggested that Mitch phone his friend now, instead of calling through El Ciudad's switchboard. Mitch said that he couldn't.

"The guy works late, see? He wouldn't be home yet. I'll call him from that phone booth out on the golf course. That'll keep anyone from listening in."

"I see," Babe repeated. "You think of everything, don't you, darling?"

They had dinner at a highway drive-in. Around dusk, Mitch brought the car to a stop on El Ciudad's parking lot. Babe reached hesitantly for the briefcase. Mitch told her to go right ahead and take it with her.

"Just don't forget, sweetheart. I can see both entrances to the joint, and I've got the keys to this buggy."

"Now, don't you worry one bit," Babe smiled at him brightly. "I'll be right inside waiting for you."

She headed for the hotel, waving to him gaily as she passed through the entrance. Mitch sauntered out to the phone booth and placed a call to Bette. Rather, since she hung up on him the first two times, he placed three calls.

At last she stayed on the wire and he was able to give her the pitch. The result was anything but reassuring. She said she'd be seeing him—she'd be out just as fast as she could make it. And he could depend on it. But there was an ominous quality to her voice, a distinctly unwifely tone. Before he could say anything more, she slammed up the receiver for the third and last time.

Considerably disturbed, Mitch walked back across the dead and dying grass and entered the hotel. The manager-clerk's eyes shied away from him. The elevator-bellboy was similarly furtive. Absorbed in his worry over Bette, Mitch didn't notice. He got off at his floor and started down the hall, ducking around scaffolding, wending his way through a littered jungle of paint cans, plaster, and wallpaper.

He came to the door of his room. He turned the knob, and entered.

And something crashed down on his head.

3

It was dark when Mitch regained consciousness. He sat up, massaging his aching head, staring dizzily at the shattered glass on the floor—the remains of a broken whiskey bottle. Then he remembered; realization came to him. Ripping out a curse, he ran to the window.

The Cad was still there on the parking lot. Yes, and the keys were still in his pocket. Mitch whirled, ran through the bath and kicked open the door to the other room.

It was empty, in immaculate order, sans Babe and sans baggage. There was nothing to indicate that it had ever been tenanted. Mitch tottered back into his own room, and there was a knock on the door and he flung it open.

A man walked in and closed it behind him. He looked at Mitch. He looked down at the broken bottle. He shook his head in mild disapproval.

"So you are supposedly a sick man, Marty," he said gutturally. "So you have a great deal of money—my money. So drunk you should not get."

"H-huh? W-what?" Mitch said. "Who the hell are you?"

"So I am The Pig," the man said. "Who else?"

The name suited him. Place a pecan on top of a hen's egg and you've got a good idea of his appearance. He was perhaps five feet tall and he probably weighed three hundred pounds. His arms were short almost to the point of deformity. He had a size-six head and a size-sixty waistline.

Mitch stared at him blankly, silently. The Pig apparently misunderstood his attitude.

"So you are not sure of me," he said. "So I will take it from the top and give you proof. So you are The Man's good and faithful servant through all his difficulties. So The Man passes the word that you are to pay me fifty thousand dollars for services rendered. So you are a very sick man anyway, and have little to lose if detected while on the errand—"

"Wait a minute!" Mitch said. "I—I'm not—"

"So you are to transport the money in small traveler's checks. So you cannot be robbed. So they can be easily cashed without attracting unwanted attention. So you have had a day to cash them. So"—The Pig concluded firmly—"you will give me the fifty thousand."

Mitch's mouth was very dry. Slowly, the various pieces of a puzzle were beginning to add up. And what they added up to was curtains—for him. He'd really stepped into something this time: a Grade A jam, an honest-to-hannah, double-distilled frammis. The Pig's next words were proof of the fact.

"So you know how I earned the fifty G's, Marty. So you would not like me to give you a demonstration. It is better to die a natural death."

"N-now-now, listen!" Mitch stammered. "You've got the wrong guy. I'm not Martin Lonsdale. I'm—I'm . . . Look, I'll show you." He started to reach for his wallet. And groaned silently, remembering. He had thrown it away. There was a risk of being caught with two sets of identification, so—

"So?" The Pig said.

"I! Look! Call this Man whoever he is. Let me talk to him. He can tell you I'm not—"

"So," The Pig grunted, "Who can call Alcatraz? So—" he added, "I will have the money, Marty."

"I don't have it! My wife—I mean the dame I registered in with—has it. She had the room next to mine, and—"

"So, but no. So I checked the registry myself. So there has been no woman with you."

"I tell you there was! These people here—they're hungry as hell, see, and she had plenty of dough to bribe them . . ." he broke off, realizing how true his words were. He resumed again, desperately, "Let me give you the whole pitch, tell you just what happened right from the beginning! I was trying to thumb a ride, see, and this big Cadillac stopped for me. And . . ."

Mitch told him the tale.

The Pig was completely unimpressed.

"So that is a fifty-grand story? So a better one I could buy for a nickel."

"But it's true! Would I make up a yarn like that? Would I come here, knowing that you'd show up to collect?"

"So people do stupid things." The Pig shrugged. "So, also, I am a day early."

"But, dammit!—" There was a discreet rap on the door. Then it opened and Bette came in.

This Bette was a honey, a little skimpy in the chin department, perhaps, but she had plenty everywhere else. A burlesque house strip-teaser, her mannerisms and dress sometimes caused her to be mistaken for a member of a far older profession.

Mitch greeted her with almost hysterical gladness. "Tell this guy, honey! For God's sake, tell him who I am!"

"Tell him . . . ?" Bette hesitated, her eyes flickering. "Why, you're Martin Lonsdale, I guess. If this is your room. Didn't you send for me to—"

"N-nno!" Mitch burbled. "Don't do this to me, honey! Tell him who I really am. Please!—"

One of The Pig's fat arms moved casually. The fist at the end of it smashed into Mitch's face. It was like being slugged with a brick. Mitch stumbled and fell flat across the bed. Dully, as from a distance, he heard a murmur of conversation . . .

". . . had a date with him, a hundred-dollar date. And I came all the way out here from Los Angeles . . ."

"So Marty has another date. So I will pay the hundred dollars myself . . ."

There was a crisp rustle, then a dulcet, "Oh, aren't you nice!" Then the door opened and closed, and Bette was gone. And The Pig slowly approached the bed. He had a hand in his pocket. There was a much bigger bulge in the pocket than a hand should make.

Mitch feigned unconsciousness until The Pig's hand started coming out of his pocket. Then Mitch's legs whipped up in a blur of motion. He went over backwards in a full somersault, landed on the other side of the bed, gripped and jerked it upward.

Speed simply wasn't The Pig's forte. He just wasn't built for it. He tried to get out of the way, and succeeded only in tripping over his own feet. The bed came down on him, pinning him to the floor. Mitch set him to sleep with a vicious kick in the head.

Mitch realized he had been moving in a blur. But now his mind was crystal clear, sharper than it ever had been.

Where was Babe? Simple. Since she couldn't have ridden away from the place, she must have walked. And Mitch knew where she had walked to.

What to do with The Pig? Also simple. The materials for taking care of him were readily at hand.

Mitch turned on the water in the bathtub. He went out into the hall and returned with two sacks full of quick-drying plaster . . .

He left The Pig very well taken care of, sitting in plaster up to his chin. Then, guessing that it would be faster, he ran down the stairs and out to the Cadillac. Wheels spinning, he whipped it down the horseshoe driveway and out onto the highway.

He slowed down after a mile or two, peering off to his right at the weed-grown fields which lay opposite the ocean. Suddenly, he jerked the car onto the shoulder and braked it to a stop. He got out; his eyes narrowed with grim satisfaction.

He was approximately parallel now with the place where he had assumed the identity of Martin Lonsdale. The place where Martin Lonsdale had supposedly committed suicide. And out there in this fallow field was an abandoned produce shed.

From the highway, it appeared to be utterly dark, deserted. But as Mitch leaped the ditch and approached it, he caught a faint flicker of light. He came up on the building silently. He peered through a crack in the sagging door.

There was a small stack of groceries in one corner of the room, also a large desert-type water bag. Blankets were spread out in another corner. Well back from the door, a can of beans was warming over a Sterno stove. A man stood over it, looking impatiently at the food.

Mitch knew who he was, even without the sunglasses and cap. He also knew who he was *not*—for this man was bald and well under six feet tall.

Mitch kicked open the door and went in. The guy let out a startled "Gah!" as he flung himself forward, swinging.

He shouldn't have done it, of course. Mitch was sore enough at him, as it was. A full uppercut, and the guy soared toward the roof. He came down, horizontal, landing amidst the groceries.

Mitch snatched him to his feet, and slapped him back into consciousness. "All right. Let's have the story. All of it and straight, get me? And don't ask me what story or I'll—"

"I w-won't—I mean, I'll tell you!" the man babbled frantically. "We—tied into Lonsdale at a motor-court. Figured he was carrying heavy, so Babe pulled the tears for a ride. We was just going to hold him up, you know. Honest to Gawd, that's all! But—but—"

"But he put up a fight and you had to bump him."

"Naw! No!" the man protested. "He dropped dead on us! I swear he did! I'd just pulled a knife on him—hadn't touched him at all—when he keeled over! Went out like a light. I guess maybe he must have had a bad ticker or something, but anyway . . ."

Mitch nodded judiciously. The Pig had indicated that Lonsdale was in bad health. "So okay. Keep singing."

"W-well, he didn't have hardly any dough in cash like we thought he would. Just that mess of checks. But we'd pumped him for a lot of info, and we figured if we could find the right kind of chump—excuse me, Mister—I mean, a guy that could pass for Lonsdale—"

"So you did a little riding up and down the highway until you found him. And you just damned near got him killed!"

He gave the guy an irritated shake. The man whimpered apologetically. "We didn't mean to, Mister. We really figured we was doing you a favor. Giving you a chance to make a piece of change."

"I'll bet. But skip it. Where's Babe?"

"At the hotel."

"Nuts!" Mitch slapped him. "You were going to hole up here until the heat was off! Now, where the hell is she?"

The man began to babble again. Babe hadn't known how soon she could scram. There'd been no set time for joining him here. She had to be at the hotel. If she wasn't, he didn't know where she was.

"Maybe run out on me," he added bitterly. "Never could trust her around the corner, I don't see how she could get away, but—"

Mitch jerked a fist swiftly upward.

When the guy came to, he was naked and the room had been stripped of its food, water and other supplies. His clothes and every-thing else were bundled into one of the blankets, which Mitch was just lugging out the door.

"Wait!" The man looked at him fearfully. "What are you going to do?"

He departed. A mile or so back up the road, he threw the stuff into the ditch. He arrived at the hotel, parked and indulged in some very deep thinking.

Babe had to be inside the joint. This money-hungry outfit was hiding her for a price. But exactly where she might be—in which of its numerous rooms, the countless nooks and crannies, cellars, and sub-cellars that a place like this had—there was no way of telling. Or find-ing out. The employees would know nothing. They'd simply hide themselves if they saw him coming. And naturally he couldn't search the place from top to bottom. It would take too long. Deliverymen—possibly other guests—would be showing up. And then there was The Pig to contend with. Someone must have driven him out here, and he

would not have planned to stay later than morning. So someone would
be calling for him, and—

Well, never mind. He had to find Babe. He had to do it fast. And
since he had no way of learning her hiding-place, there was only one
thing to do. Force her out of it.

Leaving the hotel, Mitch walked around to the rear and located a
rubbish pile. With no great difficulty, he found a five-gallon lard can
and a quantity of rags. He returned to the parking lot. He shoved the
can under the car's gas tank and opened the petcock. While it was
filling he knotted the rags into a rope. Then, having shut off the flow of
gasoline, he went to the telephone booth and called the hotel's switchboard.

The clerk-manager answered. He advised Mitch to beat it
before he called the cops. "I know you're not Lonsdale, understand?
I know you're a crook. And if you're not gone from the premises in
five minutes—"

"Look who's talking!" Mitch jeered. "Go ahead and call the
cops! I'd like to see you do it, you liver-lipped, yellow-bellied—"

The manager hung up on him. Mitch called him back.

"Now get this," he said harshly. "You said I was a crook. All
right, I am one and I'm dangerous. I'm a crib man, an explosives ex-
pert. I've got plenty of stuff to work with. So send that dame out here
and do it fast, or I'll blow your damned shack apart!"

"Really? My, my!" The man laughed sneeringly, but somewhat
shakily. "Just think of that!"

"I'm telling you," Mitch said. "And this is the last time I'll tell
you. Get that dame out of the woodwork, or there won't be any left."

"You wouldn't dare! If you think you can bluff—"

"In exactly five minutes," Mitch cut in, "the first charge will be
set off, outside. If the dame doesn't come out, your building goes up."

He replaced the receiver, went back to the car. He picked up the
rags and gasoline, moved down the hall to the red-and-white mailbox.
It stood in the deep shadows of the porte-cochere and he was not
observed. Also, the hotel employees apparently were keeping far back
from the entrance.

Mitch soaked the rag rope in the gasoline and tucked a length of
it down inside the mailbox. Then he lifted the can and trickled its
entire contents through the letter slot. It practically filled the box to
the brim. The fluid oozed through its seams and dripped down upon
the ground.

Mitch carefully scrubbed his hands with his handkerchief. Then, he ignited a book of matches, dropped them on the end of the rope, and ran.

His flight was unnecessary. For the "bomb" was an almost embarrassing failure. There was a weak rumble, a kind of a growl—a hungry man's stomach, Mitch thought bitterly, would make a louder one. A few blasts of smoke, and the box jiggled a bit on its moorings. But that was the size of it. That was the "explosion." It wouldn't have startled a nervous baby. As for scaring those rats inside the joint, hell, they were probably laughing themselves sick.

Oh, sure, the box burned; it practically melted. And that would give them some trouble. But that didn't help Mitch Allison any.

From far down the lawn, he looked dejectedly at the dying flames, wondering what to do now. He gasped, his eyes widening suddenly as two women burst through the entrance of El Ciudad.

One—the one in front—was Babe, barelegged, barefooted, dressed only in her bra and panties. She screamed as she ran, slapping and clawing wildly at her posterior. And it was easy to see why. For the woman chasing her was Bette, and Bette was clutching a blazing blowtorch.

She was holding it in front of her, its long blue flame aimed straight at the brassy blonde's flanks. Babe increased her speed. But Bette stayed right with her.

They came racing down the lawn toward him. Then, Bette tripped and stumbled, the torch flying from her hands. And at practically the same instant, Babe collided head-on with the steel flagpole. The impact knocked her senseless. Leaving her to listen to the birdies, Mitch sat down by Bette and drew her onto his lap. Bette threw her arms around him, hugging him frantically.

"You're all right, honey? I was so worried about you! You didn't really think I meant the way I acted, did you?"

"I wouldn't have blamed you if you had," Mitch said.

"Well, I didn't. Of course I was awfully mad at you, but you *are* my husband. I feel like murdering you myself lots of times, but I'm certainly not going to let anyone else do it!"

"That's my girl." Mitch kissed her fondly. "But—"

"I thought it was the best thing to do, honey. Just play dumb and then go get some help. Well—"

"Just a minute," Mitch interrupted. "Where's your car?"

"Over by the ocean." Bette pointed, continued. "Like I was saying, I found her listening out in the hall. I mean, she ducked away real fast, but I knew she had been listening. So I figured you'd probably be all right for a little while, and I'd better see about her."

"Right," Mitch nodded. "You did exactly right, honey."

"Well, she had a room just a few doors away, Mitch. I guess they had to move her nearby because they didn't have much time. Anyway, she went in and I went right in with her . . ."

She had asked Babe the score. Babe had told her to go jump, and Bette had gone to work on her, ripping off her clothes in the process. Babe had spilled, after a time. Bette had learned, consequently, that there would be no help for Mitch unless she provided it.

"So I locked her in and went back to your room. But you were gone, and I guessed you must be all right from the looks of things. That guy in the bathtub, I mean." Bette burst into giggles, remembering. "He looked so funny, Mitch! How in the world do you ever think of those stunts?"

"Just comes natural, I guess," Mitch murmured modestly. "Go on, precious."

"Well, I went back to her room, and the clerk called and said you were threatening to blow up the place. But she wouldn't go for it. She said she was going to stay right there, no matter what, and anyway you were just bluffing. Well, I was pretty sure you were, too, but I knew you wanted to get her outside. So I went out in the hall again and dug up that big cigar lighter—"

Mitch chuckled and kissed her again. "You did fine, baby. I'm really proud of you. You gave her a good frisk, I suppose? Searched her baggage?"

Bette nodded, biting her lip. "Yes, Mitch. She doesn't have the money."

"Don't look so down about it—" he gave her a little pat. "I didn't figure she'd keep it with her. She's ditched it outside somewhere."

"But, Mitch, you don't understand. I talked to her, and—"

"I know. She's a very stubborn girl." Mitch got to his feet. "But I'll fix that."

"But, Mitch—she told me where she put the money. When I was chasing her with the torch."

"Told you! Why didn't you say so? Where is it, for Pete's sake?"

"It isn't," Bette said miserably. "But it was." She pointed toward the hotel. "It was up there."

"Huh? What are you talking about?"

"She . . . she mailed it to herself."

4

Sick with self-disgust, Mitch climbed behind the wheel of Bette's car and turned it onto the highway. Bette studied his dark face. She patted him comfortingly on the knee.

"Now, don't take it so hard, honey. It wasn't your fault."

"Whose was it, then? How a guy can be so stupid and live so long! Fifty grand, and I do myself out of it! I do it to myself, that's what kills me!"

"But you can't expect to be perfect, Mitch. No one can be smart all the time."

"Nuts!" Mitch grunted bitterly. "When was I ever smart?"

Bette declared stoutly that he had been smart lots of times. Lots and lots of times. "You know you have, honey! Just look at all the capers you've pulled! Just think of all the people who are trying to find you! I guess they wouldn't be, would they, if you hadn't outsmarted them."

"Well . . ." Mitch's shoulders straightened a little.

Bette increased her praise.

"Why, I'll bet you're the best hustler that ever was! I'll bet you could steal the socks off a guy with sore feet, without taking off his shoes!"

"You-uh-you really mean that, honey?"

"I most certainly do!" Bette nodded vigorously. "They just don't make 'em any sneakier than my Mitch. Why—why, I'll bet you're the biggest heel in the world!"

Mitch sighed on a note of contentment. Bette snuggled close to him. They rode on through the night, moving, inappropriately enough, toward the City of Angels.

The Frightening Frammis

Teleplay by

Jon Robin Baitz &

Howard A. Rodman

Cast

Peter Gallagher	Mitch Allison
Isabella Rossellini	Babe
Nancy Travis	Bette
John Reilly	Martin Lonsdale
Joe Viterelli	Ugolino
Bill Erwin	Chick
Jean Speegle-Howard	Dolly

Executive Producer: Sydney Pollack
Producers: William Horberg, Lindsay Doran, Steve Golin
Co-Producer: David Wisnievitz
Directed by: Tom Cruise
Director of Photography: Peter Suschitzky
Production designed by: Armin Ganz
Costumes designed by: Shay Cunliffe
Casting by: Owens Hill and Rachel Abroms
Fallen Angels theme by: Elmer Bernstein
Music by: Peter Bernstein
Edited by: David Siegel
Story Editor: Geoffrey Stier

EXTERIOR: BLACKTOP ROAD. NIGHT.

Dark, grainy, almost black-and-white:

MITCH ALLISON *is seen walking along the side of the road. His suit is wrinkled, stained, matted, battered, and torn; his face cut, scabbed, stubbled. He trudges wearily, as if every ounce of life has been beaten out of him . . . which it has.*

We hear his voice:

MITCH *(voice-over):* Two days ago, you were strolling down Easy Street, tipping your hat to strangers. But it wasn't good enough for you, was it. *(Pausing:)* Well, my friend. How do you like yourself now? *(A car seems to be approaching, heading right for him.)* Two days ago, you had a wife, you had a home, you had twenty thousand in cash on the bedroom dresser. *(The car's headlights stab* MITCH *in the face. Strangely, it seems to be accelerating. Mitch's face: weary, blank, resigned.)* Yeah, that's me. Mitch Allison. (As the car tears straight at him:) Maybe it was Destiny. Maybe it was the sucker *inside. (Pause.)* Maybe both. *(Pause.)* They got together, shook hands, had a drink . . . And decided to give poor Mitch the merry ha ha . . . (MITCH ALLISON, *broke, bruised, battered, without a cent to his name or a friend in the world . . . transfixed by the car that's about to run him over.)* Two days ago. Two sweet, dumb days ago . . .

(Now we hear a terrible screech of brakes. The car stops—with MITCH *frozen in the headlights.* FREEZE FRAME. Dissolve to:)

INTERIOR: MITCH AND BETTE'S HOUSE. EARLY MORNING.

Four empty bottles of Veuve Cliquot—clearly, somebody has been celebrating in style. Several ashtrays, full up. Half the butts are stained with deep red lipstick. And a three-year-old wedding picture: a younger, happier MITCH, *dressed to the nines, with* BETTE, *his glowing, blushing bride.*

We pan to MITCH. *Looking ten times more together than he did in the previous scene. He's busy right now—scooping that aforementioned stack of small bills into a leather Gladstone bag.*

As he glances in the dresser mirror, we see a woman, BETTE, *under the sheets, dead to the world, beautiful to behold.*

MITCH *(voice-over):* I bought a big case of the bubbly—the good stuff. Then we stayed up all night, in the nicest possible way. I made sure she was good and exhausted. I should have been, too. *(Pausing:)* But of course I had something else on my mind.

(His loving point of view: BETTE, *in all her splendor, her naked body tangled tantalizingly in the bedclothes.)*

BETTE: *(in her sleep):* Oh Mitchy, the way you touch me . . .

MITCH *(voice-over):* Bette, my beauty. Everything I ever wanted in a woman and a hell of a lot more than I ever expected. She'd spent three months setting it up—then pulled an intricate double double-cross on the madam of a parlor house. The proceeds were in our personal possession. Twenty grand, to be exact.

(Now he stops to tape a note on the mirror. We hear him read the note in voice-over.)

Bette. I'm heading for the trains to duble yr money. Better con man than husband.

xxx yr one & only
Mitchy

P.S. Left $20 plse pick up my mohair jkt cleaners, tkt. on dresser.

(The mirror reflects the empty dresser top where the cash used to be.

Now BETTE *stirs in her sleep.)*

MITCH *(voice-over):* It had taken Bette three months to make that kind of money. In three hours, I could double it. *(Pausing:)* Skill. The Mitch Allison kind of skill.

(He prepares to walk out the door, Gladstone in hand, of course.)

INTERIOR: TRAIN. DAY.

An early-50s vintage private compartment. Big enough for six, now occupied by three: MITCH, *and an elderly couple,* CHICK *and* DOLLY. *They have the appearance of being in fragile health and of farm stock.*

We find the three engaged in a friendly game of poker. Or, more accurately, the two men play, while the woman looks on. Over the clack of the train and the murmur of shuffling cards we hear MITCH:

MITCH *(voice-over):* Chick, and *Dolly,* if you can believe it. They were from *Oxnard,* if you can believe it.

*(*CHICK *coughs, and reaches inside his suitcase for a vial of little red pills. As he opens the suitcase, we see a large green stack of money.* MITCH *presents the deck for a cut, then deals.)*

MITCH *(voice-over):* They'd sold their citrus grove to Uncle Sam who wanted the land for a radar base. They were on their way to Vegas. They had the cash with them. Sweet old Chick and Dolly.

CHICK: You know, it's watchin' this country go red that's killing me. Blood red. Used to be red, white, 'n' blue. Now it's all gone red, black, and Jew.

*(*DOLLY *giggles.* MITCH *is disgusted.*

Now MITCH *wins the hand. He has a tidy little pile in front of him.)*

MITCH *(voice-over):* It was the hot ticket. It was perfection itself. You could work the trains for a lifetime and not run into a Chick and a Dolly. And when I proposed raising the stakes—you know, to give them a chance to win a little bit back . . .

DOLLY: I hope you know what you're doing, Chick.

CHICK: Hell, Doll. Why not live a little? *(He smiles.)* I'm a tricky old dog, sweetie, it'll be fine. Your deal, young man.

(Close on MITCH *as he deals the cards.)*

MITCH *(voice-over):* Bingo. *(The clack of the train.)* I realized that right about now, Bette would probably be having some differences of opinion with what I'd done—

INTERIOR: MITCH AND BETTE'S HOUSE. BEDROOM. DAY.

An empty bottle hurtles at the wall near the dresser where it shatters into sad, green shards. We pan to reveal BETTE, *who has just thrown the bottle. She is dressed in a bathrobe now, sitting on the side of the bed. Her eyes are red from crying. Looking at the big, wide, empty dresser top, she is angry.*

BETTE *(scared, scary, furious):* MIT-CHY-Y-Y-Y!!!

INTERIOR: TRAIN COMPARTMENT. LATER. DAY.

MITCH *(voice-over):* —but I also knew that when I came home with the money, well . . . Forty grand buys a lot of amnesia.

(An astonishing amount of money on the table. Mitch's twenty thou and Chick and Dolly's twenty thou, all in cash, all in the pot. CHICK *and* DOLLY *sit grimly.* MITCH *is very intense: an addict just before his rush.)*

MITCH: Hold on, I just want to . . . feel it for a sec, Pops. The thrill, you know? *(*MITCH *holds out his arm to put down his hand: goosebumps.)* See that . . . See that . . . My hair is standing up. *(Pausing.)* Okay. Let's do it.

(He lays down his cards and lets them see his full house, aces over eights. He looks up, waiting for Chick's reaction . . . as CHICK *lays down four sevens—the winning hand.)*

DOLLY *(disbelieving):* Did we *win?*

*(*CHICK *grins and reaches over to hug his wife.)*

CHICK: Yes we did! Yes we did, my darlin'.

(Now CHICK *reaches across the table to take the pot and with it, all Mitch's money—or really, all Bette's money.* MITCH *looks at the couple, watching them carefully, without expression. And then: the dawning of a horrified recognition.)*

CHICK: Another hand, young man? I'd hate to leave you without the chance—

MITCH: I don't have any more money. But I guess you know that, dontcha? *(Pausing:)* It's a scam, isn't it? It's a first-class frammis. *(Pausing:)* Man, you guys are good.

(CHICK *and* DOLLY, *of course, look as innocent as churchmice.)*

DOLLY: Frammis? Why I don't believe I know that word.

MITCH: You're a pair of grifters. Workin' the trains, conning the cons. Christ, and me thinking I was so smart . . .

CHICK: Well. I guess this just isn't your day.

MITCH *(considers. Then:)*: The sad thing is, it's not your day either, Pops. *(Low, unwavering:)* Because you ain't gonna keep the dough.

DOLLY: Ohh . . . Sore loser, huh kid? *(All smiles:)* I'd like to know where you got *your* twenty thou.

(MITCH *puts his hand over Dolly's as she is about to slide the money into a carpet bag. She lets forth with a world-splitting scream—so loud, it shocks even* MITCH.)

DOLLY: Help! Help! Help! Help us someone!

(Freeze: Upright, frail, old CHICK *and* DOLLY, *in their best Grant Wood pose.)*

MITCH *(voice-over)*: Look at them . . . *(Another freeze: The sharply dressed* MITCH ALLISON, *looking like he's about to rip their heads off.)* Look at me. Who would *you* believe?

EXTERIOR: DIRT. DESERT. DAY.

MITCH *abruptly rolls into frame, plummeting to the ground. He breaks his fall, rolling, tucked-up, in the dirt.*

EXTERIOR: DESERT. DAY.

MITCH, *walking down the two-lane blacktop, into the red sun. The road comes to a shimmering point in the middle of nowhere under a red sun. There is nothing anywhere save for the odd Joshua tree, the dying cactus, the remains of a tire or two.*

Every cactus has a wavy edge around it, every object lined up in strange, forced perspective: a fever dream.

MITCH *(voice-over):* If I ever saw them again when the odds were even, I'd kill Dolly fast, Chick slow, until the living envied the dead.

(Mitch's point of view: the tar surface of the road beneath Mitch's unmoving feet. He has run out of steam. Poor, dusty, bedraggled not-so-handsome-now MITCH ALLISON *standing numbly with his thumb out, next to a colorful billboard reading:*

LOS ANGELES 210 MILES BUT
HADLEY'S DATE SHAKES 50 MILES!

MITCH *is heading back to Los Angeles—arms down, head down, lost in thought. The sun beats down relentlessly.)*

MITCH *(voice-over):* They talk about the heat in the desert, dry heat, like it was clean and pure, and wouldn't you want some? That's the way they talk, "A hundred ten, but so dry that you don't mind it at all." *(Pausing:)* Well I just never bought it.

(A black Cadillac convertible passes in the opposite direction. Probably the only car Mitch will see all day—but he wasn't able to get his thumb up in time.

He turns around to look for it and it's already far away, way down the road. He watches it rippling fiercely in the desert heat-shimmer.

He starts walking again, but from behind now comes another black convertible—it couldn't possibly be the same one, could it? The car's black lacquer gleams under the dust. Its occupants: a handsome young couple, BABE *and* MARTIN.

Babe *turns slowly. She looks over the top of her sunglasses, straight at* MITCH, *as the car slows down. She stares.)*

MITCH *(voice-over):* I do believe that no woman in my memory had ever given me such a going over—and seemed to like so well what she saw—as the one sitting next to the Cad's driver.

BABE *(to* MITCH*):* Need a ride? *(To the driver:)* Stop the car, stupid.

(On MITCH *as the car pulls to a stop.)*

MITCH *(voice-over):* It was a break. And just when I was beginning to think that I had no luck at all.

INTERIOR: CAR. MOVING SHOT. LATER. THAT DAY.

Tight on MITCH, *in the back of the car, miserable. He is listening to the couple in the front seat claw and bicker, bicker and claw.*

BABE: You're so damned tight you squeak, you know that, Mister Martin Lonsdale?

MARTIN *(wearily):* Babe, please . . .

MITCH *(voice-over):* Oh it was a break, all right.

BABE: If only I'd known what you were like before I married you!

MARTIN: Same here.

MITCH *(voice-over):* I should have jumped out then and there. Sitting in the back seat of that Cadillac, listening to the two of them—I tell you, it was the Ninth Circle.

BABE: Jerk! Jealous! Stingy! Selfish!

MARTIN *(simply):* This is sup*posed* to be our *honey*moon.

BABE *(right back at him):* I always wanted to honeymoon in a ghost town!

MARTIN *(patiently):* It's a *resort hotel.*

BABE: It's a ghost town. You're just too cheap and jealous to live it up a little!

MARTIN: I just want to be alone with you. Is that a crime?

(BABE *just ignores him. The tension is so thick you could cut it with a dull butter knife.*

MITCH *can't stand it. He breaks in, trying to strike a cheery note:)*

MITCH: What do you *do*, Mr. Lonsdale?

MARTIN: What's that?

MITCH: For a living.

MARTIN: I'm a printer.

BABE *(cutting in):* Yeah, he prints all those hotel room bibles they have in hotel rooms all over the world. It's so sexy when he talks about typefaces and bindings. It's why I married him. *(She lets this sink in.)* Do you want a drink?

(Some time has passed. At least two-thirds of the booze is gone. BABE *is now in the back seat, with* MITCH. *An increasingly enraged* MARTIN LONSDALE *sits alone in the driver's seat.)*

MITCH *(voice-over):* Babe had made quite a dent in the booze—but it didn't seem to make her any nicer. Now she was driving him from the *back* seat.

EXTERIOR: CAR. DAY.

Zooming down the desert blacktop.

EXTERIOR/INTERIOR: CAR. MOVING SHOT. DAY.

The radio blares and the Southwestern twangs of an EVANGELIST *fill the car and the arid desert landscape.*

RADIO EVANGELIST: —and who knows about evil? Only the bible does. Why, folks, in my booklet, *Revelations Revealed,* you too can learn the secrets of salvation for the small sum of . . .

BABE: Oh, Martin. Turn that off! You want to spoil the honeymoon?

MITCH *(voice-over):* Newlyweds. *(Pausing:)* I tell you, if Bette ever talked to me like that—

MARTIN: If I'm going to be a chauffeur at least let me have the radio.

MITCH *(to* BABE*):* What would it hurt to be a little nice? You don't want Martin here to send us over a cliff, do you?

BABE: Oh he'd never do anything that exciting. He likes things kind of—limp.

(The car abruptly stops inches away from a scenic overlook, at right angles to the edge. MITCH *and* BABE *are slammed into the back of their seats.* MARTIN *turns, white-faced, to* BABE.*)*

BABE *(bored):* Oh quit the cry-baby act and drive.

MARTIN: This entire marriage has been a mistake. I see that now. I see that now.

(He turns up the volume with a furious twist. Organ music fills the air. He gets out of the car in a blind rage, stomps towards the front grille, and glowers at BABE *through the windshield.*

BABE *puts an arm on Mitch's shoulder. When he turns to meet her gaze:)*

BABE *(intimately):* Do you know what this is? This is a sulk. It's what
   Martin does best. We've been married for—*Ohmygod!*

   (MITCH *follows her gaze to the front of the car—where* MARTIN *is
   no more! They sit, stunned. Then* MITCH *slowly gets out of the car and
   walks over to the canyon rim.* BABE *follows.)*

BABE: Martin? Martin?

   (*Mitch's and Babe's point of view: There crumbled at the base of the
   canyon, straight down, several hundred feet below, is a body—its limbs
   splayed at an awful, broken-doll angle, and quite clearly dead.)*

BABE *(flat, affectless):* I guess I rode hubby a little too hard.

   (*Over the radio, the evangelical organ music swells.* MITCH *shakes
   his head.)*

MITCH: Yeah, I guess you did.

   (BABE *turns away.)*

MITCH *(looking down):* Hey, pal, you know, you get used to it. That's
   what wives do, but you don't throw yourself over a cliff because
   they boss you around a little.

   (*Behind him,* BABE *grabs a red briefcase from the front seat and
   flips the latch. Inside is an extraordinary number of traveler's checks.)*

BABE: I got a problem here.

MITCH *(turning around):* I'll say . . .

   (*He stops and stares as he sees the money.)*

BABE: Fifty thousand dollars in traveler's checks. Do you know anyone
   who could help me cash them? Someone with dark hair and a
   medium build? Someone who could wear his *suit?*

   (*When* MITCH *finally speaks, his tone is not a pleasant one.)*

MITCH: I should have known you were working some angle on the
   kid.

   (*Her reply is as cold as the wind from the canyon.)*

BABE: I bet you know a little something about working the angles.
   Quite the little something, I would say.

MITCH *(voice-over):* She offered me twenty-five percent, so we talked. We ended up at fifty-fifty. If you want my opinion, she was gettin' herself a bargain.

EXTERIOR: LA CASA DEL CONDOR. DUSK.

It might have been a grand hotel twenty years back, but now it's a ghost town—a colonnaded building the same parched, dry color as the surrounding desert.

MITCH *(voice-over):* I felt bad about Martin, but not that bad. A guy who would end his life over a dame like this one—well, the world hadn't lost much, had it.

(The Cadillac pulls up to the main building. It's the only car in sight. As MITCH *and* BABE *get out, we realize* MITCH *is wearing one of Martin's suits.*

An old bearded man—the PROPRIETOR*—gets up from his rocking chair on the porch and comes forward to take their bags.)*

INTERIOR: HOTEL ROOM. LA CASA DEL CONDOR. NIGHT.

About what you'd expect from a place called La Casa del Condor.

MITCH *is at the little escritoire, practicing his signature:* Martin Lonsdale. Martin Lonsdale. Martin Lonsdale. *He pours Scotch into a glass from a big bottle and drinks. We follow the glass up to his face, then down to the desk where it rests next to his handiwork.*

Compared to the signature on the traveler's checks, Mitch's work gets better and better. Suddenly, Babe's hand enters the frame, pours some Scotch into Mitch's glass, and we follow the glass to her lips. She is looking over Mitch's shoulder, in her honeymoon negligee, staring at his work.

BABE: You're very good, aren't you?

*(*MITCH *just keeps on signing and drinking, his signature growing closer and closer to Lonsdale's.)*

BABE: You can't use any of the branch banks, you know. *(Managing to make it sound sultry.)* The branch banks. They have a Central Referral System. You try to push paper, they'll nail you on your second try.

*(*MITCH *looks at her.)*

MITCH *(voice-over):* She was throwing everything she had at me, and what she had was plenty. Still, she was a bum: a hundred-ten pounds of pure rat poison. *(Pausing:)* I didn't want to be the rat.

(He goes back to his work.)

BABE: You think badly of me, don't you. *(Pausing:)* You don't like me. *(Pausing again:)* I can understand that. I grew up by myself and for most of my life I've been a woman alone in this world and a woman alone has to learn to take care of herself. I *am* alone— but you don't have to make me feel so . . . lonely.

(She looks at him: a moment of true feeling. She puts her drink down and touches his face lightly. MITCH looks back for a long moment.)

MITCH *(knocking her hand away):* Let's clear somethin' up. I'm married. And I actually love my wife. But maybe that's too hard a concept to grasp for a woman who drives her husband over a cliff. *(Turning back to the desk.)* Now beat it, sister. I got work to do.

(He goes back to practicing his signature. BABE turns away.)

(Extreme close-up on: Mitch's near-perfect reproduction of Martin Lonsdale's signature. Tilt up to reveal the face of a lovely California-girl teller who does not even look once *at the traveler's checks that have just been signed in front of her. Rather, smitten by MITCH ALLISON who looks like a million dollars, she hands over the dough as if hypnotized.)*

MITCH *cashing checks.*

The action is the same, except the teller is an elderly woman. MITCH *winks at her. She giggles coltishly.*

MITCH *getting into the car.*

BABE *is at the wheel, the money in a red briefcase, right next to Babe's long and beautiful thighs.*

MITCH *cashing.*

The teller is a very queeny young thing, stuck out in the middle of nowhere, MITCH *the most beautiful thing he's ever seen.*

He is suddenly replaced by a stern bank official dressed in a conservative suit. The Martin Lonsdale IDs are scrutinized. There is a tense moment, but then the official nods. MITCH *receives ten thousand dollars in big bills, a stoic expression on his face.*

EXTERIOR: LA CASA DEL CONDOR. AFTERNOON.

MITCH *and* BABE *pull up and get out of their car. The same laconic* PROPRIETOR *rocks in his rocking chair on the front porch.* MITCH *carries the red briefcase full of money. As he and* BABE *arrive on the porch,* MITCH *stops.*

MITCH *(to* BABE*):* I have to make a call.

(BABE *twirls the car keys, holding them at arm's length in front of his face.)*

BABE: Don't worry, I trust you.

(She goes inside. We hear the sound of a phone ringing as we cut to:)

INTERIOR: MITCH AND BETTE'S HOUSE. AFTERNOON. BETTE.

It has been thirty-six hours since her man done left and took the money with him. She's on the bed—red-eyed, heartbroken, and angry.

The phone keeps ringing. She considers. Finally, without putting it to her ear, BETTE *picks it up and slams it down.*

It rings again. This time, she speaks.

BETTE *(into the phone):* You lost it, didn't you! You lost my money! You no-good two-bit chiseler!

(But before she can slam the receiver down again:)

MITCH *(voice-over):* Excuse me, Bette, am I to understand that you are angry at me for *doubling* your money?

BETTE: What the *hell* are you talking about?

EXTERIOR: LA CASA DEL CONDOR. PHONE. AFTERNOON.

The PROPRIETOR *saunters slowly past.* MITCH *pitches his voice low, so as not to be overheard.*

MITCH: Because I *literally* have fifty thousand dollars *literally* in my hands as we speak—and if you're angry with me for working a decent grift—

BETTE *(voice-over; still angry):* You doubled the money? Right!

MITCH: —then I suggest we seriously re-evaluate this entire relationship.

INTERIOR: MITCH AND BETTE'S HOUSE. BEDROOM. AFTERNOON.

BETTE: This better not be another one of your—

MITCH *(voice-over):* Just come and get me, Bette. La Casa del Condor, outside Desert Hot Springs. I'm here under the name of Martin Lonsdale.

BETTE: Mitchy? If you are *lying,* it is the *end.* It will be *over* this time. Did you hear that? I hope you heard that. *(She slams down the phone.)*

EXTERIOR: LA CASA DEL CONDOR. PHONE. AS BEFORE. AFTERNOON.

As he hangs up:

MITCH *(voice-over):* Half of fifty was twenty-five. Not enough for me. *Certainly* not enough for Bette. I would have to gain possession of Babe's share. I would have to give her the slip. But, hell, that shouldn't be too tough a job—

INTERIOR: HOTEL ROOM. LA CASA DEL CONDOR. EVENING.

MITCH *(voice-over):* —not for Mitch Allison.

(The door begins to open. We see Mitch's cheerful silhouette. And . . . WHAM! BABE *smashes* MITCH *full on the noggin with the fifth of Scotch.*

MITCH *crumples. Bending carefully,* BABE *picks up the briefcase. She looks at him on the floor—slacked-mouthed, collapsed, and dilapidated.)*

BABE: I'll never forget you, Mitch. You were the one that got away.

(She—and the money—walk out the door. With his last shred of consciousness, he watches her go. Then he's out.)

MITCH *(voice-over):* Maybe it was gonna be a little tougher than I thought.

INTERIOR: HOTEL ROOM. LATER THAT NIGHT.

Mitch's point of view: the room, beginning to come into focus. On MITCH, *bound hand-and-foot to a wooden chair. Now he hears some movement, and sees a blurry figure in front of him, just out of focus.*

MITCH: Bette? Honey? I have a splitting headache. Something happened, Bette, and I—

(The figure, as it comes into focus, is a large and frighteningly solid-looking man of late middle age, dressed in a black suit and tie, and oddly, wearing surgical gloves. The figure peering at him, stony-faced, is not BETTE—*not* BETTE *at all. But rather:)*

UGOLINO: Hello Mr. Lonsdale. And where is Mr. Vegas's money? I don't see it anywhere and have looked—everywhere.

MITCH: I'm sorry? I think, uh . . . I don't . . . who? Martin Lons—I'm not—I'm . . . huh?

*(*MITCH *looks up at the man, still not fully clear-headed. He squints and shakes his head as it starts to become evident that he's in terrible, terrible trouble.)*

UGOLINO: Perhaps you are unclear about who I am. I am Mr. Ugolino. And you, Mr. Lonsdale, have fifty thousand dollars belonging to my employer Mr. Vegas. Is that not the case?

*(*MITCH *groans in pain and shakes his head.)*

UGOLINO: You were told to deliver a briefcase *containing* that fifty thousand dollars to a Mr. Salmonelli in Palm Springs. And when Mr. Salmonelli says you did not show, you did not show.

UGOLINO *fondles a small black leather case—fondles it menacingly.*

MITCH: I'm not Lonsdale! I'm—just—I'm someone else, okay?!

UGOLINO: Mr. Lonsdale, if you would be saying you are not Mr. Lonsdale because you had already spent Mr. Vegas's money, we would be having a serious problem right now. *(*UGOLINO *grabs him by the lapel. The jacket's lining bears the label,* Tailored for Martin Lonsdale.*)* So.

MITCH *(scared, but slightly annoyed):* Look, when you found me, was I rolling in the green? No! Was I cold-cocked on the linoleum? Yes! Doesn't that tell you something? It's the girl who has the money. It's the girl! *(*UGOLINO *opens his small black leather case.)*

UGOLINO: The teller at First Indio. She didn't mention anything about a girl.

(We see now that the case contains several gleaming surgical instruments. UGOLINO *picks up one polished scalpel after another, as if trying to decide which might be most appropriate.)*

UGOLINO: You know, of course, what I am paid for? And do you think, Mr. Lonsdale, that I might walk away from this?

(He holds a scalpel up to Mitch's face. FREEZE.)

MITCH *(voice-over):* Oh God. I'd really stepped into something this time. It was a Grade-A, honest-to-hannah, double-distilled *frammis.*

(UNFREEZE.)

MITCH: Hey, wait a second! Take it easy, buddy!

UGOLINO *(quiet, dreamy, psychotic):* I am not a man who likes his work, Mr. Lonsdale. I am going to quit this vile profession as soon as I've amassed a certain sum. Which you *impede!* I do not kill because it gives pleasure, sir. I kill because it will pay for me to go to medical school. And how do I kill? *(He grabs Mitch's hair to hold his head steady.)* I do autopsies on the living.

(And with that, he makes a small, exploratory cut which will leave a permanent scar on the still-somewhat-beautiful face of MITCH ALLISON, hapless con.)

MITCH: My God, you're a lunatic!

UGOLINO *(whispers):* Yes, and there are so many of us, too. The money, Mr. Lonsdale. The money.

MITCH: If I had your fifty thousand, I'd give it to you. But I don't *have* it. I don't have the fifty thousand!

BETTE *(voice-over):* What do you *mean* you don't have the fifty thousand?

(Standing in the doorway is Mitch's salvation: BETTE, holding a .32 Colt in her right hand. But the .32 is pointed at MITCH.

Reacting to the voice, UGOLINO slowly turns. BETTE moves the gun back and forth between captor and captive.)

MITCH: Oh, Bette, thank God . . .

BETTE *(to MITCH):* You don't *have* the money? *(To UGOLINO:)* On your stomach, pal. And lose the knife.

UGOLINO: Please. Miss. Do not play games with a gun.

(BETTE *cocks the gun. Her fury is a thing to behold.*)

BETTE: I said get down!

(UGOLINO *looks at her and realizes that she is just gone enough to mean it.*)

BETTE: Now! (*In compliance, he gently places the scalpel back on its velvet bed, and carefully lies down on the floor.*) Nobody, *nobody,* kills Mitch Allison—

(*She walks over and holds the gun to Mitch's forehead. Intimately, to* MITCH:)—nobody but me.

MITCH: Bette, sweetpea, can we talk about this later?

BETTE: You lied to me!

MITCH: Bette, just take it easy. I *had* the money . . . I just . . . *lost* it.

BETTE: You *lost* it? I work three months setting up a grift and you *lose* it?

UGOLINO (*interrupting*): Madame, if I may—It was not his money in the first place. It belonged to—

BETTE (*turning the gun on* UGOLINO): Stay out of it!

MITCH (*to* BETTE): You're a little upset. And I respect that. But we can't talk if I'm tied up like this. (*Sing-song.*) *Un*-tie the rope, and *give* me the gun. We'll talk about it in the car . . .

(BETTE *looks him in the eye. There's murder in that look. Then slowly she begins to crack, her eyes filling with tears.*)

BETTE: Mitch.

(*She keeps* UGOLINO *covered as she picks up the scalpel with her left hand and uses it to cut* MITCH *free—nicking him in the process, of course.*)

MITCH (*as though dealing with a mental patient*): Okay. There we go . . . Can I have the gun now? (*He gently reaches up and takes the gun out of her hand.*) Atta Bette. (*He gives her a kiss. She doesn't respond.*) You just go wait in the car now.

BETTE (*total dejection*): I'm leaving.

MITCH *(oblivious):* That's fine. I'll finish up with this guy and be right out.

(MITCH *turns to* UGOLINO *and kicks him in the side.* BETTE *stands in the doorway, watching him with an overwhelming sadness.*)

BETTE *(a final whisper):* Good-bye, Mitchy.

(MITCH *is busy and doesn't really hear her. She leaves.*)

MITCH *(without turning around):* We'll talk all about it in the car.

INTERIOR: HOTEL BATHROOM. NIGHT. A FEW MINUTES LATER.

MITCH *is tying* UGOLINO *to the toilet with a bed sheet. Ugolino's feet are bare, his socks having been stuffed in his mouth. Now, gun in hand,* MITCH *considers his life, considers his marriage—considers* UGOLINO.

MITCH *(yanking the sheet):* Her name is Babe. Five nine, dark hair, accent. She drives a black Cadillac and watch out, because she's pretty handy with a whiskey bottle. But, hell, you're a professional. *(He catches sight of his face in the bathroom mirror.)* I was gonna quit the grift. I was gonna be an *actor.* You think anyone will hire me with *this? (Indicates the cut on his face.)* You know what sort of parts I'll get? Playing people like *you,* you psychotic, pre-med quack!

EXTERIOR: FRONT ENTRANCE. LA CASA DEL CONDOR. NIGHT.

MITCH *comes out of the hotel. He looks around:* No BETTE. *No car.*

MITCH *(yelling):* Bette! Bette! Bette!

(Faintly, from a doorway at the side of the hotel, we hear the muffled rural twangs of the RADIO EVANGELIST.*)*

MITCH *(voice-over):* She was gone. I had a suit of clothes belonging to the late Martin Lonsdale. I had a .32 Colt that I'd given my wife as a first-anniversary present. Nothing else in the world to call my own.

RADIO EVANGELIST: Where may you find the secret of this repentance? You may find it in our exclusive guide. The postal order in the sum of five dollars may be sent to God, care of L. L. Lenoir, Post Office Box—

MITCH *(dawning recognition):* Don't tell me. Please.

(MITCH *heads for the doorway, gun in hand.*)

INTERIOR: LA CASA DEL CONDOR. ANOTHER DINGY ROOM. NIGHT.

MARTIN *sits in a corner.* MITCH *kicks the door open and walks in.* MARTIN *turns around, startled and scared.* MITCH *turns off the blaring radio.*

MITCH: Where is she?

MARTIN: I don't know.

(MITCH *punches him.* MARTIN *doubles over, making an oomph sound as the air goes out of him.*)

MITCH: Hey, Mister Lonsdale—you know what? I've been lied to, knocked out, laughed at, *cut* up, humiliated, and cheated—okay? I've lost my wife and my self-respect. So just *don't.*

MARTIN *(pathetic):* Look, I'm *not* Lonsdale. My name is Christopher Shaw. *(Pausing:)* The real Lonsdale was some guy . . . Babe hooked up with him at a motor court. Then something happened . . .

MITCH: "Something"? You bumped him, didn't you?

MARTIN: No. Nobody *bumped* him. I guess he had a bad heart. He and Babe were fighting, and somehow he just dropped dead. I don't know. It happened.

MITCH: Oh, I love this story. So the two of you dump his body and drive back and forth, all day, waiting for just the right chump to come along who could cash his checks. (MARTIN *nods.*) Why didn't you cash 'em yourself?

MARTIN: Couldn't. *(Demoralized.)* Spastic colon.

MITCH: Boy, where'd she get a hold of *you?*

MARTIN: I'm from Salt Lake. I print Bibles. That part was true. I was in Las Vegas, for the annual convention.

MITCH: When all you Bible printers get together?

MARTIN *(missing the irony):* Exactly. I met Babe. And everything *changed.* My mind must have just . . . I forgot about my wife, about my kids . . . *(Pausing:)* I never meant to hurt anyone! I just—*(He collapses in sobs.)* She told me to wait here. I guess she's not coming back.

(MITCH *tucks the .32 back under his belt.*)

MITCH: Go home, kid. People love to forgive—it gives 'em power. Your wife, sure she bugs you sometimes, they all do, but *they're* the ones who forgive, not women named *Babe.* Women named *Babe,* they eat you for breakfast with a bowl of Wheatina. Go back to Salt Lake. Print Bibles. That's grift enough for you. (MITCH *turns to leave. Halfway out the door, he turns back.)* Hey, kid. One thing. How'd you pull the stunt at the canyon?

MARTIN: The, um, body at the bottom of the Canyon? That was the real Lonsdale. I just dropped to the ground and went under the car. You almost rolled over me when you pulled out.

MITCH: Nice.

(MITCH *goes out the door.*)

EXTERIOR: TWO-LANE BLACKTOP. NIGHT.

This is where we came in. MITCH—*desolate, broke, broken—walking back to* L.A.

MITCH *(voice-over):* There I was, two pockets full of nothing. My wife, *gone.* Fifty grand of what shoulda been my money, *gone.* I had a great future and it was all behind me. *(A car is heading straight toward him.)*

(MITCH *is frozen in the headlights.*

The car doesn't swerve, doesn't veer—in fact, it seems to accelerate.

MITCH *jumps back, diving and rolling in the dry desert dirt. Now the car screeches to a stop.* MITCH *stares at the driver who just tried to run him over. It's* BETTE. *She rolls down the window. Doesn't look at him.)*

BETTE: Did you really have the fifty thousand?

MITCH: Right in my hands.

(She thinks about it, looks at his pitiful battered face, and then:)

BETTE: Get in.

(MITCH looks down at her for a moment and then gets in the car. He sinks down low in the seat beside her.)

MITCH: Take me home, Bette . . . I feel all funny. I think I'm getting a cold.

INTERIOR/EXTERIOR: BETTE'S CAR. MOVING SHOT.

MITCH: I don't know. I don't think I have it in me anymore.

BETTE: Aah, nobody can be smart all the time.

MITCH: When was I *ever* smart?

BETTE: Oh, c'mon. Just think of all the people who want to kill you. Would they want to kill you so bad if you hadn't outsmarted them?

MITCH *(straightens his shoulders a bit):* Well . . .

BETTE: I bet you could steal the socks off a guy with sore feet—without taking off his shoes. *(She puts her arm around him, pulling his head into her shoulder. She holds him there, kissing him on the top of his head.)* Ah, Mitchy. I bet you're the biggest heel in the world.

(MITCH smiles at the compliment.)

EXTERIOR: DESERT. NIGHT.

As the car disappears into the distance, we pan over to a sign: Welcome to Los Angeles County.

MITCH *(voice-over):* You can live your life safe, you can live your life boring, nothing ever happens, then you die. Or you can take some chances. Have some fun. *(Pausing:)* One minute you're so high you've got goosebumps, the next minute you're rolling in the dirt. It can be hard to take. But that's the Mitch Allison way.

(The car zooms onward to the City of Angels.)

Dead-End for Delia

William

Campbell Gault

The only light in the alley came from the high, open windows of the faded dancehall bordering its east length. From these same windows the clean melody of a tenor sax cut through the murky air of the alley. There was nothing else around that was clean.

The warehouse running the west border of the alley was of grimy red brick, the alley itself littered with paper and trash, cans, and bottles. It was a dead-end alley, no longer used.

The beat officer was at its mouth, keeping the small crowd back, and now the police ambulance came from the west, its siren dying in a slow wail.

The beat officer said, "Better swing out and back in. Sergeant Kelley with you?"

"No. Why?" The driver was frowning.

"It's his wife," the beat officer said. "She really got worked over."

"Dead?"

"Just died, two minutes ago. How she lived that long is a wonder."

The driver shook his head, and swung out to back into the mouth of the alley.

From the west again, a red light swung back and forth, and the scream of a high-speed siren pierced the night. The prowl car was making time. It cut over to the wrong side of the street and skidded for fifteen feet before stopping at the curb.

The man opposite the driver had the door open before the car came to rest, and he was approaching the beat patrolman while the driver killed the motor.

"Barnes? I'm Kelley. My wife—?"

"Dead, Sergeant. Two minutes ago."

Sergeant Kelley was a tall man with a thin, lined face and dark brown eyes. He stood there a moment, saying nothing, thinking of Delia, only half hearing the trumpet that was now taking a ride at Dreamland, the Home of Name Bands.

Delia, who was only twenty-three to his thirty-seven, Delia who loved to dance, Delia of the fair hair and sharp tongue—was now dead. And that was her dirge, that trumpet taking a ride.

He shook his head and felt the trembling start in his hands. He took a step toward the other end of the alley, and the patrolman put a hand on his arm.

"Sergeant, I wouldn't. It's nothing to see. Unless you're a Homicide man, it's nothing you'd—Sergeant, don't."

Sergeant Kelley shook off the hand and continued down the alley.

Dick Callender of Homicide was talking to the M.E. He turned at the sound of Kelley's footsteps.

Dick said, "It's nothing to see, Pat."

Pat Kelley didn't answer him. There was enough light from the dancehall for him to see the bloody face of his wife and the matted hair above it. He hadn't seen her for four months.

Then he looked at Callender. "She say anything, Dick?"

"Just—*Tell Pat I'm sorry. Tell Pat Lois will know.* Make sense to you; the second sentence, I mean?"

"None," Pat lied. The band was playing a waltz now.

Callender said, "We'll give it a lot of time. Homicide will shoot the works on this one."

Pat looked at him and used his title, now. "I want a transfer, Lieutenant. To Homicide." His voice was very quiet. "You can fix it."

A piece of dirty newspaper fluttered by, stirred by the night breeze. The white-coated men were laying the stretcher alongside the body.

Callender said, "We've got a lot of good men in Homicide, Pat." He didn't say, *And we want our suspects brought in alive.*

But Pat could guess he was thinking it. He said, "She left me, four months ago. I'm not going to go crazy on it, but I'd like the transfer."

"We'll see, Pat." The lieutenant put a hand on his shoulder. "Come on. I'll ride back to headquarters with you."

They went in the lieutenant's wagon. About halfway there, Pat said, "It could have been one of those—pick-up deals, some mug out of nowhere who'll go back to where he came from." Shame burned in him, but he had to get the words out.

Callender didn't look at him. "I've got Adams and Prokowski checking the dancehall. They're hard workers, good men."

Pat said nothing.

Callender went on, quietly. "There must be some angle you've got on it. Your wife must have thought you knew this—this Lois, or she wouldn't have mentioned it. She didn't have enough words left to waste any of them on some trivial matter."

"My wife knew a lot of people I didn't," Pat said. "My statement will include everything I know, Lieutenant. Have her sent to the Boone Mortuary on Seventh Street, will you? I'll talk to her mother tonight."

"She—was living with her mother, Pat?"

"No. I don't know where she's been living these past four months. But it wasn't with her mother. I wish to God it had been, now."

They made the rest of the trip in silence.

It was a little before midnight when Sergeant Pat Kelley, of the pawn shop and hotel detail, climbed the worn stairs of the four-story building on Vine. The place was quiet; these were working people and they got to bed early.

Mrs. Revolt lived on the third floor, in two rooms overlooking the littered back yard and the parking lot beyond. Pat knocked and waited.

There was the sound of a turning key, and then Mrs. Revolt opened the door. Her lined, weary face was composed, but her eyes quickened in sudden alarm at the sight of Pat.

"Pat, what is it?"

"I'd better come in," he said. "It's Delia, Mrs. Revolt. Something's happened . . ."

She pulled her wrapper tightly around her, as though to stiffen her body against his words. "Come in, come in. But what—? Pat, she's not—it's not—"

He came into the dimly lighted room with the rumpled studio couch, the gate-leg table with the brass lamp, the worn wicker chairs, the faded, dull brown rug. In this room, Delia Revolt had grown from an infant to the beauty of the block. In this room, Papa Revolt had died, and Pat had courted the Revolt miracle.

"Sit down, Mrs. Revolt," Pat said now.

She sat down in the wicker rocker. "She's dead, I know. She's dead. My Delia, oh Lord, she's dead." She rocked, then, back and forth, her eyes closed, her lips moving, no decipherable words coming out.

Pat sat on the wicker lounge. "She was found in an—she was found near the Dreamland dancehall. She's dead. There'll be detectives coming to see you; other detectives, Mrs. Revolt."

Her eyes opened, and she stopped rocking. "Murdered—Delia? It wasn't an accident? Murdered—Delia?"

He nodded. Her eyes closed again, and a strangled sound came from her tight throat, and she toppled sideways in the chair.

Pat got to her before she hit the floor. He put her on the studio couch, and was waiting with a glass of water when her eyes opened again.

Her voice was a whisper. "How did it happen?"

"She was hit with something blunt, concussion. Nobody knows anything else. But there's something I wanted you to know."

Fear in her eyes, now. She said nothing.

"Before she died, Delia mentioned a name. It was Lois. I told the officer in charge the name meant nothing to me. I told him I didn't know any Lois."

The frightened eyes moved around Pat's face. "Why did you say that?"

"Because they're going after this one. She's a cop's wife and they won't be pulling any punches. This man in charge, Callender, can be awful rough. I'd rather talk to Lois, myself."

"But why should they bother Lois?"

"Delia mentioned the name, before she died. They're not going to overlook anything and they're not going to be polite."

"All right, Pat. I had a feeling, when you knocked, something had happened. I've had a feeling about Delia for years. You can go now; I'll be all right. I'll want to be alone."

She was under control, now, this woman who'd met many a tragedy, who'd just met her biggest one. The fortitude born of the countless minor tragedies was carrying her through this one.

Pat went from there to Sycamore. He was off duty, and driving his own car. On Sycamore, near Seventh, he parked in front of an old red-brick apartment building.

In the small lobby, he pressed the button next to the card which read: *Miss Lois Weldon*.

Her voice sounded metallic through the wall speaker. "Who's there?"

"It's Pat, Lois. Something has happened."

He was at the door when it buzzed.

She was waiting in her lighted doorway when he got off the self-service elevator on the fourth floor. She was wearing a maroon flannel robe piped in white, and no make-up. Her dark, soft hair was piled high on her head.

Her voice was quiet. "What's happened?"

"Delia's been murdered."

She flinched and put one hand on the door frame for support. "Pat, when—how—?"

"Tonight. In the alley next to the Dreamland ballroom. Slugged to death. She didn't die right away. She mentioned your name before she died."

"My name? Come in, Pat." Her voice was shaky.

There wasn't much that could be done about the apartment's arrangement, but color and taste had done their best with its appearance. Pat sat on a love seat, near the pseudo-fireplace.

Lois stood. "Now, what did she say?"

Pat frowned. "She said, 'Tell Pat I'm sorry. Tell Pat Lois will know.' She told that to Lieutenant Callender of Homicide, before she died. He asked me who Lois was, and I told him I didn't know."

"Why?"

"I was trying to protect you. It might have been dumb. But they're going to be rough in this case."

She sat down in a chair close by, staring at him. "I saw Delia two days ago, Thursday afternoon. She told me then that she was sorry she'd left you. Could it have been that, Pat?"

"It could have been. Yes, that's probably what she meant. What else did she tell you?"

"N-nothing. She was very vague. She'd—been drinking, Pat."

"Drinking? That's a new one for her. Was she working?"

"I didn't get that impression. She didn't tell me where she was living, either. Do you know?"

Pat shook his head, staring at the floor. The three of them had grown up in the same block on Vine, though they weren't of an age. Delia had been twenty-three, and Lois was—let's see, she was thirty and the fairly well paid secretary to a vice president of a text publishing firm. When Pat was twenty-two and freshly in uniform, he'd been Lois's hero, who'd been fifteen. At thirty-three, in another kind of uniform, U. S. Army, he'd been Delia's hero, and she'd been nineteen.

At the moment, he was an old man, and nobody's hero.

Lois said, "I guess you need a drink." She rose. "Don't try to think tonight, Pat. It won't be any good."

"I was without her for four months," he said, mostly to himself. "I got through that. I don't know about this. I don't seem to have any feelings at all. It's like I'm dead."

Her back was to him. "I know. That's the way I felt four years ago." She poured a stiff jolt of rye in the bottom of a tumbler.

"Four years ago?" He was only half listening.

"When you married her." She had no expression on her face as she walked over to him. Her hand was steady, holding out the drink.

He looked up to meet her gaze. "Lois, what are you—?"

"I just wanted you to know," she said, "and now. I'm glad you didn't tell that officer you knew me. That's a gesture I can hang on to. It will warm me, this winter."

"Lois—" he protested.

"Drink your drink," she said quietly. "Bottoms up."

He stared at her, and at the glass. He lifted it high and drained it. He could feel its warmth, and then he started to tremble.

"You're one of those black Irishmen," Lois said softly, "who can go all to hell over something like this. And wind up in the gutter. Or examine yourself a little better and decide she was a girl headed for doom from the day of her birth and all you really loved was her beauty."

"Stop talking, Lois. You're all worked up. I'd kill anybody else who talked like that, but I know you loved her, too."

"Who didn't love her? She was the most beautiful thing alive. But she was a kid, and she'd never be anything else. Even now you can see that, can't you?"

Pat stared at his empty glass, and rose.

"Thanks for the drink," he said, and walked to the door. There he paused, faced her. "It was probably a silly gesture, covering you. There'll be a million people who can tell them who Lois is. I'm sorry I got you up."

"Pat," she said, but he was through the door.

He caught a glimpse of her as he stepped into the elevator. She was like a statue, both hands on the door frame, watching him wordlessly. . . .

The Chief called him in, next morning. He was a big man and a blunt one. He said, "Callender tells me you want a transfer to Homicide for the time being."

Pat nodded, "Yes, sir."

"How is it you didn't tell Callender about this Lois Weldon last night? A half dozen people have told him about her since."

"I wasn't thinking last night, sir."

The Chief nodded. "You're too close to it, Sergeant. For anybody else, that would be withholding evidence. I'm overlooking it. But I'm denying your request for a temporary transfer to Homicide."

Pat stared at him, saying nothing.

The Chief stared back at him. "You'll want a few days leave."

"Maybe more." He omitted the "sir."

The Chief frowned and looked at his desk top. His eyes came up, again. "I don't like to hammer at you at a time like this. But why *more*? Were you planning to work on this outside of the department?"

Pat nodded.

"If I gave you a direct order not to that would be insubordination, Sergeant."

Pat said nothing.

The Chief said, "Those are my orders."

Pat took out his wallet and unpinned the badge. He laid it on the Chief's desk. "This isn't easy, sir, after fifteen years." He stood up, momentarily realizing what a damn fool speech that had been.

"You're being dramatic," the Chief said evenly. "The thing that makes a good officer is impartiality. Last night you tried to cover a friend. In your present mood, you might go gunning on a half-baked lead and do a lot of damage. This department isn't run that way. But it's your decision, Sergeant." He picked up the badge.

Pat started for the door, and the Chief's voice stopped him. "It would be smart to stay out of Lieutenant Callender's way."

Pat went out without answering. He stood there, in the main hall of headquarters, feeling like a stranger for the first time in fifteen years. It was then he remembered Lois saying, *You're one of those black Irishmen who can go all to hell. . . .*

He wasn't that complicated, whether she knew it or not. His wife had been killed and it was a personal business with him. His job for fifteen years had been to protect the soft from violence and fraud and chicanery, and this time it was closer to home. Only a fool would expect him to continue checking pawn shops; he hadn't thought the Chief was a fool. But then, it wasn't the Chief's wife.

Detective Prokowski came along the hall and stopped at the sight of Pat.

Pat asked, "What did you find out at Dreamland last night, Steve?"

Prokowski licked his lower lip, frowning.

"Orders, Steve?" Pat asked quietly. "From the lieutenant?"

Prokowski didn't answer that. "Did your transfer go through?"

"No. I've left the force. Don't you want to talk about Dreamland? I won't remind you how long we've known each other."

"Keep your voice down," Prokowski said. "I'll see you at Irv's, at one-thirty."

"Sure. Thanks, Steve."

Irv's wasn't a cops' hangout. Prokowski was a Middle Westerner originally, and a perfectionist regarding the proper temperature of draught beer. Irv had it at the proper temperature.

It was a hot day, for fall, and the beer was cool enough to sweat the glass without being cold enough to chill the stomach. Pat drank a couple of glasses, waiting for Steve.

Steve came in at a quarter to two and Irv had a glass waiting for him by the time he reached the bar.

He was a big man, Steve Prokowski, and sweating like a college crew man right now. "Nothing," he said wearily. "Lots of guys danced with her. Nothing there. Shoe clerks and CPAs and punk kids. There was a guy they called Helgy. That name mean anything to you, Pat?"

Pat lied with a shake of the head. "This Helgy something special?"

"Danced with her a lot. Took her home. Brought her a couple of times. The way it is, I guess, if you really *like* to dance there's only one place to do it where you've got the room and the right music. That's a place like Dreamland.

"I mean you can't catalogue a guy because he goes to a public dancehall any more than you can catalogue people because you saw them in Grand Central Station. All kinds of people like to dance. This Helgy drove a smooth car, a convertible. That's nightclub stuff, right? But he liked to dance, and the story is, he really could."

Steve finished his beer and Irv brought another. Steve said casually, "Now, what do you know, Pat?"

"I'm out of a job. I don't know anything beyond that. The Chief acted on Callender's recommendation, I suppose?"

"I don't know. The lieutenant doesn't always confide in me. What can you do alone, Pat?"

"It wasn't my idea to work alone." Pat climbed off his stool and put a dollar on the bar. "Out of that, Irv, all of them." He put a hand on Steve's shoulder. "Thanks for coming in."

"You're welcome. Thanks for the beer. I still work for the department, remember, Pat."

"I didn't forget it for a minute."

He could feel Steve's eyes on him in the mirror as he walked out.

Once at breakfast, Delia had been reading the paper and she'd said, "Well, imagine that!"

"I'll try," he'd said. "Imagine what?"

"This boy I used to dance with at Dreamland, this Joe Helgeson. He's a composer, it says here. He likes to dance, and always has, and he knows very little about music, but he's composed. And he must be rich. Helgy, we always called him."

"You should have married him," Pat told her, "so you could have your breakfast in bed."

"There's always time," she told him. "But right now I'm happy with you."

After that, Pat had been conscious of the name. He saw it on sheet music, and it disturbed him. He heard Delia talk to friends about the composer she knew, Helgy, as though that was her world.

He swung his coupe away from the curb and headed toward the Drive. He knew the building, Delia had pointed it out to him once.

It was about eleven stories high with terrace apartments overlooking the bay. Helgy had one of the terrace apartments.

There was a clerk in the quiet lobby, too, and his glance said Pat should have used the service entrance.

Pat said, "Would you phone Mr. Helgeson and tell him Delia Kelley's husband would like very much to talk to him?"

The clerk studied him for a moment before picking up the phone.

He looked surprised when he said, "Mr. Helgeson will see you, sir."

The elevator went up quickly and quietly, and Pat stepped out onto the lush, sculptured carpeting of the top floor. There was a man waiting for him there, a thin man with blond hair in a crew cut, and alert blue eyes.

"Sergeant Kelley?"

Pat nodded.

"I've—been reading the papers. It's—I really don't know what to say, Sergeant."

"I don't either," Pat said, "except to ask you what you might know about it."

They were walking along the hall, now. They came to the entry hall of the apartment, and Helgeson closed the door behind them. There he faced Pat honestly.

"I've seen her a few times, Sergeant, since she—she left you. There was nothing, well, nothing wrong about it."

"That part doesn't matter," Pat said. "I'm not looking for the men who flirted with her. I'm looking for the man who killed her."

They went into a low, long living room with a beamed ceiling, with floor-length windows facing on the terrace. Helgeson sat in a chair near the huge, bleached mahogany piano.

"I can't help you with that," he said. "I danced with her, at Dreamland. I don't know what attraction the place had for me, except it was the only magic I knew as a kid. I never probed myself for any reasons. She was—a wonderful dancer. I didn't think of her beyond that. That sounds phony, I know, but—" His voice died.

"I'm surprised the Homicide section hasn't sent a man to see you, or have they? You said you'd been reading about it."

"Homicide? No. Why should they?"

"You're pretty well known, and they have your nickname."

"I'm not known down there, not generally. Not as the composer. I'm just another punk, just Helgy, down there. A rather aging punk." He stared at Pat. "But if you know, they know."

Pat shook his head. "I've left the force. I asked to be assigned to this case and was refused."

"Oh," Helgeson rubbed his forehead frowningly. "She told me, when she phoned to break a date yesterday, that she was going back to you. I thought—"

"Yesterday?" Pat interrupted. "She told you *that*, yesterday?"

Helgeson nodded, studying Pat quietly.

Pat could see the pulse in his wrist and he had a passing moment of giddiness. "Where was she living?"

"The Empire Court, over on Hudson."

"Working, was she?"

"I don't think so. She never mentioned it, if she was. She was kind of reticent about all that."

Pat looked at Helgeson levelly. "Was she—living alone?"

Helgeson took a deep breath. "I don't know. I never went in, over there. She was always ready when I called for her." He seemed pale and his voice was unsteady.

Pat felt resentment moving through him, but he couldn't hate them all. Everybody had loved Delia.

He said quietly, "There's nothing you know? She must have mentioned some names, or what she was doing. What the hell did you talk about?"

"We didn't talk much. We danced, that's all. Sergeant, believe me, if I could help I would." His voice was ragged. "If you knew how much I—wanted to help." He shook his head. "There isn't anything I know, not a damned thing."

"All right. I can believe that. If there's anything you hear or happen to remember, *anything at all,* phone me." He gave him the number.

He went from there to the Empire Court, on Hudson. It was a fairly modern, U-shaped building of gray stone, set back on a deep lot. There was a department car among the cars at the curb.

The name in the lobby read: *Delia Revolt.* Pat pressed the button and the door buzzed.

It was on the second floor and he walked up. There were some technical men dusting for prints, and there was Lieutenant Callender, his back to the doorway, standing in the middle of the living room.

He turned and saw Pat. His face showed nothing.

"Anything?" Pat asked him.

"Look, Pat, for the love of—"

"You look," Pat said. "She was my wife. You got a wife, Lieutenant?"

"I'm married to my second, now." He shook his big head and ran a hand through his hair. "The Chief said you'd resigned."

"That's right."

"You've been a cop for fifteen years. You're acting like a rookie."

"I've only been a husband for four years, Lieutenant. I'm not getting in your way."

"We'll probably get a million prints, all but the right ones. We found a dressing robe we're checking, and some pajamas." The lieutenant's eyes looked away. "I'll talk to the Chief, Pat. I'll see that you get your job back."

"I don't want it back—yet. Thanks, anyway, Lieutenant." He kept seeing Delia in the room and somebody else, some formless, faceless somebody, and the giddiness came again and he knew he wouldn't have the stomach to look in any of the other rooms.

He turned his back on the lieutenant and went down the steps to the lobby and out into the hot, bright day. They were right about it, of course. A cop shouldn't be on a family case any more than a surgeon should. Emotion was no asset in this business.

He sat in the car for minutes, trying to get back to reality, trying to forget that cozy apartment and the lieutenant's words. The brightness of the day seemed to put a sharp outline on things, to give them a sense of unreality, like a lighted stage setting.

He heard last night's trumpet again, and started the motor.

The alley was bright, now, but no cleaner. The voices of the freight handlers on the street side of the warehouse were drowned by the racket of the huge trucks bumping past. He walked to the alley's dead end and saw, for the first time, the door that led from the dance-hall, a fire exit.

It was open, now, and he could see some men in there, sprinkling the floor with some granulated stuff. There was the sound of a huge rotary brush polisher, but it was outside his line of vision.

He went in through the open door, along a wide hall that flanked the west edge of the bandstand. The men looked at him curiously as he stood there, imagining what it must have been like last night. He could almost hear the music and see the dim lights and the crowded floor.

Along this edge the floor was raised and there were seats up here, for the speculative males, looking over the field, discussing the old favorites and the new finds, wondering what happened to this transient queen and that one. Some had married and not retired.

One of the workers called over, "Looking for the boss, mister?"

"That's right."

"Won't be in this afternoon. The joint's been full of cops and he went out to get some fresh air."

"Okay." Pat turned and went out.

It was nearly five now. He turned the car in a U-turn and headed for Borden. He parked on a lot near Borden and Sixth, and walked the two blocks to Curtes-Husted, Publishers.

Lois was busily typing when he opened the door to the outer office. She looked up at his entrance, and her face seemed to come alive suddenly.

"Pat!" She got up and came over to the railing.

"I was pretty rough last night. I thought a drink and dinner might take us back to where we were. Part way, anyway."

"It will, it will. Oh, Pat, if you knew what last night—" She put a hand on his on top of the railing.

The door to Pat's right opened, and a man stood there. He had a masculine, virile face and iron-gray hair. He said, "You can go any time, Lois. I guess Mr. Curtes won't be back."

"Thank you, Mr. Husted," she said. "I'll be going in a minute."

He smiled, and closed the door.

"My boss, the VP," she whispered. "Isn't he handsome?"

"I suppose." Pat could feel her hand trembling.

She said quietly, "You're better, aren't you? You're coming out of it."

"I'm better," he said. "This whole case is one blind alley."

"Delia knew a lot of men—of people. I'll be with you in a minute."

They went to the Lamp Post, an unpretentious restaurant nearby.

They had a martini each, and Lois told him, "Their spare ribs are the best in town."

He ordered the spare ribs.

She seemed animated. She said, "It's going to be all right. It's going to take some time, and then you're going to be really happy, Pat. I'm going to see that you're happy."

He ordered another pair of drinks, and they finished those before the ribs came. They went from the Lamp Post to a spot on the west side, and Pat tried very hard to get drunk. But it didn't work; the alcohol didn't touch him.

They went back to Lois's place. He sat with her in the car in front of her apartment.

"Come on up," she said. "I'll make some coffee."

He shook his head. "I know Husted was paying for that apartment Delia was living in. I've known it for two months, Lois. And you did, too, didn't you?"

Her silence was his answer.

"You probably thought Husted killed her, and yet you've told the police nothing. Delia probably told you yesterday or the day before that she was coming back to me. But you didn't tell me that. Was it yesterday you saw her?"

"The day before. I didn't want her to come back, Pat. And I didn't tell you about my boss because he's got a family, because he's a fundamentally decent man."

"You didn't want her to come back. Because of me?" Pat's voice was hoarse. "You poor damned fool, you don't know me, do you? No matter what she was, Lois, I'll be married to her the rest of my life. But you were the one who could have told me she was coming back. You could have saved her life."

"Pat—"

"Get out, Lois. Get out—quick!"

She scrambled out.

The liquor was getting to him a little now. He finished the note, there on his dinette table, and then went to unlock the front door. Then he called headquarters, gave them the message, and went to pick up the note. He read:

Lieutenant Callender:
        I wanted to work with Homicide because I thought
it would be safer that way. I could see how close you boys
were getting. But it doesn't matter now, because I've no
desire to escape you. I killed my wife with a wrecking bar
which you'll find in the luggage deck of my car. I couldn't
stand the thought of her loving anyone else and I wasn't
man enough to rid myself of her. The checking I've done
today reveals to me I would probably have escaped
detection. I make this confession of my own free will.
                                Sergeant Patrick Kelley

He waited then, .38 in hand. He waited until he heard the wail of the siren, and a little longer. He waited until he heard the tires screeching outside.

Then he put the muzzle of his .38 to the soft roof of his mouth, and pulled the trigger.

Dead-End for Delia

Teleplay by

Scott Frank

Cast

Gary Oldman	Pat Kelley
Meg Tilly	Lois Weldon
Gabrielle Anwar	Delia
Paul Guilfoyle	Steve Prokowski
Vondie Curtis Hall	David O'Connor
Dan Hedaya	Lt. Calender
Wayne Knight	Leo Cunningham
Patrick Massett	Joe Helgeson
John Putch	Officer Barnes

Executive Producer: Sydney Pollack
Producers: William Horberg, Lindsay Doran, Steve Golin
Co-Producer: David Wisnievitz
Directed by: Phil Joanou
Director of Photography: Declan Quinn
Production designed by: Armin Ganz
Costumes designed by: Shay Cunliffe
Casting by: Owens Hill and Rachel Abroms
Fallen Angels theme by: Elmer Bernstein
Music by: Peter Bernstein
Edited by: Stan Salfas
Story Editor: Geoffrey Stier

BLACK. EXTERIOR: ALLEYWAY. NIGHT.

A tenor sax cuts through the humdrum noises of the city. A siren wails, getting closer as we then:

Fade In: Close-Up of DELIA KELLEY.

Perfection. Twenty-three years of beautiful, staring right at us with alluring, dark eyes. A half-smile . . .

The camera rotates and pulls back and we see that DELIA *is actually lying on her side. A bit of trash blows past her face. The siren gets louder.*

Continuing to pull back, we see that DELIA *is actually dead, lying in the middle of a dead-end alleyway, the only light coming from the open windows of the old dancehall bordering one side.*

It's from these high windows that the clean sound of the tenor sax floats through the murky air of the alley. Nothing else is clean.

JACK CALENDER, *the Homicide man, stands a few steps from the corpse, talking with his partner,* STEVE PROKOWSKI. *The siren gets louder and* CALENDER *looks to:*

THE MOUTH OF THE ALLEY.

An OFFICER *keeps a small crowd back as a police ambulance pulls up, its siren dying in a slow wail. The* OFFICER *walks to the driver's side.*

OFFICER: It's a dead end. Better swing out and back in. *(Then:)* Sergeant Kelley with you?

DRIVER: No. Why?

OFFICER: It's his wife. Someone really knocked her into next week. Cracked her head open like a coconut. I was walkin' my beat, almost tripped over her.

(The DRIVER *shakes his head, then swings out and backs into the alley. We hear the scream of another siren as a prowl car cuts across traffic to the wrong side of the street and pulls into the mouth of the alley.*

A big man, SERGEANT PAT KELLEY, *gets out before the cop at the wheel has even stopped the car. He crosses to the patrolman in a few quick strides.)*

PAT: Barnes. I'm Kelley. My wife?

OFFICER: Dead, Sergeant. Just now.

*(*PAT, *thirty-seven, stands there a moment staring into the alley, only half hearing the trumpet that now takes a ride at Dreamland. He looks up at the windows, below which an old, painted sign on the wall reads* Dreamland, the Home of Name Bands.

He takes a step towards the other end of the alley. The OFFICER *puts a hand on his arm.)*

OFFICER: Sergeant, I wouldn't. It's nothing to see. Unless you're a Homicide man. It's nothing you'd wanna—

*(*PAT *shakes off the hand and continues down the alley.* CALENDER *steps in front of the body as he approaches.)*

CALENDER: Pat. Maybe you shouldn't . . .

(There's enough light from the dancehall for PAT *to see her blood-matted hair, and the now-big puddle of red goo behind her head.)*

PAT: Delia. Jesus.

PROKOWSKI: I'm sorry, Pat.

(PAT *looks at* CALENDER *and* PROKOWSKI, *just now noticing them.*)

CALENDER: We'll give it a lot of time, Pat. We'll shoot the works on this one.

(PAT *just nods, and turns to go.*)

CALENDER: She said some things, Pat. (PAT *pauses, looks back at* CAL-ENDER.) Right before she died.

(*Beat.*)

PAT: What . . . things?

CALENDER: She said, "Tell Pat I'm sorry. Tell Pat Lois will know." Make sense to you? The second sentence, I mean.

PAT: None.

(PAT *watches as two white-coated men load the body onto the stretcher. A piece of dirty newspaper flutters by, stirred by the night breeze. It gets caught on Delia's face a moment and we see the headline, "Stan the Man and His Magic Bat Smack #20 for the Season!"*

One of the men pulls the paper away, cuts an uncomfortable look at PAT.)

CALENDER: Come on, I'll give you a lift back to the station.

INTERIOR: CALENDER'S CAR. NIGHT.

CALENDER *drives.* PAT *stares out the window.*

PAT: I want a transfer, Lieutenant. You can fix it.

CALENDER: We've got a lot of good men in Homicide, Pat. We want him as bad as you do.

PAT: You mean, you want him *alive.* (*Turns to* CALENDER.) She left me four months ago. I went through what I had to back then. I'm sayin', I'm not gonna go crazy on you.

CALENDER: We'll see. The meantime, I've got Prokowski checking the dancehall.

PAT: Prokowski could't find his ass with both hands.

CALENDER (*looking over at him*): There must be some angle you've got on this. Your wife must've thought you knew this Lois or she wouldn't've mentioned it. I mean, she just didn't have enough words to waste on something like that.

PAT: My wife knew a lot of people I didn't.

INTERIOR: APARTMENT BUILDING HALLWAY. NIGHT.

PAT *is knocking on a door.*

LOIS *(voice-over):* All right already, I'm coming.

(An attractive woman, fresh out of the shower, a towel still around her, opens the door. Her face lights up.)

PAT: Hello, Lois.

LOIS: Pat. What a surprise . . . *(She widens the door a bit so he can see a little better, and takes a healthy sip from a highball glass.)* What an absolutely swell surprise. *(She studies him and the light goes out.)* What's wrong?

INTERIOR: LOIS'S APARTMENT. NIGHT.

A working-woman's studio. She's done the most with what she has. LOIS *sets her drink down on the counter, which she leans against for support.*

LOIS: Dead . . . I just can't believe it . . .

PAT: When was the last time you saw her?

LOIS: Two days ago.

PAT: She mentioned your name before she died.

LOIS: My name? What'd she say?

*(*PAT *sits in the love seat near the pseudo-fireplace.)*

PAT: She said, "Tell Pat I'm sorry. Tell Pat Lois will know."

LOIS: I'll know *what?* *(*PAT *studies her face for a reaction. She just shrugs.)* I don't know what she meant by that.

PAT: Lieutenant Calender, the Homicide man, asked if I knew who Lois was. I told him I didn't.

LOIS: Why would you do that?

PAT: I was trying to protect you.

LOIS: From what? *(He doesn't say. She looks at him, sighs, and crosses to an oriental screen.)* Pat, I told you. I don't know what Delia meant. And for the record, I've been at work since four this afternoon. I can't believe you'd even—

PAT: When I saw you yesterday, you didn't mention anything about seeing Delia the day before.

LOIS *(caught):* I guess I forgot.

PAT: In fact, I even asked you if you'd seen her recently and you said no.

LOIS: I don't always tell you every time I see her. *(Beat.)* You know how you get.

(We see through the screen as she lets the slip fall from her body. She cuts a look at PAT, making sure he's watching.)

PAT: She seeing anyone? *(No answer.)* She was, wasn't she?

(She moves against the screen and peers at him over the top.)

LOIS: Look, I don't know any names, Pat, but I know one guy was a doctor.

PAT: A doctor?

LOIS: That's what she said. Said he specialized in feet or something.

PAT: Feet?

(She pulls a dress over her head.)

LOIS: You know how she is. Never gives you a straight answer. *(Realizes her mistake.)* I mean, how she *was*.

PAT: Was she working?

LOIS: No. She didn't say where she was living either.

(LOIS comes out from behind the screen, a knock-out in a black dress. PAT swallows, forgets to blink.)

LOIS: What do you think? I bought it for Betty's tonight. *(Pause.)* Zip me up?

(She comes over to him. The zipper's on the side of the dress. She doesn't need any help. PAT looks at her a moment, then zips her up. She smiles at him.)

LOIS: I guess you need a drink.

(*He watches as she walks to a liquor cabinet.*)

LOIS: Don't try to think tonight, Pat. It won't do you any good.

PAT: That's just it, I don't seem to have any feelings at all. It's like I'm dead.

(*Her back is to him as she pours them each a drink.*)

LOIS (*after a momentary pause*): I know. That's the way I felt four years ago.

PAT: Four years ago?

LOIS: When you married her. (*No expression on her face, she walks back over and hands him his drink. Her hand is perfectly steady.*) Bottoms up.

(*She sits down on the arm of the love seat, keeping an eye on him as they drink.*)

PAT: What?

(*She leans close, moving in on him.*)

LOIS: You're one of those black Irishmen who can go all to hell over something like this. And wind up in the gutter. Or you can examine yourself a little better and decide she was a girl headed for doom from the day of her birth and all you really loved was her beauty.

(*Her face is just inches from his now; she leans still closer. He gets up.*)

PAT: Shut up, Lois—you're all worked up. I'd kill anybody else who talked like that, but I know you loved her, too.

(*She gets up and follows him—pins him against the liquor cabinet.*)

LOIS: Who didn't love her? She was the most beautiful thing alive. But she was a tramp and she'd never be anything else. Even now you can see that, can't you?

(*She's right in front of him. He looks at her a moment, then slips around her and moves to the door.*)

PAT: That was probably a dumb move, covering for you. There'll be a million people who can tell them you two were friends.

LOIS: That's okay. I'm glad you did it. It's a gesture I can hang on to. It will warm me this winter.

(He pauses near the door and gives her a look.)

PAT: Thanks for the drink.

INTERIOR: HALLWAY. NIGHT.

As PAT *steps out into the hallway, he shuts the door behind him. He stares at Lois's door a moment.*

DELIA *(voice-over):* I don't drink . . .

INTERIOR: DREAMLAND DANCEHALL. NIGHT.

PAT *stands with a decked-out* DELIA *at the bar. Couples are dancing all around them.*

DELIA: I don't trust myself.

PAT: You come here just to dance?

DELIA: "Just to dance"? That's like saying I go to church just to pray.

PAT: You go to church? *(She looks at him: he's serious.* PAT *grips the bar, unable to look away. He extends his hand.)* Pat Kelley.

DELIA: Uh-oh. *Irish. (He doesn't know what to say. She helps him out.)* Guess *my* name.

(He keeps looking at her. She sips from a soda. He finally shrugs.)

DELIA: You must know a *few* girls' names.

PAT: None good enough.

(She looks at him and sees that PAT *is actually sincere. This catches her off guard. She's about to speak when* LOIS—*younger, all dolled-up, and bored—pushes through the crowd.)*

LOIS: Come on Delia, let's get out of here.

*(*DELIA *looks at* PAT *and smiles: the game's over.* LOIS *notices* PAT *now, smiles at him, elbows* DELIA.*)*

DELIA: Pat, Lois. Lois, Pat.

(But PAT *stares at* DELIA.*)*

INTERIOR: HALLWAY. NIGHT.

PAT *stands there, shaking.*

PAT *(whispering):* Delia.

(He hurries down the hallway.)

INTERIOR: POLICE DEPARTMENT. CORRIDOR. DAY.

PAT *stops* DETECTIVE PROKOWSKI, *one of the Homicide men in the alley the other night.*

PAT: What'd you find out at Dreamland last night, Steve?

(Beat.)

PROKOWSKI: I can't find my ass with both hands?

PAT: Come on, Steve. We've known each other a long time. You know how I get.

PROKOWSKI: Yeah, well *I* would never say somethin' like that about *you.* *(He sighs, looks around.)* Your transfer go through?

PAT: I quit.

PROKOWSKI: You *what?*

PAT: Just now. The chief won't let me work homicide.

PROKOWSKI: Fifteen years . . . just like that? I can't believe you'd do that.

PAT: Yeah, I know, I'll miss you, too, but we can cry about it later. Right now I wanna hear about Dreamland.

*(*PROKOWSKI *looks around nervously.)*

PROKOWSKI: Why didn't you tell Calender about Lois Weldon last night? Least a half dozen people have told him about her since.

PAT: I wasn't thinking last night.

PROKOWSKI: That's withholding evidence.

PAT: I need to know about Dreamland.

*(*PROKOWSKI *sighs, studies* PAT *a moment.)*

PROKOWSKI: Man, I don't know, Pat. That look on your face, I've seen it before. Somebody's liable to end up dead.

PAT: Somebody already has. *(Softens.)* Please. She was my wife.

(PROKOWSKI *eyes* PAT *a moment, then takes* PAT *aside.)*

PROKOWSKI: There's nothing to tell. She went there all the time. Lots of guys danced with her. Nothing there. Just coloreds, zoot suiters, and rich kids lookin' to score a little reefer. There was a guy called Helgy. That name mean anything to you, Pat?

PAT *(shakes his head):* This Helgy something special?

PROKOWSKI: I don't know. He brought her a couple of times. Real smooth guy. Drives a red convertible.

PAT: Anything else?

PROKOWSKI: Story is, he can really dance.

PAT: I meant, forensic-wise.

PROKOWSKI: Oh. Just that the coroner says she was most likely hit with something metal, like a pipe or a crowbar.

PAT: I owe you one. *(He starts off down the corridor.)*

PROKOWSKI: Pat? *(PAT pauses, turns back to PROKOWSKI.)* I know what she was to you, but man . . . Don't quit.

(PAT *considers his friend—then turns and walks off.)*

INTERIOR: PAT'S CAR. DAY.

PAT *gets in, but doesn't start the car. He sits there a moment, staring out the windshield.*

DELIA *(voice-over):* Well, imagine that . . .

INTERIOR: PAT'S APARTMENT. MORNING.

Bright sunshine streams onto the breakfast table. PAT *sits there drinking a cup of coffee.*

PAT: I'll try. Imagine what?

(DELIA *lowers the newspaper to reveal her smiling, ever-beautiful face.)*

DELIA: This boy I used to dance with at Dreamland. Joe Helgeson. Says here he's a composer. Says he likes to dance and always has. He knows very little about music, but he's composed. *(She folds up the paper and takes a bite of Pat's toast.)* He must be rich. Helgy, we always called him.

PAT: You should have married him. So you could have your breakfast in bed.

DELIA: There's always time. But for now I'm happy having breakfast right here *(takes a sip of Pat's coffee)* with you.

(DELIA looks over at the radio as we hear the opening bars of "I Can't Get Started." She smiles, gently pulls PAT to his feet, and starts dancing with him right there in the kitchen.)

PAT: I got two left feet.

DELIA: No. You dance swell.

(She rests her head on his shoulder as they keep on dancing. The music gets louder as we cut to:)

INTERIOR: A RECORDING STUDIO. DAY.

A large piano sits in the center of the room. A group of musicians are jamming as PAT enters. They stop.

PAT: I'm looking for Joe Helgeson.

HELGESON *(voice-over):* Sergeant Kelley?

(JOE HELGESON, a thin man with blond hair in a crew cut, stands up at the piano. PAT moves to him.)

HELGESON: I've been reading the papers. It's—I really don't know what to say, Sergeant.

PAT: You can start with telling me what you know about it.

HELGESON: I don't know anything about it. *(Adds quickly:)* I mean, yes, I've seen her a few times since she, she left you. There was nothing, well, nothing wrong about it. I used to dance with her at Dreamland. I was there the day Dave O'Connor first opened the doors. So was Delia. She was a wonderful dancer. She was . . .

(HELGESON cuts a look at the musicians, sits down at the piano.)

PAT: When was the last time you saw her?

HELGESON: Two nights ago. We were supposed to go out last night, but she broke our date.

PAT: She say why?

HELGESON: She said she couldn't keep on going the way she had been. She said she was ready to settle down. She said she was in love with someone.

(PAT *turns away, watches as the back-up guys begin to jam a little bit.*)

PAT: This "someone" have a name?

HELGESON: I didn't ask. Tell you the truth, I didn't want to know.

PAT: Where was she living?

HELGESON: The Empire Court over on Hudson.

PAT: Nice place. She live alone?

HELGESON: I don't know. We hardly spoke. We danced, that's all. Sergeant, believe me, if I could help I would.

(PAT *nods, puts a cigarette in his mouth.*)

PAT: One last question. (*He lights up.*) What'd you do last night? After Delia broke your date, after she told you she was in love with someone else?

HELGESON: I was here all night, composing.

PAT: Alone, I take it?

HELGESON: That's right. Sergeant, you don't think I—My God I couldn't. I—I just couldn't.

(*His hands are shaking as he stares at the keyboard.* PAT *studies him a moment, then starts for the door.*)

PAT: It's okay, Helgy. (*Looks back at him.*) Everybody loved Delia.

EXTERIOR: EMPIRE COURT APARTMENTS. DAY.

A U-shaped building in a nice neighborhood. PAT *walks to the entrance.*

INTERIOR: DELIA'S APARTMENT. DAY.

The place is full of policemen. PROKOWSKI *goes through drawers; lab guys dust for prints.* LT. CALENDER, *going through a closet, looks up when* PAT *walks in.*

CALENDER: I hear you quit.

PAT: You got a wife, Lieutenant?

CALENDER: I'm on my second. *(Looks away from the closet.)* What the hell were you thinking? You were a cop for fifteen years.

PAT: Yeah, well, I was only a husband for four.

*(*PAT *stares into the closet where a man's black silk robe now hangs.* PAT *pulls the robe out, runs his hand over where the letters* DOC *have been sewn onto the pocket.)*

PAT: Doc.

CALENDER: Mean anything to you?

PAT: No, but I'd lay odds he was the one payin' for this place.

CALENDER *(nods, looks around):* Nice digs. That's for sure.

LANDLORD *(voice-over):* And I expect it to stay that way.

(They look over as a fat man in a double-breasted suit enters the apartment.)

CALENDER: Who the hell are you?

LANDLORD: I the hell am the owner of this apartment; of this whole building, for that matter. As well as the one next door.

CALENDER: Well, good for you, Mr . . . ?

LANDLORD: Cunningham. Leo Cunningham.

PAT: Can you tell us who was paying the rent, Mr. Cunningham?

*(*CALENDER *gives* PAT *a look that clearly says: stay out of this.)*

LANDLORD: The renter's name is on the mailbox downstairs. If you cops can't read it, I'd be happy to get my four-year-old daughter to read it for you.

PAT: I got a better idea: Why don't you have your four-year-old call an ambulance.

LANDLORD: What for?

PAT: To come scrape your fat ass off the sidewalk after I throw it out that fuckin' window.

(PAT *grabs the guy and runs him across the room. He rams the Landlord's head through the glass window. The man screams. The other cops hurry over but* CALENDER *stops them.*)

PAT: Who paid for the apartment?

LANDLORD: I don't know.

(*Terrified, the* LANDLORD *stares down the three stories at the street.* PAT *grabs him by the belt, pushes him out a little farther.*)

PAT: *Who paid for the apartment?*

LANDLORD: All I know is, Miss Revolt always paid in cash, and always put the bills in the same kind of envelope . . .

(PAT *pulls the guy back inside.*)

PAT: What kind of envelope?

LANDLORD: They all had the name *Dreamland* printed on them.

(*The* LANDLORD *jerks away from* PAT, *touches a cut on his forehead, looks over at* CALENDER, *sees that he and the other cops are just standing there, bemused.*)

LANDLORD (*to* CALENDER): Jesus Christ, you just gonna stand there, let him get away with that?

CALENDER (*shrugs*): He quit.

(PAT *pushes the guy away from him. The* LANDLORD *brushes himself off, and goes and stands near* CALENDER.)

LANDLORD: You're gonna pay for that window. In fact, I want this whole place in the exact condition in which you found it.

CALENDER: We found it a mess.

(*The* LANDLORD *gives* CALENDER *a look, and gets the hell out of there.*)

PAT: You hear what he said? About Dreamland?

CALENDER: Yeah, I heard it. *(Lights a cigarette.)* I gotta be honest with you, Pat. The more time I spend on this one, the more I see it as a pick-up deal. A one-night stand. Guy's probably blown the state by now.

(PAT looks at the Lieutenant. PROKOWSKI takes a step away from the window, knowing what's coming.)

PAT: You saying some guy picked her up?

CALENDER: Come on, Pat. Girl like her. The way she was. Hell, I don't have to tell *you*, you were married to her, for chrissake—

PROKOWSKI: Pat, no—

(PAT throws a straight punch to Calender's face. The cop drops to the floor, taking out a coffee table and a floor lamp. CALENDER sits up, touches his jaw.)

CALENDER: Arrest that bastard!

(As one of the uniforms makes a move for PAT, he hits him once in the chin, shoves him into PROKOWSKI, and takes off out of there.)

EXTERIOR: ALLEY BEHIND DREAMLAND. DAY.

The same trash-laden alley as in the opening. PAT steps into frame, pausing to consider the spot where he saw DELIA lying the other night.

He looks up at the row of windows, flicks away his cigarette and enters Dreamland through the fire exit.

INTERIOR: DREAMLAND. DAY.

PAT steps inside, remains in the doorway, staring at the dance floor. He watches DELIA dancing with HELGY without music.

PAT takes a step closer and we see that he's really watching a JANITOR as he buffs the dance floor with a polisher. He looks up as PAT walks to the bandstand and stares at it.

JANITOR *(voice-over):* I help you with somethin', mister?

(PAT looks over at the JANITOR, now leaning against the polisher.)

PAT: Boss around?

JANITOR *(voice-over):* Upstairs. Takin' a break from all you cops.

(PAT *moves to the staircase.*)

INTERIOR: OWNER'S OFFICE. DAY.

(*Dancing-feet wallpaper.* O'CONNOR, *a handsome black man in his thirties, is just about to begin humping a lovely topless woman on his desk when Pat bursts inside.*)

O'CONNOR: Hey—

PAT (*takes it in, smiles*): What's up—Doc?

O'CONNOR: Who the fuck are you? Get the hell outta here!

PAT (*doesn't budge, lights a cigarette*): I'm Pat Kelley, Delia's husband.

(O'CONNOR *reacts.* PAT *tosses the woman her blouse.*)

PAT: Get some air, sister.

(*The woman looks at* O'CONNOR. *He nods; she grabs the blouse and hurries out of there.* O'CONNOR *takes a silver flask from his desk and takes a long drink.*)

O'CONNOR: Nobody's called me *Doc* since the service.

PAT: Nobody, except Delia.

(O'CONNOR *looks at* PAT, *takes another long drink.*)

O'CONNOR: Everybody thinks I got the nickname *Doc* after my initials—D, O, C—but it was because I used to help guys in my unit, you know, teach 'em how to dance whenever they had a hot date. They started callin' me "Doctor Feet." Been a while . . . (*Takes another drink.*) Whatta you want? Take a swing at me or something? Go ahead.

PAT: You saw Delia yesterday, didn't you?

O'CONNOR (*looks away*): I said all I had to say to the cops.

PAT: So you're the mystery man.

(O'CONNOR *looks at him, confused now.*)

PAT: Funny, I pictured somebody . . . younger.

O'CONNOR: Mystery man—what the hell you talkin' about?

PAT: Delia was in love. Friend of hers tells me she was even talkin' about settling down. Seems the last time this friend saw her, she was on her way to see the guy. That was last night.

O'CONNOR: Man, I think you got things a little mixed up. Yeah, I saw Delia last night, right before it happened. But she didn't come to tell me she loved me, she came to tell me *good-bye.*

(This catches PAT *off guard.* O'CONNOR *shrugs.)*

O'CONNOR: I knew it wasn't gonna be forever. Delia loved my bread, not me. She even said so to my face. She said she wanted to "move up" and that I was gonna help her. Now it ain't often I let a lady take a ride like that, but Delia . . . man, she had *that much* . . . *(His smile fades.)* Then last night, she comes in here and tells me she's been wrong the past four months. That she doesn't care about movin' up or money or any of that no more. She said the right man was there and she wasn't gonna let him go.

PAT: Sounds like a real romance. She say who this guy was?

*(*O'CONNOR *looks at* PAT *a moment.)*

O'CONNOR: You mean you really don't know?

PAT: The hell you think I'm doing here?

(Beat.)

O'CONNOR: Man, it was you. She said she was going back to *you.*

PAT: What—

O'CONNOR: She said she'd made a big mistake by leaving you. That she loved you and wanted to give it a try again. If you would still have her.

PAT: She told you *that? Yesterday?*

O'CONNOR: Yes. Right before . . . it happened. *(*PAT *sits up straight and looks around the room, dazed.* O'CONNOR *tosses him the flask.)* Here. You look like you could use a little. *(Then:)* She came up here around seven. Band started playing and all of a sudden she lights up, says she wants to have one last dance. So we stand up and—

*(*PAT *isn't listening anymore. He gets to his feet, almost falling over.)*

O'CONNOR: Kelley? You okay?

(PAT *hangs on to the flask and walks out the door.*)

EXTERIOR: ALLEYWAY. DAY.

As PAT *stumbles out the fire exit, he tosses the flask aside and leans against the wall for support.*

PAT: Oh, God . . . (*He falls to his knees on the spot where* DELIA *was lying the night before and cries out . . .*) Delia!

(*His voice booms and echoes.*)

INTERIOR: DINER. NIGHT.

A *busy downtown grease spot.* LOIS *comes out of the kitchen balancing a couple of blue-plate specials.* PAT *steps over and grabs her by the arm. He doesn't look so good.*

LOIS: Pat.

PAT: We have to talk.

LOIS (*sees that he's in a state*): Okay. Just let me drop these—

PAT: *Now.*

(PAT *drags her back into the kitchen.* LOIS *sets the plates down on a metal counter.*)

PAT: What'd Delia tell you, Lois?

LOIS: Pat—you're hurting me.

PAT: What'd she tell you?

LOIS: I don't know what you're talking about.

(LOIS *tries to pull her arm free, but he holds on.*)

PAT: She told you she was coming back to me, didn't she? (*Shakes her.*) Didn't she? (*Then, gently:*) Am I right? Was it yesterday that you saw her?

LOIS (*crying*): She didn't say anything—

PAT: Come on, you were her best friend, Lois. And Delia's last words were, "Tell Pat Lois will know."

(LOIS's BOSS *sticks his head in the door.*)

BOSS: Girlie, let's go! I'm buried out here! *(Sees* PAT.*)* Hey, who the hell are—

PAT *(pulls his gun, kicks the door closed):* She's busy.

   (The DISHWASHER *looks over as* PAT *holds the door closed with his foot and grabs* LOIS.*)*

LOIS: I didn't want her to come back.

PAT: Why? Because of me? *(He releases her, pushing her away.)* Don't you get it, Lois? Don't you understand? No matter what she was, I'll always love her. *She's dead* and I'm still married to her.

BOSS *(through the window in the door):* I'm callin' the cops!

PAT: When I saw you yesterday, you could have told me she was coming back. *(Beat.)* You could have saved her life.

LOIS: What're you talking about? How? Pat, please. I just wanted— *(She takes a step toward him.)*

PAT: Get away from me—

   (He shoves her hard, and she stumbles backwards onto a pile of pots and pans. PAT *gives her an icy look, and walks out.)*

   EXTERIOR: POLICE STATION. NIGHT.

   The COP *from the opening scene looks on as* PAT *screeches his car to a stop out front. As he opens the front door, an empty bottle tumbles out of the car and shatters on the pavement. He pulls a package bundled in newspaper from the front seat.*

PAT: Evening, Barnes.

COP *(nervous):* Sergeant Kelley.

PAT: Calender in?

COP: He's uh, out looking for *you.*

   (The two men stand considering each other in the dark a moment. The COP *inches his hand toward the butt of his gun.)*

PAT: You pull it, kid, you're gonna have to use it. Sure you wanna do that? *(Before the* COP *can decide,* PAT *shoves the package at him, and the* COP *grabs it on reflex.* PAT *smiles.)* Give this to Calender when he gets back. *(The* Cop *stares at the package.* Pat *claps the guy on the shoulder.)* Don't worry, Barnes, it ain't ticking.

EXTERIOR: PAT'S APARTMENT. NIGHT.

Pat *gets out of the car and stumbles up the walk.*

INTERIOR: PAT'S APARTMENT. NIGHT.

Sad. Spare. Now lacking Delia's touch. Pat *enters and walks to the kitchen. He walks to a cupboard and takes down a bottle of bourbon and takes a long pull.*

INTERIOR: CALENDER'S OFFICE. NIGHT.

Calender *enters and takes off his jacket. He walks to his desk and is about to sit down when he notices the package on his chair.*

We hear a loud, metallic CLUNK as Calender *drops the newspaper bundle onto the desk. He eyes it a beat, then begins unwrapping it.*

As he rips it open, we begin to see that some of the inside layers are stained with blood.

Calender *finishes unwrapping the newspaper, stares a moment at what's inside. He then slowly lifts a black crowbar into frame. It's caked with dried blood and matted hair.*

He sets the crowbar down and then rifles through the newspaper until he finds what he's looking for.

An envelope. He opens it, his eyes widening as he reads it. He grabs his coat.

Calender: *Steve!*

INTERIOR: PAT'S APARTMENT. NIGHT.

Pat *walks to the phonograph and puts on a record. We hear the first few bars of "I Can't Get Started." He stands there a moment, listening.*

EXTERIOR: EMPIRE COURT APARTMENTS. NIGHT.

In a flashback, we see Delia, *dressed to the nines, come out and hail a taxi. We pull back and realize we've been watching from Pat's car.* Pat *follows the cab.*

INTERIOR: PAT'S APARTMENT. NIGHT.

PAT *pulls his .38 from his holster, and walks over and sets it down on the table.*

EXTERIOR: DREAMLAND. NIGHT.

In a flashback, the cab pulls up and DELIA *gets out.* PAT *pulls to the curb just as she goes inside.*

INTERIOR: PAT'S APARTMENT. NIGHT.

PAT *checks the revolver, making sure it's loaded.*

EXTERIOR: ALLEY BEHIND DREAMLAND. NIGHT.

Flashback. PAT *stands in the shadows smoking a cigarette, looking up at the lighted windows where we see* DELIA *talking with* DAVE O'CONNOR.

INTERIOR: CALENDER'S CAR. NIGHT.

The siren blares. CALENDER *drives as* PROKOWSKI *reads the note aloud.*

PROKOWSKI *(reading):* "Lieutenant Calender, I wanted to work Homicide because I thought that way I could see how close you were getting."

(Prokowski's voice fades, and we hear PAT *in* voice-over.)

EXTERIOR: ALLEY BEHIND DREAMLAND. NIGHT.

Flashback. An anguished PAT *watches as* DELIA *dances her last dance with* O'CONNOR *up in his office.*

PAT *(voice-over):* "But it doesn't matter now, because I no longer have any desire to escape you. I killed my wife with a crowbar which you now have in your possession. I killed her because I simply couldn't stand the thought of her loving anyone else."

(We move down Pat's body to see that he repeatedly bangs the crowbar against his leg as he watches them dance.)

INTERIOR: CALENDER'S CAR. NIGHT.

PROKOWSKI *reads the note aloud.*

PAT: *(voice-over):* "The checking I've done today reveals to me I would have probably escaped detection. I make this confession of my own free will."

(He looks up at CALENDER.*)*

EXTERIOR: ALLEY BEHIND DREAMLAND. NIGHT.

Flashback. DELIA *comes out of the dancehall. She walks up to the camera and stops, startled. Then she smiles.*

DELIA: Hi.

INTERIOR: PAT'S APARTMENT. NIGHT.

The record ends. We hear the needle scratching on the label and something else now—sirens. We then hear the sound of screeching tires as several patrol cars pull up outside.

PAT picks up the gun and moves to the center of the room. He faces the door and waits.

Waits until we hear the cops coming up the stairs, hear them bang on Pat's door.

PAT *(raising the gun):* It's open.

*(*CALENDER *bursts inside, then stiffens as* PAT *shoves the gun muzzle under his own chin.)*

PROKOWSKI: Pat! Don't!

EXTERIOR: ALLEY BEHIND DREAMLAND. NIGHT.

Flashback. The band strikes up "I Can't Get Started" and DELIA *takes a step forward, smiling.*

DELIA: You hear that, darling? They're playing our song.

(And then her smile goes away and we . . . CUT TO BLACK.)

DELIA *(voice-over):* Pat—?

(We hear a gunshot.)

Murder, Obliquely

Cornell Woolrich

The other night at a party I met my last love again. By last, I don't mean latest, I mean my first and yet my final one. We said the things you say, holding tall glasses in our hands to keep us company.

"Where've you been?"

"Around. And you?"

"Here and there."

Then there wasn't anything more to say. Love is bad for conversation; dead love, I mean. We drifted on. In opposite directions, not together.

It isn't often that I see him any more. But when I do, I wonder whatever really *did* become of her.

I first met him through Jean. Jean collects people, as a velvet evening wrap collects lint. People she has no emotional need for. She is very happily married. In an insulting, slurring way. I've never heard her speak a civil word to, or of, him. Example: "Oh, I don't know why." (Shrug.) "I had a spare twin bed and it seemed a shame to let it go to waste." She is the most gregarious one-man woman I know. Or else she keeps going through brambles, I can't say. Possibly it has to do with her face. She is not beautiful by wide-screen standards. But there is a winsome, elfin quality to her expression of face. I am not beautiful, either. The similarity ends there, right there.

Even when I was young, I was always the fifth wheel on the wagon. The other girl they had to ring in an extra man for, on dates. She never brought one of her own along. Never had one to bring. And these telephone-directory swains never repeated themselves. It was always someone else, the next time around. Once had been enough, for the one before.

Jean and her husband, the Cipher, stopped by for me in a cab at six thirty, and the three of us went on together from there. The Cipher wore glasses, was beginning to show baldness, and grew on you slowly. You found yourself beginning to like him after a time lag of about six months. The nickname, Jean's creation, was not inappropriate at that. The Cipher was singularly uncommunicative, on any and all subjects, after five o'clock in the afternoon. He was resting from business, she and I supposed. "He *has* a voice," she had once assured me. "I called for him one day, and I heard it through the office door. I wasn't at all certain until then."

He said, on the present occasion, " 'Lo, Annie," in a taciturn growl as I joined them in the cab; and that, we knew, was all we were likely to get for the next hour to come, so it had to do. But " 'Lo, Annie," when it's sincere and sturdy and reliable, isn't bad, either. In fact, it may be better than a lot of facile patter. Jean had settled for it, and Jean was smarter when it came to men than I could ever hope to be.

Number 657 was one of the tall monoliths that run along Park Avenue like a picket fence from 45th to 96th; but a picket fence that doesn't do its job. It doesn't seem to keep anyone out; everyone gets in.

"Mr. Dwight Billings," Jean said to the braided receptionist.

"Sixth floor," he said.

We entered an elevator that was a trifle small. Space, presumably, was so expensive in this building that only a minimum could be spared for its utilities. We stepped out into a foyer, and there was only a single door facing us. A colored man opened it. His accent was pure university. "Good evening, Mrs. Medill, Miss Ainsley, Sir. If you'll allow me." He took the Cipher's hat. "If you ladies would care—" He indicated a feminine guest room to one side.

Jean and I went in and left our wraps there, and looked at our faces in a wide, triple-winged vanity mirror. She unlidded a cut-crystal powder receptacle, being Jean, and sniffed at it. "Quite good," she said. "Coty's, unless I'm slipping. Rachel for brunettes, and"—she unlidded a second one on the opposite side—"flesh for blondes. Evidently there are no redheads on his list."

I didn't answer. I've been redheaded since I was twenty.

We rejoined the Cipher in the central gallery. It ran on for a length of about three rooms, cutting a wide swath through the apartment, and then you stopped, and turned to your left, and came down two steps onto the floor of the drawing room. It was artfully constructed for dramatic entrances, that room.

Overhead hung two rock-crystal chandeliers. One was lighted and sparkled like a rhinestone hornet's nest inhabited by fireflies. The other was unlighted, and showed cool blue with frosty crystalline shadow. A man was sitting behind the upturned ebony lid of a grand piano. Desultory notes of "None but the Lonely Heart," played with one hand alone, stopped short at the bustle of our coming down the two steps. Then he stood up and came forward, one hand out for Jean.

I like to study people. Even people that I think I'm going to see only once.

He was tall and he was thirty-five; brown eyes and lightish hair, blond when he was still a boy. He was like—how shall I say it? Everyone's glimpsed someone, just once in her life, that she thought would've been just the right one for her. I say would've, because it always works out the same way. Either it's too late and he's already married, or if he isn't, some other girl gets across the room to him first. But it's a kindly arrangement, because if you *had* got across the room to him first yourself, then you would have found that he wasn't just the right one for you after all. This way, the other girl is the one finds it out, and you yourself don't get any of the pain.

What's the good of trying to describe him? He was—well, how *was* that man that you didn't quite get over to in time?

I like to study people. People that I know I'm going to see lots more than just once. That I want to, that I've got to.

"This is Annie," Jean was saying in that careless way of hers. Nothing could be done about that. I'd given up trying. All the "Anyas" and "Annettes" when I was seventeen and eighteen hadn't helped any. I was back to plain Annie again, this time to stay. Good old Annie, there's a good girl.

We all sat down. He looked well sitting; not too far forward, not too far back. Not too straight, not too sunken. Couldn't he do anything wrong? He should do something wrong. This wasn't good for me.

We talked for a while, as people do, entering on the preliminaries of social intercourse. We said a lot of things; we said nothing. His man brought in a frost-clouded shaker and poured Bacardis and offered them to us. The talk that was talk for the sake of making talk went on, at quickened pace now, lubricated by the cocktails.

"How did you happen to get hold of all this?" Jean blurted out in that pseudonaive way of hers. We were at the table now.

"An aunt," he smiled. "The right kind."

"Old and rich," she quickly supplied.

"Fond of me," he contributed.

"Dead," She topped him.

"It's a co-operative, she owned it, and when she died two years ago, I found it on my hands."

"Why don't I find things like that on my hands?" Jean wondered innocently.

"I didn't know what to do about it, so I moved in here, along with Luthe. He's my man. The estate takes care of the upkeep, so that what it amounts to practically is I'm living here rent-free."

I kept wondering what he did. I didn't know how to go about asking, though. Jean did. It was a great convenience having her along, I couldn't help reflecting.

"Well, what do you do?" she pressed him.

"Nothing," he said bluntly. "Simply—nothing."

She burst out with enthusiasm. "Now, there's a man after my own heart! Let me shake hands with you." And she proceeded vigorously to do so.

"I did have a job until this—this windfall descended upon me," he said. "I even kept it up for a while afterwards—at first. And then I got up too late for work one day after a party, and it felt good not to go to work, so I said to myself 'Why haven't I done this before?' and I never did go back from then on."

The Cipher made his hourly utterance at this point. "I admire you," he stated emphatically. "That's the way all of us have felt at one time or another. Only, you had spunk enough to go ahead and carry it out."

"Do you always carry out the things you feel like doing, stray impulses that come along?" Jean asked him mischievously. "If you do, I'd hate to be the lady in front of you in a theater seat wearing one of those tall, obliterating hats."

"Pretty nearly always," he said with grim determination. "Pretty nearly always."

And you could tell he wasn't joking.

We left early. He closed the door, and we could hear his step going away down the corridor inside. He had a fine, firm, crisp tread; clean-cut, without any slurring. He even walked right.

She stood there looking at me with her brows raised.

"Why are your brows up?" I asked, finally.

"Are they up?"

"Well, they don't grow that way."

She let them down at length. Presently she remarked, as if to herself, "He's unhappy." She turned back to me for corroboration. "Don't you think so? Couldn't you notice?"

"Women," observed the Cipher, eyeing the cab ceiling light.

She ignored him. "Some girl, probably." She pondered the matter. Then she nodded confirmation of her own line of reasoning. "He's the broody type, would let it get him."

"I couldn't see anything the matter with him," the Cipher put in. "What did you expect the poor fellow to do, stand on his hands?"

"Men," she said crushingly.

"I think I saw her," I told her.

"What was she like?" she wanted to know eagerly.

"Not good for him," I said somberly. "Or anyone else. She was inside a frame in one of the rooms there. He had the door closed, I guess so we wouldn't look in, but the key was still in it on the outside. It said: 'To my Dwight,' down in a lower corner, but her own name wasn't signed. As though," I went on resentfully, "there could be no possible danger of confusion, there was only one of her in his life."

"Ho, you were busy!" she reveled.

"She must use the room sometimes. Stay over," I said bitterly. "It was all in peach and marabou."

"He's a big boy now," Jean drawled extenuatingly. "And he is a bachelor. And they do say there's an awful lot of it going on."

"That will do," said the Cipher with mock primness.

And so we began to know him, the little that you could. The little that he would let you. Or perhaps I should say, the little that we were capable of.

I had him at my place, and then Jean had him at hers. It went better there. Anything always did at Jean's place. Even a funeral would have been lively. We were all even now. I don't know why you have to be, but you have to be. Then he called, in about a week, and invited us to dine with him again, starting the thing over.

Jean, it was obvious, already didn't view the prospect with any great enthusiasm. "I'm not going to stay too late," she remarked. "You come away blue. I don't mind anyone being lovesick, but not if I have to sit and watch it."

I didn't answer. I was trying to decide what I was going to wear.

The dinner was just as good as the first time. He was just as hard to get to know as ever.

After we'd left the table, Luthe kept coming to the door with telephone calls. Effect without cause; you never heard it ring. Dwight just shook his head in refusal each time. I counted about five or six times it happened. It got on Dwight's nerves finally.

"Not anyone, understand?" he said sharply. "Not anyone at all."

Jean looked into her drink as though she were wondering whether it were big enough to drown herself in.

The next thing, Luthe had come back to the door again, in spite of the recent blanket injunction he'd been given.

Dwight turned his head abruptly. "I thought I told you—"

Luthe beamed at him. Wordlessly a message passed between them. I don't know how they did it, but it was sent and it was understood.

"No!" Dwight gasped incredulously. And then I saw his face light up as I'd never seen it light up yet. There was only one way to describe it. It was the face of a man deliriously in love. The face of a man who had thought all along he'd lost something, and now found it was being returned to him. That it was his once more.

It hurt me a little to see that light on his face. Second-degree burns, most likely, from foolishly trying to get too near.

The telepathic currents continued to flow back and forth between the two of them. Luthe was all white teeth. "Sure enough," he grinned.

Dwight choked on some sort of too-turgid happiness brimming up all over him. "Luthe, you're not fooling me? Don't do that."

"Don't I know the right voice?"

"When did she get back?"

"You better find that out for yourself."

He went into a sudden flurry of—I don't know what you'd call it—altruistic ecstasy. "More drinks for everybody! Annie, Jean, another. Champagne this time, Luthe. I'll join you in it, be right back!" And as he zigzagged to get out of the room in the shortest time possible, he passed close by where I was sitting, and in a sudden blind effusion—it must have been blind, it must have been—he bent and elatedly kissed the top of my head.

He didn't walk down the gallery out there. You could hear him running. It was a long thing, and he ran the whole length of it; then his footsteps stopped, and he'd arrived; he was there, he was talking to her.

I sat very still, as though I were afraid of spilling a drop of the champagne Luthe had just poured for me.

Nothing was said.

There was a muffled thud, outside there, about where the footsteps had ended. As when a chair goes over, perhaps. A little less sharply defined than that. Or when you sway unexpectedly and bump your head upon a table or against a doorframe.

Luthe looked up sharply. Then he hastened over and looked out, down the gallery. He hurried from sight, in that direction.

We waited there, holding our champagne.

He took a long time to come back to us.

Jean got up and wandered over to the radio console, and studied it. But then she didn't turn it on. There was more and better drama here, on the outside of it. I'd been hoping she wouldn't. She came back again presently and reseated herself about where she'd been before.

It must have been about ten minutes. Then he came walking in again. A little tiredly, a little inertly. There was a neat little patch of adhesive up on his temple, back from the eye.

"I got a little bump on the head," he smiled. "Luthe insisted on giving me first aid. Sorry I was so long."

His face was too white for that. It was drawn, it was sick. You don't get that look on your face even when you half knock yourself out. It was behind the eyes, mostly; inside them.

"She's said good-bye—whoever she is," I said to myself.

I took a sip of champagne. Funny how quickly it worked through you, making you glow, making you feel happy, even such a small sip.

Luthe had come in with a drink for him. It was straight brandy. It was a giant. It wasn't a drink for conviviality; it was a restorative.

He looked at it dubiously while Luthe stood there holding it for him. Then he looked up into Luthe's face, as though appealing to some superior wisdom, more than he himself had at the moment. "That won't help much, will it?" I heard him say almost inaudibly.

"No, that won't help much," Luthe agreed ruefully.

Luthe turned away with it, set it aside someplace, went out without it.

We tried to pick up the pieces of the conversation. Even Jean chipped in now, her humanitarian instincts aroused.

I kept watching his flayed face. I wondered if we were being cruel or kind.

"Don't you think we'd better be getting along," I suggested.

"No, don't go yet," he said, almost alarmedly. "Wait a little while longer, can't you? It's good to have you here. I feel sort of—"

He didn't finish it, but I knew the word: lonely.

We stayed on, by common consent. Even the Cipher forbore looking at his watch, that gesture with which he had a habit of harrying Jean, any evening, anywhere—but home.

It would have been a case of leaving just as the curtain was about to go up, though we didn't know it.

Suddenly drama had come fuming in around us, like a flash flood.

Luthe reappeared, went to him, bent down and said something. This time wholly inaudibly.

Dwight looked up at him, first in complete disbelief. Then in consternation. Then he pointed to the floor. I caught the word. *"Here?"*

Luthe nodded.

I caught the next two words too. *"With him?"* I saw him wince, as if in imminence of unendurable pain.

"All right," he said finally, and gave his hand an abrupt little twist of permission. "All right."

I got it then. There's somebody else; that was her first message, the one that floored him. But not only that: she's come right here with the somebody else.

He was a bad actor. No, I shouldn't say that. We were in the wings, watching him; we were backstage. All actors are bad when you watch them from behind-scenes. He was a good actor from out front. And that was from where he was meant to be seen.

He got up and he went over quickly to where Luthe had parked
that brandy bombshell. And suddenly the glass was empty. I never saw
a drink go down so fast. It must have flowed in a steady stream, without a stop for breath between. He did it with his back to us, but I saw
him do it just the same. Then he wagged his head and coughed a little,
and it was all down.

It wasn't a restorative now, it was more an anesthetic.

Then he slung himself to the arm of the settee I was on, and
lighted a cigarette, not without a little digital difficulty, and he was
ready for the curtain to go up. On the last act of something or other.

His timing was good, too.

Luthe showed up at the gallery opening, announced formally:
"Mr. and Mrs. Stone."

She came out onto the entrance apron, two steps above the rest of
us. She, and a husband tailing her. But what it amounted to was: *she*
came out onto the entrance apron. He might just as well not have been
there.

She was familiar with the stage management of this particular entryway, knew just how to get the most out of it. Knew just how long to
stand motionless, and then resume progress down into the room.
Knew how to kill him. Or, since she'd already done that pretty successfully, perhaps I'd better say, knew how to give him the shot of adrenaline that would bring him back to life, so that she could kill him all over
again. To be in love with her as he was, I couldn't help thinking, must
be a continuous succession of death throes. Without any final release. I
imagined I could feel his wrist, hidden behind me, bounce a little, from
a quickened pulse.

She stood there like a mannequin at a fashion display modeling a
mink coat. Even the price tag was there in full view, if you had keen
enough eyes; and mine were. Inscribed *"To the highest bidder, anytime,
anywhere."*

She had a lot of advantages over the picture I'd seen of her. She
was in color; skin like the underpetals of newly opened June rosebuds,
blue eyes, golden-blonde hair. And the picture, for its part, had one
advantage over her, in my estimate: it couldn't breathe.

She had on that mink she was modeling, literally. Three-quarters
length, flaring, swagger. She was holding it open at just the right place,
with one hand. Under it she had on an evening gown of white bro-
caded satin. The V-incision at the bodice went too low. But evidently
not for her; after all, she had to make the most of everything she had,

and not leave anything to assumption. She had a double string of pearls close around her neck, and a diamond clip at the tip of each ear.

They have the worst taste in women, all of them. Who is to explain their taste in women?

She came forward, down the steps and into the room. Perfume came with her, and the fact that she had hip sockets. The bodice incision deepened, too, if anything.

I kept protesting inwardly. But there must be something more than just what I can see. There *must* be something more. To make him fall and hit his head at the telephone; to make him down a glass of brandy straight to keep from moaning with pain. To make his pulse rivet the way it is against the back of this settee. As though he had a woodpecker hidden in it.

I kept waiting for it to come out, and it didn't. It wasn't there. It was all there at first glance, and beyond that there was nothing more. And most of it, at that, was the mink, the pearls, the diamonds and the incision.

She was the sort of girl who got whistled at, passing street corners. Her two hands went out toward him, not just one. A diamond bracelet around one wrist shifted back a little toward the elbow, as they did so.

"Billy!" she crowed. And her two hands caught hold of his two, and spread his arms out wide, then drew them close together, then spread them wide again. In a sort of horizontal handshake.

So she called him Billy. That would be about right for her, too. Probably "Billy-boy" when there were fewer than three total strangers present at one time.

"Well, Bernette!" he said in a deep, slow voice that came through hollow, as from inside a mask.

One pair of hands separated, then the other. His were the ones dropped away first, so the impulse must have come from him.

"What happened?" she said. "We were cut off." I saw her glance at the court plaster. "Billy!" she squealed delightedly. "You didn't *faint*, did you? Was it that much of a shock?" She glanced around toward her oncoming fellow arrival, as if to say: "See? See what an effect I still have on him?" I read the look perfectly; it was a flicker of triumphant self-esteem.

The nonentity who had come in with her was only now reaching us; he'd crossed the room more slowly.

He was a good deal younger than either one of them; particularly

Dwight. Twenty-three perhaps, or five. He had a mane of black hair, a little too oleaginous for my taste, carefully brushed upward and back. It smelled a little of cheap alcoholic tonic when he got too near you. He had thick black brows, and the sort of a beard that leaves a bluish cast on the face even when it is closely shaven. He was good-looking in a juvenile sort of way. His face needed a soda-jerk's white cocked hat to complete it. It was crying for something like that; it was made to go under it. And something told me it had, only very recently.

Her hand slipped possessively back, and landed on his shoulder, and drew him forward the added final pace or two that he hadn't had the social courage to navigate unaided.

"I want you to meet my very new husband. Just breaking in." Then she said, "You two should know each other." And she motioned imperiously. "Go on, shake hands. Don't be bashful. Dwight. Harry. *My* Dwight. *My* Harry."

Dwight's crisp intelligent eyes bored into him like awls; you could almost see the look spiraling around and around and around as it penetrated into the sawdust. You could almost see the sawdust come spilling out.

It's not the substitution itself, I thought; it's the insult of *such* a substitution.

The wait was just long enough to have a special meaning; you could make of it what you willed. Finally Dwight shook his hand. "You're a very lucky—young fellow, young fellow."

I wondered what word he would have liked to use in place of *young fellow*.

"I feel like I know you already," the husband said sheepishly. "I've heard a lot about you."

"That's very kind of Bernette," Dwight said dryly.

I wondered where she'd got him. He had the dark, slicked-back good looks that would hit her type between the eyes.

Then again, why differentiate? They went well together. They belonged together.

The line of distinction didn't run between him and her; it ran between her and Dwight. And part of her, at that, belonged on one side of the line, and part belonged on the other. The mink coat and the pearls and the diamond clips belonged on Dwight's side of the line; and she herself belonged on the other side of it. She wasn't even an integrated personality. The husband, with all his cheapness and callowness, at least was.

Dwight introduced the rest of us; introduced us, after I already knew her better than he ever had or ever would, with a pitiless clarity that he would never have.

Jean might have aroused her antagonistic interest, I could see that, but the married title deflected it as quickly as the introduction was made. Then when it came to myself, one quick comprehensive look from head to foot, and she decided, you could tell, there was nothing to worry about *there*.

"Drinks for Mr. and Mrs.—" Dwight said to Luthe. He couldn't get the name yet. Or didn't want to.

"Stone," the husband supplied embarrassedly, instead of letting the embarrassment fall on Dwight, where it rightfully belonged.

She at least was perfectly self-possessed, knew her way around in this house. "My usual, Luthe. That hasn't changed. And how are you, anyway?"

Luthe bowed and said coldly that he was all right, but she hadn't waited to hear. The back of her head was to him once more.

Their drinks were brought, and there was a slow maneuvering for position. Not physical position, mental. She lounged back upon the settee as though she owned it, and the whole place with it; as she must have sat there so very many times before. Tasted her drink. Nodded patronizingly to Luthe: "As good as ever."

Dwight, for his part, singled out the husband, stalked him, so to speak, until he had him backed against a wall. You could see the process step by step. And then finally, "By the way, what line are you in, Stone?"

The husband floundered badly. "Well, right now—I'm not—"

She stepped into the breach quickly, leaving Jean, with whom she had been talking, hanging on midword. "Harry's just looking around right now. I want him to take his time." Then she added quickly, just a shade too quickly. "Oh, by the way, remind me; there's something I want to speak to you about before I leave, Billy." And then went back to Jean again.

That told me why she'd dragged him up here with her like this. Not to flaunt him; she had no thought of profitless cruelty. The goose that had laid its golden yolks for one might lay them for two as well. Why discard it entirely?

"Where'd you go for your honeymoon, Bernette?" Dwight asked her.

She took a second, as though this required care. She was right, it did. "We took a run up to Lake Arrow."

He turned to the husband. "Beautiful, isn't it? How'd you like it?" Then back to her again, without waiting for the answer he hadn't wanted anyway. "How *is* the old lodge? Is Emil still there?"

She took a second. "Emil's still there," she said reticently.

"Did you remember me to him?"

She took two seconds this time. "No," she said reluctantly, mostly into the empty upper part of her glass, as though he were in there. "He didn't ask about you."

He shook his head and clicked with mock ruefulness. "Forgetful, isn't he? Has he done anything about changing that godawful wallpaper in the corner bedroom yet?" He explained to me, with magnificent impartiality: "He was always going to. It was yellow, and looked as though somebody had thrown up at two-second intervals all over it." He turned and flicked the punch line at her. "Remember, Bernette?"

It was now she who addressed the husband.

"We were both up there at the same time, once. I went up there on my vacation. And Billy went up there on his vacation. At the same time. And the room that Billy had, had this godawful wallpaper."

"At the same time," I thought I heard Dwight murmur, but it wasn't a general remark.

"I know, you told me," the husband said uneasily.

I saw the way his eyes shifted. It's not that he doesn't know, I translated; it's that he doesn't want to be forced into admitting publicly that he knows.

I watched them at the end, when they were about to go. Watched Dwight and her. When the good-bye had been said and the expressions of pleasure at meeting had been spoken all around—and not meant anywhere. They reversed the order of their entry into the room. The husband left first, and passed from sight down the gallery, like a well-rehearsed actor who clears the stage for a key speech he knows is to be made at this point. While she lingered behind a moment in studied dilatoriness, picking up her twinkling little pouch from where she had left it, pausing an instant to see if her face was right in a mirror on the way.

Then all at once, as if a random afterthought: "Could I see you for a minute, Billy?"

They went over to the side of the room together, and their voices faded from sound. It became a pantomime. You had to read between the attitudes.

I didn't watch. I began talking animatedly to Jean. I didn't miss a

gesture, an expression of their faces, a flicker of their eyes. I got everything but the words. I didn't need the words.

She glanced, as she spoke, toward the vacant gallery opening, just
once and briefly.

Talking about the husband.

She took a button of Dwight's jacket with her fingers, twined it a
little.

Ingratiation. Asking him something, some favor.

She stopped speaking. The burden of the dialogue had been
shifted to him. He began.

He shook his head almost imperceptibly. You could scarcely see
him do it. But not uncertainly, definitely. Refusal. His hand had
strayed toward his billfold pocket. Then it left it again still empty.

No money for the husband.

The dialogue was now dead. Both had stopped speaking. There
was nothing more to be said.

She stood there at a complete loss. It was something that had
never happened to her, with him, before. She didn't know how to go
ahead. She didn't know how to get herself out of it.

He moved finally, and that broke the transfixion.

They came back toward us. Their voices heightened to audibility
once more.

"Well—good night, Billy," she said lamely. She was still out of
breath—mentally—from the rebuff.

"You don't mind if I don't see you to the door, do you?" He
wanted to avoid that unchaperoned stretch between us and it, wanted
to escape having to pass along there alone with her, and being subject
to a still more importunate renewal of the plea.

"I can find the way," she said wanly.

She left. I had him all to myself for a moment, at least the exterior
of him.

Not for long, just between the acts. It wasn't over yet. Suddenly,
over his shoulder, I saw she'd reappeared at the lower end of the room,
was standing there.

"Billy, talk to Luthe, will you? What's the matter with him? Has
he had a drink or something? I can't get him to give me my coat." And
her whole form shook slightly with appreciative risibility.

He called and Luthe appeared almost instantly there beside her in
the gallery opening, holding the mink lining-forward in both arms.
Like someone who has been waiting in the wings the whole time and
takes just a single step forward to appear and play his part.

"Luthe, what are you doing?" he said amiably. "Is that Mrs. Stone's coat you're holding?" And before she could interject "Of course it is!" which it was obvious she was about to do, he added: "Read the label in the pocket lining and see what it says."

Luthe dutifully peered down into the folds of satin and read, "Miss Bernette Brady."

There was a pause, while we all got it, including herself. It was Miss Brady's coat, but not—any longer—Mrs. Stone's. Dwight stepped over to a desk, lowered the slab, and hastily inked something on a card. And then he went to her with it and handed it to her. "Bernette," he said, "take this with you."

It was an ordinary visiting or name card. She held it bracketed by two corners and scanned it diagonally, puzzled.

"What's this for?"

"I'll call him and make an appointment for you," he said quietly. "Go in and talk to him. The whole thing'll be over in no time."

"What do I need a lawyer for?" she blurted out.

I understood then, without the aid of the card. An annulment.

Anger began to smolder in her eyes. She gave him warning, but a warning that was already too late to avert the brewing storm. "That isn't funny."

"I'm not trying to be funny."

Her fingers made two or three quick motions and pieces of cardboard sputtered from them.

"Think it over," he urged, a second too late.

"I just did," she blazed. "Just then." She quirked her head sideward, then back toward him again. "Is Luthe going to give me my coat?"

"Come back for it," he drawled soothingly. "It'll be here—waiting for you—any time you say. . . ."

Her voice was hoarse now, splintered. "Then let's be consistent, shall we? How about it?"

Her hands wrestled furiously at the back of her neck. The pearls sidled down the bodice incision. She trapped them there with a raging slap, balled them up, flung them. They fell short of his face, they were probably too light, but they struck the bosom of his shirt with a click and rustle.

"Bernette, I have people here. They're not interested in our private discussions."

"You should have thought of that sooner." Her hands were at her earlobes now. "You want them to know you gave me things, don't you? You don't have to tell them! *I'll* tell them!" The ear clips fell on the carpet at his feet, one considerably in advance of the other.

"You can't carry that out down to its ultimate . . ."

"I can't, hunh? You think these people being here is going to stop me, hunh? The hell with them! The hell with you yourself! I'll show you! I'll show you what I think of you!"

She was beside herself with rage. There was a rending of satin, and suddenly the dress peeled off spirally, like a tattered paper wrapper coming off her. Then she kicked with one long silk-cased leg, and it fluttered farther away.

She had a beautiful figure. That registered on my petrified mind, I recall. We sat there frozen.

"Keep your eyes down, ducky," I heard Jean warn the Cipher in a sardonic undertone. "I'll tell you when you can look up."

For a moment she posed there, quivering, a monotoned apparition all in flesh tints, the undraped skin and the pale-pink silk of vestigial garments blending almost indistinguishably.

Then she gave a choked cry of inexpressible aversion, and darted from sight.

Dwight raised his own voice then, but not in rage, only for it to carry to a distance. "Luthe, that raincoat in the hall! Put it over her."

A door slammed viciously somewhere far down the gallery.

None of us said anything. What is there that can be said following such a thing?

Jean was the first one to speak, after the long somewhat numbed silence that followed. And, probably unintentionally, her matter-of-fact minor-keyed remark struck me as the most hilariously malapropos thing I had ever heard. I wanted to burst out laughing at it.

She stirred and said with mincing politeness: "I really think we should be going now."

A six-week interval, then. It must have been fully that; I didn't time it exactly. Oh, why lie? Why write this at all, if not truthfully? I counted every week, every day, every hour. I didn't tally them up, that was all. At least once every day I had to remind myself, unnecessarily, "I haven't seen him since that explosive night. That makes it a day more, that I haven't seen him." It worked out at something like six weeks.

Nothing happened. No word. No sight. No sign.

Was he with her once more? Was he with somebody else entirely

different? Was he alone, with nobody at all? Where was he? What was
he doing? Was he still in New York? Had he gone somewhere else?

I had it bad. Real bad.

Finally I sent him a little note. Just a little note. Oh, such a very
little note. *". . . I haven't heard anything from you in some time now—"*

A coward's note. A liar's note; a liar even to myself.

The phone rang the next afternoon. I made a mess of it. I
dropped the phone. I burned myself on a cigarette. I had to trample
the cigarette out first. Then I hung onto the phone with both hands,
when I'd once retrieved it.

He said things. The words didn't matter; it was just the voice they
were pitched in.

Then he said: "I don't dare ask you and the Medills to come up
here after what happened that last time."

"Dare," I said faintly. "Go on, dare."

"All right, would you?" he said. "Let's all have dinner together
and—"

When I told Jean that he had called, about fifteen minutes later,
she said the strangest thing. I should have resented it, but she said it so
softly, so understandingly, that it never occurred to me until later that
I should have resented it.

"I know," Jean said. "I can tell."

She murmured presently, "I think we should. I think it'd be good
for us."

How tactful of her, I thought gratefully, to use the plural.

So back we went, the three of us, for another glimpse at this real-
life peepshow that went on and on with never an intermission, even
though there was not always someone there to watch it.

He was alone. But my heart and my hopes clouded at the very
first sight of him as we came in; they knew. He was too happy. His face
was too bright and smooth; there was love hovering somewhere close
by, even though it wasn't in sight at the moment. Its reflection was all
over him. He was animated, he was engaging, he made himself pleasant to be with.

But as for the source of this felicity, the wellspring, you couldn't
tell anything. If I hadn't known him as he'd been in the beginning, I
might have thought that was his nature. He was alone, just with Luthe.
We were only four at the table, one to each side of it, with candles and
a hand-carved ship model in the center of it.

Then when we left the table, I remember, we paired off unconventionally. I don't think it was a deliberate maneuver on anyone's part, it just happened that way. Certainly, I didn't scheme it; it was not the sorting of partners I would have preferred. Nor did he. And the Cipher least of all. He never schemed anything. That left only Jean; I hadn't been watching her. . . .

I think I do recall her linking an arm to mine, which held me to her. And then she leaned back to the table a moment and reached for a final grape or mint, which resulted in reversing the order of our departure. At any rate, the two men obliviously preceded us, deep in some weighty conversation; she and I followed after. We gave them a good headstart, too. She walked with deliberate slowness, and I perforce had to follow suit.

She stopped short midway down the gallery, well before we had emerged into view of the drawing room, which the two men had already entered.

"I have premonitions of a run," she said. "I don't trust these sheers." But what she did was jog her elbow into my side, in a sort of wordless message or signal, as she turned aside and went in through the nearest doorway. *That* doorway.

I turned and followed her; that was what her nudge had summoned me to do.

Lights went on, and the big bed leaped into view in the background.

She went toward the full-length mirror in a closet door. She went through the motions of validating her excuse for stepping in here; raised her skirt, cocked her leg askew toward the mirror, dropped her skirt again. Then she reached out and purposefully took hold of the faceted glass knob of the closet door.

"Jean," I said with chaste misgivings. "Don't do that."

I saw she was going to anyway.

She swept it wide, the door, with malignant efficiency, and stood back with it so that I could see, and looked at me, not it, as she did so.

Satins and silks, glistening metallic tissues, flowered prints; and in the middle of all of them, like a queen amidst her ladies in waiting, that regal mink.

Then there was a blinding silvery flash as the electric light flooded across the mirror, and the door swept back into place.

"Back again," she said, brittlely. "This time, for keeps." And, I thought, what an apt word.

But for long moments afterward, long after the other things had faded and been effaced, it still seemed as if I could see the rich darkness of that mink, through glass and all, as if shadowed against some X-ray apparatus. Then finally it, too, dimmed and was gone, and there was just clear mirror left. With somebody's woeful, heartsick face on it. My own.

She put out the light as she shepherded me across the threshold; I remember the room was dark as we left it behind. I remember that so well. So very well.

She held her arm around me tight as we walked slowly down the remainder of the gallery.

I needed it.

"Tune in the Stadium concert, Luthe," he suggested at one point. "It must be time for it."

I wondered what he wanted that for.

Some very feverish dance-band drumming filtered out.

"If that's the Stadium concert," Jean said, "they've certainly picked up bad habits."

"Luthe," he said good-naturedly, "what're you doing over there? I said the open-air concert, at the Lewisohn Stadium."

"I can't seem to get it. What station is it on?"

"ABC, I think."

"I'm on ABC now. Doesn't seem to be it."

"Does it?" agreed Jean, pounding her ear and giving her head a shake to clear it, as a particularly virulent trombone snarl assailed us.

"Call up the broadcasting station and find out," he suggested.

Luthe came back.

"No wonder. It's been called off on account of rain. Giving it tomorrow night instead."

"It's not raining down here," Jean said. She returned from the window. "It's bone-dry out. Do you even have special weather arrangements for Park Avenue?" she queried.

"Look who we are," he answered her. A little distraitly, I thought, as though he were thinking of something else. "What time is it now, Luthe?" he asked.

She arrived about an hour and a half later. Perhaps even two hours. I don't know; since I hadn't been expecting her, I wasn't clocking her exactly. If he was, he'd kept it to himself; you couldn't notice it. No more parenthetic requests for the time, after that first one.

There was one thing noticeable about her arrival. I mean, even over and above the usual flashlight-powder brilliance of her arrival anywhere, anytime. It was that she was not announced. She simply entered, as one does where one belongs. Suddenly, from nowhere, she had taken her stance there on the auction block (as I called it after that first time). Then, after flamboyant pause and pose there, she was coming down the steps to join us.

He'd made a few improvements in her. Surface ones only; that was the only part of her he could reach, I suppose. Or maybe he needed more time. Her dress was a little higher at the neck, now, and the phantom price tag had been taken off. You got her value after awhile, but not immediately, at first sight.

She'd even acquired an accent. I mean an accent of good, cultivated English; and since it was false, on her it was an accent.

When she walked, she even managed to use the soles of her feet and not her hips so much any more. I wondered if he'd used telephone directories on her head for that, or just clouted her there each time one of them swayed, until she'd stopped it.

Or maybe she was just a good mimic, was getting it all by suction, by being dunked into the company of the right people more and more often. For my money, she'd had all the other makings of a good sponge right from the start; why not in that way, too?

"You remember Annie and Jean, and Paul," he said.

"Oh yes, of cowass; how are you?" she leered affably. She was very much the lady of the manor, making us at home in her own domain. "Sorry I'm so late. I stayed on to the very end."

"Did you?" he said.

And I thought, Where? Then, No! It can't be! This is too good to be true. . . .

But she rushed on, as though speaking the very lines I would have given her myself. She wanted to make a good impression, avoid the cardinal social sin of falling mute, not having anything to say; all those unsure of themselves are mortally afraid of it. So the fact of saying something was more important than the content of what it was she said.

"Couldn't tear myself away. You should have come with me, Billy. It was heavenly. Simply heavenly." Business of rolling the eyes upward and taking a deep, soulful breath.

"What'd they play first?" he said tightly.

"Shostakovich," she said with an air of vainglory, as when one has

newly mastered a difficult word and delights in showing one's prowess with it.

You couldn't tell she'd said anything. His face was a little whiter than before, but it was a slow process; it took long minutes to complete itself. Until finally he was pale, but the cause had long been left behind by that time, would not have been easy to trace any more.

She caught something, however. She was not dense.

"Didn't I pronounce it well?" she asked, darting him a look.

"Too well," he said.

She was uneasy now.

She didn't like us. She was hampered by our being there; couldn't defend herself properly against whatever the threat was. And although she didn't know what it was herself, as yet, she couldn't even make the attempt to find out, because of our continuing presence.

She sat for a moment with the drink he'd given her, made a knot with her neck pearls about one finger, let it unravel again. Then she stood up, put her drink down over where they originally came from.

"I have a headache," she said, and touched two fingers to the side of her head. To show us, I suppose, that that was where it was, in her head.

"Shostakovich always gives me a headache, too," Jean said sweetly to her husband.

She shot Jean a quick look of hostility, but there was nothing she could do about it. There was nothing to get her teeth into. If she'd picked it up, that would have been claiming it for her own.

"If you'll excuse me now," she said.

She was asking him, though, not the rest of us. She was a little bit afraid. She wanted to get out of this false situation. She didn't know what it was, but she wanted to extricate herself.

"You don't have to stand on ceremony with us, Bernette." He didn't even turn to look at her, but went ahead dabbling in drinks.

I thought of the old Spanish saying, *Aquí tiene usted su casa.* My house is yours. And it probably was as little valid in the present circumstance as in the original flowery exaggeration.

"But you just came," the Cipher said. He was only trying to be cordial, the poor benighted soul. He hadn't stepped aside into that room with us.

Jean and I simply looked at each other. I could almost lip-read what she was about to say before it came out. "She hasn't far to go." I nearly died for a minute as I saw her lips give a preliminary flicker.

Then she curbed herself. That would have been going too far. I breathed again.

She made her good nights lamely, and yet with a sort of surly defiance. As if to say, I may have lost this skirmish, but I haven't even begun to fight yet. This was on ground of your choosing; wait till he's without his allies, and must come looking for me on ground of my own choosing. We'll see whose flag runs down then.

She even reached out and shook hands with him. Or at least, sought out his, took it up, then dropped it again; all the volition coming from hers.

Oh, really, I protested inwardly. You don't do that from room to room.

She climbed the steps, she turned galleryward, she passed from view. Tall and voluptuous in her black summer dress, her head held high, her chin out. A little cigarette smoke that had emanated from her on the way lingered behind her for a moment or two. Then that dissolved, too.

And that's all the trace you leave behind in this world, sometimes: a little cigarette smoke, quickly blown away.

Presently another figure passed the gallery opening, coming from farther back in the apartment, but going the same way she had. Handsome, well-dressed, almost unrecognizable for a moment in his tactfully cut suit and snap-brim hat. There wasn't a garish detail of attire from head to foot. He would have passed without obtruding himself upon us, but Dwight turned his head.

"Going now?"

"Yes, sir. Good night." He tipped his hat to the rest of us, and left.

This time you could hear the outside apartment door close after him. Not like the time before.

"Luthe goes home out to Long Island one night a week to visit his mother, and this is his night for it." He shook his head. "He's studying law. I wish I lived as quietly and as decently as he does."

We left soon afterward ourselves.

As we moved down the gallery in leisurely deliberation, I looked ahead. That room that Jean and I had been in before was lighted now, not dark as we had left it. The door was partly ajar, and the light coming from it lay on the floor outside in a pale crosswise bar or stripe.

Then as we neared it, some unseen agency pushed it unobtrusively closed, from the inside. I could see the yellow outshine narrow and snuff out, well before we had reached it.

We were kept waiting for the elevator for some time. Finally, when it appeared, it was being run by a gnarled elderly individual in fireman's overalls, quite *declassé* for this building. There was no night doorman on duty below when we got there, either.

"What happened?" Jean asked curiously. "Where's all the brass?"

"Walked off," he said. "Wildcat strike. The management fired one of the fellows, and so they all quit. Less'n 'n hour ago. They ain't nobody at all to run the back elevator. I'm practic'ly running this whole building singlehanded, right now. You'll have to get your own taxi, folks. Can't leave this car."

"She stayed," I breathed desolately, while the Cipher was off in quest of one.

"Just wait till he gets her alone, though," Jean chuckled. "She'll have a lot of explaining to do. I'd give anything to hear what's going on between the two of them right now."

He was waiting for me, the driver. I'd dropped them off first.

"I've lost something. Look, you'll have to take a run back with me a minute."

He meshed gears. "To where the other folks got out?"

"No, the first place. Where we all got in."

I'd lost something. A door key. Or pride. Or self-respect. Something like that.

"Want me to wait?" he said when we'd arrived.

"No, you'd better let me pay you. I don't want you clocking me the whole time I'm in there."

"You may have a wait for another, lady, at this hour."

He looked me too straight in the eye, I thought. The remark didn't warrant such a piercing gaze. And he had no need to crinkle the corners of his eyes like that; it gave his glance too familiarly knowing an aspect.

I dropped my own eyes primly. "Keep the rest."

The same elderly pinch hitter was still servicing the building's elevators singlehanded. "They ain't nobody at all looking after the back one," he complained unasked.

I felt like saying, "You said that before," but I didn't.

He took me up without announcing me. I got out and I knocked at Dwight's door. The car went down and left me alone there.

No one came. I knocked again, more urgently, less tentatively. I tripped the Louis XVI gilt knocker, finally. That carried somewhat better, since it had a metal sounding board, not a wooden one.

Suddenly his voice said, "Who is it?" Too quickly for this last summons to have been the one that brought him; it must have been the first one after all, and he had been waiting there behind the door.

"Annie," I whispered, as though there were someone else around to overhear.

The door opened, but very grudgingly. Little more than a crevice at first. Then at sight of me, it widened to more normal width. But not full width of passage, for he stood there in the way; simply full width enough to allow unhampered conversation.

He was in a lounging robe. His shirt was tieless above it, and the collar band was unfastened. It had a peculiar effect on me: not the robe nor the lack of tie, simply the undone collar band; it made me feel like a wife.

"Don't look so stunned. Am I that frightening?" I couldn't resist saying. "Didn't you hear me give you my name through the door?"

"No," he said, "I missed it." Then he changed that to: "I thought I heard someone whisper, but I wasn't sure."

I didn't quite believe him, somehow. If he'd heard the whisper, then he'd heard the name whispered, I felt sure. I didn't resent the implication of a fib; quite the contrary. It was complimentary. It allowed me to believe—if I chose to, and I did—that my name effected the opening of the door, that another name would not have been able to. Castles in a foyer.

"Did I get you out of bed?" I said.

He smiled. It was a sort of vacant smile. The smile with which you wait for someone to go away. The smile that you give at a door when you are waiting to close it. Waiting to be allowed to close it, and held powerless by breeding. It had no real candlepower behind it, that smile. "No," he said, "I was just getting ready, by easy stages."

His face looked very pale, I thought; unnaturally so. I hadn't noticed it the first moment or two, but I gradually became aware of it now. I thought it must be the wretched foyer light, and I hoped I didn't look as pale to him as he did to me. I take pallor easily from unsatisfactory lights. The thing to do was to get inside away from it.

"It's my outside door key," I said. "I can't get into my house."

"It couldn't have been up here," he said. "I would have—I would have found it myself right after you left." He gestured helplessly with one hand, in a sort of rotary way. "It must have been in the taxi. Did you look in the taxi?"

The light was the most uncomplimentary thing I'd ever seen. It made him look almost ghastly.

"It wasn't in the taxi," I insisted. "I looked and looked. We even picked up the seat cushions." I waited for him to shift, but he didn't. "Won't you let me come in a moment and look?"

He was equally insistent. We were both strainedly civil but extremely insistent. "But it isn't up here, I tell you. It couldn't be, Annie, don't you see? If it was, I would have come across it by now myself."

I sighed exasperatedly. "But did you look for it? Did you know it was lost, until I told you so myself just now, here at the door? Then if you didn't look for it, how do you know it isn't there?"

"Well, I—I went over the place, I—" He decided not to say that, whatever it was to have been.

"But if you didn't know *what* it was that was lost, you couldn't have had your eye out for it specifically," I kept on, sugaring my stubbornness with reasonableness. "If you'd only let me step in for a moment and see for myself . . ."

I waited.

He waited, for my waiting to end.

I tried another tack. "Oh," I murmured deprecatingly, turning my head aside, as if to myself, as if in afterthought, "you're not alone. I'm sorry. I didn't mean to . . ."

It worked. I saw a livid flash, like the glancing reflection from a sun-blotted mirror, sweep across his face. Just for an instant. If it was fear, and it must have been of a kind, it was a new fear at this point: fear of being misunderstood, and no longer fear of my entering. He stepped back like magic, drawing the door with him.

"You're mistaken," he said tersely. "Come in."

And then as I did, and as he closed the door after me and pressed it sealed with his palm in one or two places, he added, and still quite tautly, "Whatever gave you that idea?" And turned to look the question at me, as well as ask it.

"After all," I drawled reassuringly. "I'm not anyone's grandmother."

This point, however, was evidently of importance to him, for some intangible reason that escaped me. Certainly I'd never detected any trait of primness in him before. "I never was so alone in my life," he said somewhat crossly. "Even Luthe went out home."

"I know," I reminded him. "He left while we were still here."

I had been thinking mainly of somebody else, not Luthe.

We moved slowly down the gallery, I preceding him.

She was gone, just as Jean had said she would be. The door that I had seen slyly closing before, shutting off its escaping beam of light, was standing starkly open now, and the room was dark. It looked gloomy in there, unutterably depressing, at that hour of the night.

"In here, maybe," I suggested, wickedly. I wasn't supposed to have been in there.

I heard him draw some sort of a crucial breath.

"No," he said quite flatly. "You didn't."

"I may have, just the same." I took a step as though to go in.

"No," he said, tautly, almost shrilly, as though I were getting on his nerves. He reached out before me and drew the door closed in my face.

I glanced at him in mild surprise, at the use of such a sharp tone of voice for such a trifling matter. The look I caught on his face was even more surprising. For a moment, all his good looks were gone. He was ugly in mood and ugly of face.

Then, with an effort, he banished the puckered grimace, let his expression smooth out again. Even tried on a thin smile for size, but it didn't fit very well and soon dropped off again.

Meanwhile, he'd withdrawn the key and the door was now locked fast.

"Why do you do that?" I asked mildly.

"I always keep it that way," he said. "It's not supposed to be left open. Luthe must have done that."

But Luthe had gone home before we had.

"Well, won't you let me go in and look at least?" I coaxed. I thought: I still love him, even when his face is all ugly and weazened like that. How strange; I thought it was largely his looks that had me smitten, and now I see that it isn't.

"But you weren't in there, so how could it get in there?"

"I was. I was in there once earlier tonight. I don't know whether you knew it or not, but I strayed in there one time this evening."

He looked at me, and he looked at the door. "Wasn't that a breach of manners on your part?" he suggested stiffly.

"There are no manners between a man and woman," I said. "There are only manners, good or bad, between a man and a man, or a woman and a woman."

He gave the cryptic answer, "Oh?"

Why do I drive him like this, I wondered? To see how far I can go? To make him fully aware of my being here alone with him? I didn't know myself.

We stood and looked at each other for a moment, he waiting for me to make the next move.

"Well, I'll have to get along without it," I said. "My key, I mean."

"Sorry."

"He wants me to go," I said, as though speaking ruefully to a third person. "He can't wait until I do."

What could he say then? What could anyone have said, except in overt offense? And that, you see, was why I'd said it. Though it was true, my saying so forced him to deny it, obliged him to act in contradiction to it. Though he didn't want to, and I knew that he didn't want to, and he knew that I knew that he didn't want to.

"No," he said deprecatingly. "No, not at all." And then warmed gradually to his own insistence; picked up speed with it as he went along. "Come inside. Away from that door." (As though my departure from a fixed point was now what he wanted to obtain, and if he could obtain it only by having me all the way in, rather than by having me leave, then he'd have me all the way in.) He motioned the way with his arm and he turned to accompany me. And kept up meanwhile the running fire of his invitation at a considerably accelerated tempo, until it ended up by being almost staccato. "Come inside and we'll have a drink together. Just you and me. Just the two of us alone. As a matter of fact, I need company, this minute."

On the rebound, I thought. On the rebound; I may get him that way. They say you do. Oh, what do I care how, if only I do.

I went down the steps, and he went down close beside me. His swinging arm grazed mine as we did so, and it did something to me. It was like sticking your elbow into an electrical outlet.

That drawing room of his had never looked vaster and more somber. There was something almost funereal about it, as though there were a corpse embalmed somewhere nearby, and we were about to sit up and keep vigil over it. There was only one lamp lighted, and it was the wrong one. It made great bat-wing shadows around the walls, from the upraised piano lid and other immovables, and now added our own two long, willowy emanations.

He saw me look at it, and said, "I'll fix that."

I let him turn on one more, just to take some of the curse off the gruesomeness, but then when I saw him go for the wall switch that would have turned on a blaze overhead I quickly interposed, "Not too many." You don't make very good love under a thousand-watt current.

I sat down on the sofa. He made our drinks for us, and then came over with them, and then sat down in the next state.

"No, here," I said. "My eyesight isn't that good."

He grinned and brought his drink over, and we sat half-turned toward each other, like the arms of a parenthesis. A parenthesis that holds nothing in it but blank space.

I saw to it that it soon collapsed of its own emptiness, and one of the arms was tilted rakishly toward the other.

I tongued my drink.

"It was a pretty bad jolt," I admitted thoughtfully.

"What was?"

"You don't have to pretend with me."

"Oh," he said lamely.

"You're still pretending," I chided him. "You're pretending that you haven't thought of it; that I'm the one who just now brought it back to your mind for the first time. When all along it hasn't left your mind, not for a single moment since."

He tried to drown his face in his drink, the way he pushed it down into it. "Please," he said, and made a grimace. "Not now. Do we have to—? Don't let's talk about it now."

"Oh, that much it hurts," I said softly.

The parenthesis had become a double line, touching from top to bottom.

"Why don't you put iodine on it?" I suggested.

He made a ghastly shambles of a smile. "Is there any for such things?"

"Here's the bottle, right beside you," I offered. "And there's no death's head on the label."

That symbol seemed to frighten him for a moment, or at least be highly unwelcome. He screwed up his eyes tight, and I saw him give his head a shake, as though to rid it of that particular thought.

"It stings for a minute, and then you heal," I purred. "You heal clean. No festering. And then you're well again; even the mark goes away. And you have a new love." I dropped my voice to a breath. "Won't you try—iodine?"

So close his face was to mine, so close; all he had to do . . .

Then he turned it a little; oh, a very, tactful little. The wrong way; so that the distance had widened a little. And he could breathe without mingling his breath with mine. Which seemed to be what he wanted.

"Don't you understand me, Dwight? I'm making love to you. And if I'm awkward about it, it's because women aren't very good at it. Can't you help me out a little?"

I saw the look on his face. Sick horror. I wish I hadn't, but I did. I never thought just a look on a face could hurt so.

"Would it be that bad? Would it be that unbearable, to be married to me?"

"Married?"

His backbone gave a slight twitch, as though a pin overlooked in his shirt had just pricked him. I caught him at it, slight as it was. That was no compliment, either, any more than the look on his face before had been.

"You've just been proposed to, Dwight. That was a proposal, just then. The first I've ever made."

He tried, first, to carry it off with a sickly grin. The implication: You're just joking, and I'm supposed to know you are, but you make me a little uncomfortable just the same.

I wouldn't let him; I wouldn't accept the premise.

"You don't laugh when a lady proposes to you," I said gently. "You don't laugh at her. You meet her on her own ground; you give her that much, at least."

He put his hand on my knee for a moment, but it was a touch of apology, of consolation; it wasn't what I wanted.

"I'm not—cut out—" He floundered. "It would be about the dirtiest trick I could play. I couldn't do *that* to you. . . ." And then finally, and more decidedly, like a snaplock to the subject: "You'd be sorry."

"I want to be. Let me be. I'd rather be sorry—with you—than glad—with anyone else."

He looked down his nose now. He didn't say anything more. A sort of stubborn muteness had set in. That was his best defense; that was his only one. He probably knew it. Their instincts are just as valid as ours.

I had to do the talking. Someone had to. It would have been even worse to sit there in silence.

I took a sip of my drink. I sighed in feigned objectivity. "It's unfair, isn't it? A woman can refuse a man, and she doesn't have to feel any compunction. He's supposed to take it straight, and he does. But if a man refuses a woman, he has to try to spare her feelings at the same time."

He hadn't as a matter of fact made any such attempt until now; he did now, possibly because I had recalled his duty to him.

"You're a swell gal, Annie. It's you I'm thinking of. You don't know what you're asking. You don't want *me*."

"You're getting your pronouns mixed," I said sadly.

All he could repeat was: "No, I mean it, you're a swell gal, Annie."

"You're a swell gal, Annie," I echoed desolately, "but you don't ring the bell."

He made the mistake of putting his arm around my shoulder, in what was meant as a fraternal embrace, I suppose. He should have left his hands off me; it was hard enough without that.

I let my head go limp against him. I couldn't have kept it up straight if I'd tried. And I didn't try.

"Then on shorter terms," I whispered, closing my eyes. "As short as you wish."

He tried to jerk his arm away, as he realized this new danger, but I caught it from in front with mine, and held it there, around my shoulders, like a precious sable someone's trying to take away from you.

"Even just—for tonight. Just for—an hour. Do I have to speak any plainer than that? *Your* terms. Any terms at all."

He shuddered, and hit himself violently in the center of the forehead. As if there were some thought lodged in there that he couldn't bear the contemplation of. "My God," I heard him groan. "My God! Right here and now, in this apartment . . ."

"Is there something wrong with this apartment?" I asked innocently.

"Not with the apartment, with me," he murmured.

"I won't dispute you there," I said cattishly.

I let go of his arm, and he promptly called it back. I stood up. I got ready to go. I'd been rejected. To have prolonged it would have veered over into buffoonery. I had no self-respect left, but at least I still had my external dignity left. The law of diminishing returns would only have set in from this point on.

I turned and looked at him, still sitting there. "Seduction doesn't agree with you," I let him know. "You look positively harassed."

I saw him wince a little, as though he agreed with me; not only looked it, but felt it. He stood now, to do the polite thing as host.

"I'll get over it," I said, speaking out loud to keep my own courage up. "It doesn't kill you."

He blinked at the word, as though it grated a little.

I was ready to go now. He came closer, to accelerate the process. "Won't you kiss me good night?" I said.

He did it with his brakes on; used just one arm to support my back. Put his lips to mine, but with a time valve to them. Took them away again as soon as time was up. Mine tried to follow, and lost their way.

We straightened ourselves. "I'll see you out," he said.

"Never mind. Don't rub it in."

He took me at my word, turned back to pour himself another drink. His hand was shaking, and if that's a sign of needing one, he needed one.

I went down the long gallery alone. So safe. Too safe. As safe as when I'd come in. My heart was blushing and my cheeks felt white.

I came opposite that door, the door to his lady-love's room. I stopped and looked at it. And as I did, a creepy feeling all at once came over me. Like a cold, cold wind that comes from nowhere and suddenly knifes you where you stand. As if the room were not empty. As if there were something in there, some terrible revelation, waiting, crying, to be seen. There was almost a pull to it, the feeling was so strong. It seemed to draw me, the way forbidden sights do. Evil sights; sights that are death in themselves and death to behold.

I started to put out my hand toward it. Then I felt his eyes on me, and turned, and saw him standing, watching me, at the end of the gallery, where I'd just come from myself.

"Annie," he said. "Don't." His voice was toneless, strangely quiet. He didn't offer to approach, stayed where he was; but his hands strayed to the cord of his robe and, of their own accord, without his seeming to know what they were doing, fumbled there, until suddenly the knot had disheveled, fallen open. Then each one, holding a loose end of the cord, flicked and played with it, all unconsciously. The way the two ends danced and spun and snaked suggested the tentative twitching of a cat's tail, when it is about to spring.

He was holding it taut across his back, and out at each side, in a sort of elongated bow-shape. It was just a posture, a stance, a vagary of nervous preoccupation, I suppose. An odd one, but meaningless.

I flexed my wrist slightly, as if to complete the touching of the doorknob.

The cord tightened to almost a straight line, stopped moving.

His eyes met mine and mine met his, the length of the gallery.

The impulse to annoy him died.

Indifferently, I desisted. I dropped my hand slowly, and let the door be.

His hands dropped too. The taut pull of the cord slackened, it softened to a dangling loop.

I went on to the outside door and opened it.

"Good night, Dwight," I murmured wanly.

"Good night, Annie," he echoed.

I saw him reach out with one arm and support himself limply against the wall beside him, he was so tired of me by this time.

I closed the outside door.

They tell you wrong when they tell you infatuation dies a sudden death. Infatuation dies a lingering, painful death. Even after all hope is gone the afterglow sometimes stubbornly clings on and on, kidding you, lighting the dark in which you are alone. Infatuation dies as slowly as a slower love; it comes on quicker, that is all.

Twice I went by there in a taxi, in the two weeks following that night. A taxi that didn't have to go by there, that could have taken me another way; but whose way I altered, I interfered with, so that it would take me by there. And each time it stopped a moment at the door. Not of its own accord, either. "Stop here a moment."

But then I didn't get out after all. Just sat there. Perhaps to see if I could sit there like that without getting out, I don't know. Perhaps to see if I was strong enough.

I was. I just barely made it, both times, but I made it.

"Drive on," I said heroically, when the driver turned his head around inquiringly after nothing had happened. It was like leaving your right arm behind, jammed in a door; but I left it.

One of the two times, I had been on my way to a party, and the excuse would have been to ask him if he wanted to come along with me. Had I carried the stop out to its ultimate conclusion. But I don't think we would have gone on to any party, even had I put the invitation to him. It takes two to want to go to any party, when there are two, and one of us wouldn't have wanted to go—even had he said yes.

(I didn't, incidentally, even go on to the party myself, after I drove on from his door; I went home and took off the regalia it had taken me an hour's solid work to array myself in. It hadn't been meant for the general admiration of any party.)

And the second of the two times I stopped, the excuse was even more flimsy. I was supposed to be on my way somewhere else. To friends, I think, for an evening of bridge.

"Drive on," I told the driver.

But I was convalescing; it was only like leaving your hand caught in the door, not your whole arm now.

"Your game isn't what it used to be," my partner told me acidulously later that evening, after we'd gone down for a grand slam.

"No," I agreed, word for word, "my game isn't what it used to be." ("And I'm a dud at the new one," I added to myself.)

But the third time, ah the third time, I stopped down there at the door, there was no excuse at all. None whatever. Not even so fragile a one as a secondhand party or a secondhand game. I did it as a sort of test, and I found out what I wanted to.

I was practically over it. I was cured. I made the discovery for myself sitting there in the taxi, taking my own blood pressure, so to speak, holding my own pulse, listening to my own heart. I could drive away now without a wrench, without feeling that I'd left a part of me behind, caught in his door.

I lighted a cigarette and thought with a sigh of relief: It's passed. It's finished. Now I've got nothing more to worry about. That was the vaccine of love. Now I'm immune. Now I can go on and just work and live and be placid.

"Y' getting out, lady, or what?" the driver asked fretfully.

"Yes," I said coolly, "I think I will. I want to say good-bye to someone in there."

And in perfect safety, in perfect calm, I paid him and got out and went inside to visit my recent, my last, love.

But, as I have often said, they tell you wrong when they tell you infatuation dies a sudden death. It doesn't. *I* know.

I seemed to have picked an inappropriate time for my farewell visit. Or at least, a nonexclusive one.

There'd been somebody else with him. The apartment door was already open, when I stepped off at his foyer, and he was standing there talking to some man in dilatory leave-taking.

The man was heavily built and none too young. In the milder fifties, I should judge. His hair was silvering, his complexion was florid, and there were little skeinlike red blood vessels threading the whites of

his eyes. He had a hard-looking face, but he was being excessively amiable at the moment that I came upon the two of them. Almost overdo-
ing it, almost overly amiable, for it didn't blend well with the rest of his
characteristics, gave the impression of being a seldom-used, almost
rusty attribute; he had to push down hard on the accelerator to get it
working at all. And he was keeping his foot pressed down on it for all
he was worth so that it couldn't get away from him.

"I hope I haven't troubled you, Mr. Billings," he was apologiz-
ing just as the elevator panel opened.

"Not at all," Dwight protested indulgently. There was even
something patronizing in his intonation. "I know how those things
are. Don't think twice about it. Glad to—" And then they both turned
at the slight rustle the panel made, and saw me, and so didn't finish the
mutual gallantries they were engaged upon. Or rather, postponed
them for a moment.

Dwight's face lighted up at the sight of me. I was welcome. There
could be no doubt of it. Not like that other night. And yet—How shall
I put it? It was not a question of being relieved. I didn't detect that at
all. It was rather that he was already so pleased with himself, and with
everything else, this evening, that even my arrival pleased him. And I
use the adverb *even* advisedly. So that I was welcome by good-hu-
mored reflection—anyone would have been at the moment—and not
in my own right.

He shook my hand cordially. "Well! Nice of you! Where've you
been keeping yourself?" And that sort of thing. But made no move to
introduce the departing caller to me.

And his manners were too quick-witted for that to have been an
oversight. So what could I infer but that there was a differentiation of
status between us that would have made a social introduction inappropriate. In other words, that one call was a personal one and the other
was not, so the two were not to be linked.

At the same time, he did not offer to disengage himself from his
first caller, conclude the parley, and turn his attention to me. On the
contrary, he postponed my playing on his attention and returned to
the first matter, as if determined it should run its unhurried course and
be completed without any haste, first of all. He even signaled to the car
operator not to stand there waiting to take the leavetaker down, as
he'd been inclined to do. "We'll ring," he said, and motioned the
panel closed with his hand.

And to me: "Go in, Annie. Take your things off. I'll be right with
you."

I went in. My last impression of the man standing there with him was that he was slightly ill at ease under my parting scrutiny; call it embarrassed, call it sheepish, call it what you will. He turned his head aside a moment and took a deep draught of an expensive cigar he was holding between his knuckles. As if: Don't look at me so closely. I certainly wasn't staring, so it must have been his own self-consciousness.

I went down the gallery of lost loves. The room door was open now. I went past it without stopping, and down the steps to the drawing-room arena.

I took off my "things," as he'd put it, and primped at my hair, and moved idly around, waiting for him to join me.

I looked at things as I moved. One does, waiting in a room.

He'd left them just as they were, to take his visitor to the door. Probably I hadn't been announced yet, at that moment. I must have been announced after they were both already at the door, and he hadn't come all the way back in here since leaving it the first time.

There were two glasses. Both drained heartily, nothing but ice sweat left in their bottoms; the interview must have been a cordial one.

There were two strips of cellophane shorn from a couple of expensive cigars.

There was a single burned matchstick; one smoker had done that courteous service for both.

His checkbook folder was lying on the corner of the table. He must have taken it out of his pocket at one time, and then forgotten to return it again. Or perhaps thought that could wait until afterward; it was of no moment.

I didn't go near it, or touch it, or examine it in any way. I just saw it lying there.

There was a new blotter lying near it. Almost spotless; it had only been used about once.

That I did pick up, idly, and look at. As if I were a student of Arabic or some other right-to-left scrawl. I looked at it thoughtfully.

He still didn't come in.

Finally I took it over to the mirror with me and fronted it to that, and looked into that.

Part of his signature came out. *"-illings."* It was the thing he'd written last, so the ink was still freshest when the blotter'd been put to it. Above it were a couple of less distinct tracings. *"-earer."* And three large circles and two smaller ones. Like this: OOOoo.

I turned swiftly, as though that had shocked me (but it hadn't;

why should it?) and pitched it back onto the table from where I stood. Then I fixed my hair a little more, in places where it didn't need it.

He came in, looking sanguine, looking zestful. I don't remember that he rubbed his hands together, but that was the impression his mood conveyed: of rubbing his hands together.

"Who was that man?" I said indifferently.

"You'll laugh," he said. And he set the example by doing so himself. "That's something for you." Then he waited, as a good raconteur always does. Then he gave me the punch line. "He was a detective. A real, honest-to-goodness, life-sized detective. Badge and everything."

I stopped being indifferent, but I didn't get startled. Only politely incredulous, as a guest should be toward her host's surprise climaxes. "Here? What'd he want with you?"

"Asking if I could give him any information," he said cheerfully. Then in the same tone: "You've heard about Bernette, haven't you?"

I said I hadn't.

"I think you met her up here once."

I visioned a pink brassiere and pink drawers. "Yes," I said, "I seem to recall."

"Well, she's disappeared. Hasn't been heard of in weeks."

"Oh," I said. "Is that bad?"

He gave me a wink. "Good," he whispered, as if afraid she'd come in just then and overhear him. And he flung one hand disgustedly toward the doorway, meaning it for her invisible presence. She should stay away.

"Why do they come to you about it?" I asked him.

"Oh," he said impatiently, "some tommyrot or other about her never having been seen again after—after the last time she left here. I dunno, something like that. Just routine. This is the third time this same fellow's been up here. I've been darn good-natured about it." Then he said, more optimistically, "He promised me just now, though, this is the last time; he won't come back any more."

He was fixing two drinks for us, in two fresh glasses. The first two had been shunted aside. The checkbook and the blotter had both vanished, and I'd been facing him in the mirror the whole time; so maybe I'd been mistaken; they hadn't been there in the first place.

"And then there was something about some clothes of hers," he went on offhandedly. "She left some of her things here with me. . . ." He broke off to ask me: "Are you shocked, Annie?"

"No," I reassured him, "I knew she stopped here now and then."

"I was supposed to send them after her; she said something about letting me know where she could be reached." He shrugged. "But I never heard from her again myself. They're still waiting in there. . . ."

He finished swirling ice with a neat little tap of the glass mixer against the rim.

"Probably ran off with someone," he said contemptuously.

I nodded dispassionately.

"I know who put him up to it," he went on, with a slight tinge of resentment. I had to take it he meant the detective; he offered no explanation to cover the switch in pronouns. "That dirty little ex-husband of hers."

"Oh, is he ex?" I said. That was another thing I hadn't known.

"Certainly. They were annulled almost as soon as they came back from their wedding trip. I even helped her to do it myself, sent her to my lawyer—"

And paid for it, I knew he'd been about to add; but he didn't.

"I told this fellow tonight," he went on, still with that same tinge of vengefulness, "that they'd better look into his motives, while they were about it. He was only out to get money out of her—"

(And she was only out to get money out of you, I thought, but tactfully didn't say so.)

"Do they think something's happened to her?" I asked.

He didn't answer that directly. "She'll probably turn up some-place. They always do." Then he said grimly, "It won't be here. Now let's have one, you and me." And he came toward me with our drinks.

We sat down on the sofa with them. He didn't need any urging tonight.

We had another pair. Then a third. We let the third pair stand and cool off awhile.

I was the upright arm of the parenthesis tonight, I noticed presently; he was the toppled-over one.

I didn't move my head aside the way he had his; his lips just didn't affect me. It was like being kissed by cardboard.

"I want you to marry me," he said. "I want—what you wanted that night. I want—someone like you."

(That's not good enough, I thought. You should want just me myself, and not someone like me. That leaves it too wide open. This is the rebound. You want the other kind of woman now. Safety, security, tranquillity; not so much fire. Something's shaken you, and you can't stand alone; so if there was a female statue in the room, you'd propose to that.)

"Too late," I said. "I've passed that point, as you arrive at it. You got to it too late. Or I left it too soon."

He wilted and his head went down. He had to go on alone. "I'm sorry," he breathed.

"I am, too." And I was. But it couldn't be helped.

Suddenly I laughed. "Isn't love the damnedest thing?"

He laughed, too, after a moment; ruefully. "A bitch of a thing," he agreed.

And laughing together, we took our leave of each other, parted, never to meet in closeness again. Laughing is a good way to part. As good a way as any.

I read an item about it in the papers a few days afterward, quite by chance. The husband had been picked up and taken in for questioning, in connection with her disappearance. Nothing more than that. There was no other name mentioned.

I read still another item about it in the papers, only a day or two following the first one. The husband had been released again, for lack of evidence.

I never read anything further about it, not another word, from that day on.

The other night at a party I met my last love again. I don't mean my latest; by last, I mean my final one. And he was as taking and as debonair as ever, but not to me any more; a little older maybe; and we said the things you say, holding tall glasses in our hands to keep from feeling lonely, keep from feeling lost.

"Hello, Annie. How've you been?"

"Hello, Dwight. Where've you been keeping yourself lately?"

"I've been around. And you?"

"I've been around, too."

And then when there wasn't anything more to say, we moved on. In opposite directions.

It isn't often that I see him any more. But whenever I do, I still think of her. I wonder what really did become of her.

And just the other night, suddenly, for no reason at all, out of nowhere, the strangest thought entered my head for a moment. . . .

But then I promptly dismissed it again, just as quickly as it had occurred to me, as being too fantastic, too utterly improbable. The people you know never do things like that; the people you *read* about may, but never the people you *know*.

Murder, Obliquely

Teleplay by

Amanda Silver

Cast

Laura Dern	Annie Ainsley
Alan Rickman	Dwight Billings
Diane Lane	Bernette Stone
Robin Bartlett	Jean Medill
Patrick Massett	Paul "The Cipher" Medill
Michael Vartan	Harry Stone
John A. Zee	Luther

Executive Producer: Sydney Pollack
Producers: William Horberg, Lindsay Doran, Steve Golin
Co-Producer: David Wisnievitz
Directed by: Alfonso Cuaron
Director of Photography: Emmanuel Lubezki
Production designed by: Armin Ganz
Costumes designed by: Shay Cunliffe
Casting by: Owens Hill and Rachel Abroms
Fallen Angels theme by: Elmer Bernstein
Music by: Peter Bernstein
Edited by: David Siegel
Story Editor: Geoffrey Stier

INTERIOR: ANNIE'S APARTMENT. AFTERNOON.

Close on a "dummy hand" of bridge laid out across a table. A female hand reaches in and pulls out the four of spades.

ANNIE AINSLEY, *a delicate-boned blond with a vulnerable look to her shy green eyes, places the four on the table.*

JEAN MEDILL *arches a razor-sharp eyebrow.*

JEAN: Leading with a spade, huh . . .

(PAUL "THE CIPHER" MEDILL, *with a taciturn expression and a face old before its time, sneezes and follows suit with a six.* JEAN *hands him a tissue and then throws down the king.*

The three of them are sitting around a small dining table in the middle of a modest one-room apartment.

ANNIE *takes the trick matter of factly with the Ace of Spades.* JEAN *turns accusingly to* THE CIPHER.)

JEAN: I thought *you* had the ace. (THE CIPHER *ignores her.* JEAN *scowls and looks back to her hand.*) Did you read about that girlfriend of Dwight's? What was her name, Bernadette?

ANNIE: Bernette.

JEAN: Whatever. She's turned up missing.

ANNIE *(looking up)*: Missing?

JEAN: Disappeared into thin air. That ex-husband of hers has been making a lot of noise about it. The police have been up to question Dwight and everything. It seems that the last time she showed her face was at his place that last time we were there.

(ANNIE is listening intently.)

THE CIPHER: Dwight probably killed her.

(JEAN bursts out laughing.)

JEAN: My God, he speaks! That's the most words he's put together in days. Priceless!

ANNIE: Who wouldn't have wanted to kill her?

EXTERIOR: BILLINGS'S HOUSE. NIGHT.

A car pulls up in front of a large house.

ANNIE *(voice-over)*: I met him through Jean. Jean collects people like a velvet evening wrap collects lint.

(ANNIE, JEAN, and THE CIPHER step out of the car. JEAN rings the doorbell. THE CIPHER sneezes.)

JEAN *(to ANNIE)*: New dress?

ANNIE: Old dress. New buttons.

JEAN: Nice.

ANNIE *(voice-over)*: I've always been the fifth wheel on the wagon. So that night was nothing new. Or so I thought.

(The door is opened by LUTHER, a small, immaculate man wearing servant's dress. Faint music is audible within.)

LUTHER: Good evening.

JEAN: Jean and Paul Medill, and Annie Ainsley for Dwight Billings.

LUTHER: Welcome. If you'll allow me . . .

(LUTHER *takes the ladies' wraps as he steps aside, ushering them within.*)

INTERIOR: BILLINGS ENTRYWAY/HALLWAY. NIGHT.

Decorated with the muted, confident elegance of the very rich.

ANNIE, JEAN, *and* THE CIPHER *follow* LUTHER *down a very long, wide hallway. The music grows louder as they walk. Its sounds are sweet and sad.*

As if drawn by the music, ANNIE *continues alone down the hallway when* JEAN *stops and takes The Cipher's arm.*

JEAN: What's the matter with you? Why didn't you give the man your hat?

(LUTHER *doubles back to take The Cipher's hat.* ANNIE *is almost to the end of the hallway now.*)

ANNIE *(voice-over):* It was the longest hallway I'd ever seen . . . and then suddenly you turned to your left, and came down two steps onto the floor of the drawing room.

(ANNIE *makes the turn as she describes it, revealing:*)

INTERIOR: DRAWING ROOM. NIGHT.

A shadowy, warm space, lit dreamily by a single rock-crystal chandelier. Music drifts from a large radio resting on a table in the far corner of the room.

Standing beside it, out on a ledge behind large, open windows, is DWIGHT BILLINGS. *He is tall. Movie-star handsome. He's looking down at the lights, glittering below.*

ANNIE *freezes. She stands in the doorway, unseen, watching him.*

DWIGHT *continues looking out at the lights of the city.*

ANNIE *watches intently.*

JEAN *(off-screen):* My God, is there an end to this hallway?

(DWIGHT *turns and catches Annie's watching eyes. Flustered, he quickly comes in from the ledge, just as* JEAN *and* THE CIPHER *enter.*)

(ANNIE *sees Dwight's handkerchief fall to the floor. It has gold stitching on its border, and the prominent initials:* DRB.)

JEAN: Dwight!

(ANNIE *watches as* DWIGHT *greets* JEAN *and* THE CIPHER.)

ANNIE *(voice-over):* Every girl's glimpsed someone, just once in her life, that she thought would've been just the right one for her. The moment that I saw Dwight Billings, I knew he was it.

JEAN: This is Annie.

DWIGHT: *(awkward):* Hello, Annie.

ANNIE *(striving for composure):* Hello.

INTERIOR: DRAWING ROOM/SITTING AREA. NIGHT.

LUTHER *hands out drinks to* DWIGHT *and his guests.*

DWIGHT: Cigarette anyone?

(DWIGHT *lights a cigarette for* ANNIE. *Her hand is shaking.*)

JEAN: We've missed you. We were beginning to think you were becoming a recluse.

DWIGHT: *(good natured):* Now, Jean, don't let's start in on that again. Thank you, Luther.

(DWIGHT *drags deeply from a cigarette. Smoke escapes from his lips in a perfectly controlled plume.*

ANNIE *can't take her eyes off him.* JEAN *gives her a nudge.*)

JEAN: I've heard so much about your lovely home, Dwight, and it lives up to every word. How did you happen to get hold of it?

DWIGHT: An aunt. The right kind.

JEAN *(picking up the gauntlet):* Old and rich?

DWIGHT: Fond of me.

JEAN: Dead.

(*Touché.*)

DWIGHT: She owned the place forever, and when she died two years ago, I found it on my hands.

JEAN: Now why don't I find things like that on my hands?

(ANNIE *offers a nervous little laugh and tips her cigarette ash into a martini.*)

(*Following the puzzled looks of* JEAN *and* DWIGHT, ANNIE *realizes what she's done and immediately blushes.*

DWIGHT *quickly stands and whisks away the ruined drink.*)

DWIGHT: Oops.

INTERIOR: POWDER ROOM. LATER THAT NIGHT.

ANNIE *and* JEAN *straighten their lipstick lines before a triple-winged vanity mirror.* ANNIE *catches* JEAN *watching her, eyebrows raised.*

ANNIE: Why are your eyebrows up?

JEAN: Are they up?

ANNIE: They don't grow that way.

(*Beat.*)

JEAN: He looks so unhappy. Don't you think? (*Beat.*) Couldn't you notice?

ANNIE: I suppose so.

JEAN: I've never seen him so blue. Some girl, probably. Always is.

(ANNIE *doesn't answer.* JEAN *is watching her again, eyebrows and all.*)

ANNIE: What?

JEAN: Just be careful, that's all.

ANNIE: Oh, come on, Jean. I'm the most careful girl you know.

JEAN: Careful girls don't flick ashes into martinis.

(JEAN *exits.* ANNIE *stares at herself in the mirror for a beat.*)

ANNIE (*voice-over*): Jean was right, of course. Jean's almost never wrong.

(ANNIE *picks up a delicate bottle of perfume from the counter. She opens the top and smells the feminine fragrance.*)

INTERIOR: DINING ROOM. NIGHT.

DWIGHT, ANNIE, JEAN *and* THE CIPHER *sit at the table, finishing dinner in silence.* ANNIE *can't stop staring at Dwight's distracted, distant face.*

ANNIE *(voice-over):* After that I kept wondering who she was, and what she did to make him feel that way. I didn't have to wonder for long.

(LUTHER *enters, looking like the cat who swallowed the canary.*)

LUTHER: There was a telephone call, Sir.

DWIGHT: So? Did you take a message?

LUTHER: I did, Sir.

(*There is a strange sparkle to Luther's eyes.* DWIGHT *double-takes. For a moment there is a silent but intense communication between them.*)

DWIGHT *(incredulous):* No!

(LUTHER *nods. Dwight's face lights up with ecstatic happiness. There is a drastic change to his demeanor.*)

DWIGHT: When did she get back?

(ANNIE *and* JEAN *share a quick look.*)

LUTHER: You better ask her that yourself . . . She said she's on her way over.

INTERIOR: DRAWING ROOM. NIGHT.

Close on glasses being filled with the soft sparkle of champagne. DWIGHT *hands them out to his guests. He's on top of the world.*

DWIGHT: Drink up, everyone! Plenty more where that came from.

(DWIGHT *hands champagne to* ANNIE. *She accepts happily.*

Then her expression changes, as she sees, arriving behind DWIGHT *in the entryway . . .* BERNETTE. *Tall, blue eyes, perfect skin. And a silver mink coat held open with one hand, exposing healthy cleavage. She stands there, holding a perfectly timed theatrical pause.*

ANNIE *(voice-over):* She stood there like a mannequin at a fashion display. Even the price tag was there in full view. It was inscribed: "To the highest bidder, anytime, anywhere."

(DWIGHT *follows Annie's gaze and turns. At the sight of* BER-
NETTE, *his face lights up.* BERNETTE *pauses for just a fraction of a second
to check herself on a wall mirror. Then she moves toward him, arms out-
stretched.*)

BERNETTE: Billy!

DWIGHT: Well, Bernette . . .

(*They embrace. The three guests stare openly.*)

ANNIE *(voice-over):* They have the worst taste in women, all of them.
Who is to explain their taste in women?

(*Suddenly* LUTHER *appears at the gallery opening, obviously dis-
tressed. He stands in the doorway, shooting* DWIGHT *a warning look. He
clears his throat.*)

LUTHER: Mr. and Mrs. . . . *Stone.*

(*The color drains from Dwight's face.*

Then LUTHER *steps aside, revealing . . .* HARRY STONE, *young,
dark, and chinless, standing in the doorway.* DWIGHT *struggles to com-
pose himself.*)

BERNETTE *(waving* HARRY *over):* I want you to meet my very new
husband. Just breaking in. (HARRY *approaches meekly.* BERNETTE
pulls him forward.) You two should know each other. *(Imperi-
ous.)* Go on, shake hands. Don't be bashful. Dwight. Harry.

(DWIGHT *stares at* HARRY *for a moment, just long enough to make
him uncomfortable. Then he puts out a hand.*)

DWIGHT: You're a very lucky—young fellow.

HARRY: I feel like I know you already. I've heard a lot about you.

DWIGHT *(dry):* That's very kind of Bernette . . . Uh, this is Annie
Ainsley, Jean and Paul Medill.

(BERNETTE *turns to the three guests and appraises them. She puts on
a wide, false smile and holds out a limp hand.*)

BERNETTE: Very pleased to meet you.

JEAN *(even larger, falser smile):* Pleasure's ours, I'm sure.

THE CIPHER: 'Lo.

(ANNIE *nods and smiles weakly.*)

DWIGHT: Luther. Champagne for Mr. and Mrs. . . .

JEAN: Stone.

(BERNETTE *shoots* JEAN *a warning look.*)

BERNETTE: I'd rather have my usual, Luther.

(BERNETTE *hands* LUTHER *her coat, revealing a sexy satin dress beneath.*

JEAN *catches* THE CIPHER *staring at her. She kicks him in the shin. Cut to:*)

INTERIOR: DRAWING ROOM/SITTING AREA. NIGHT.

DWIGHT *and his guests sit together, having drinks.*

DWIGHT: What a wonderful surprise. Where did you two honeymoon?

BERNETTE: We took a run up to Lake Arrow.

DWIGHT *(looking at* BERNETTE*):* Beautiful, isn't it Harry? How is the old lodge? Is Emil still there?

BERNETTE: Emil's still there.

DWIGHT: Has he done anything about changing that godawful wallpaper in the corner bedroom yet? *(To* ANNIE:*)* He was always going to. It was yellow, and looked as though somebody had thrown up all over it. *(Pointedly:)* Remember, Bernette?

BERNETTE *(to* HARRY*):* We both happened to be up there at the same time once. Vacationing.

(BERNETTE *puts a hand on Harry's cheek in a loving gesture.* ANNIE *sees* DWIGHT *wince and turn away.*)

DWIGHT: At the same time.

HARRY: I know. You told me.

(Awkward pause.)

ANNIE *(voice-over):* It wasn't that the husband didn't know about them. It was that he didn't want to be forced into publicly admitting that he did.

(THE CIPHER *sneezes.* JEAN *rolls her eyes and hands him a tissue from her purse.*)

BERNETTE: Well. We just wanted to stop by and say hello . . . We probably should be going. Wonderful to have met you all.

JEAN: Oh, yes. Wonderful.

HARRY: So long.

ANNIE: 'Bye.

(HARRY *leaves the room.*)

BERNETTE: *(dramatic):* Good night, Billy.

(DWIGHT *doesn't answer.* BERNETTE *pauses, then exits.*)

JEAN: It's late. We should be going as well.

(THE CIPHER *perks up at the suggestion.*)

THE CIPHER: Yes. Look at the time.

DWIGHT *(halfhearted):* Sure you don't want a refill?

(Suddenly, BERNETTE *reappears in the doorway.*)

BERNETTE: Billy, talk to Luther, will you? I can't get him to give me my coat.

(LUTHER *appears in the doorway, carrying the mink.*)

DWIGHT: Luther, is that Mrs. . . . Stone's coat you're holding?

BERNETTE: Of course it's my coat!

(BERNETTE *grabs for the coat.* LUTHER *quickly pulls it out of her reach. He obviously knows her moves.*)

DWIGHT: Read the label in the lining and see what it says.

(LUTHER *complies.*)

LUTHER: "Miss Bernette . . . Brady."

DWIGHT: Ah, yes. Miss *Brady.*

BERNETTE: Oh come on. *(She looks from* LUTHER *to* DWIGHT.*)* Are you serious?

(DWIGHT *moves to a rolltop desk and quickly scribbles something on a business card. He hands the card to* BERNETTE.)

DWIGHT: Take this with you. Use it.

BERNETTE: What—

(HARRY *drifts back into the doorway, not sure where he should be.*)

DWIGHT: I'll call him and get you a quick appointment. The whole thing will be over in no time.

(BERNETTE *studies the card. Her eyes narrow.*)

BERNETTE: What do I need a divorce lawyer for?

(DWIGHT *says nothing.*)

BERNETTE: That isn't funny.

DWIGHT: I'm not trying to be funny.

(BERNETTE *rips up the card, anger building.* HARRY *is still in the doorway, watching. And completely ignored.*)

BERNETTE: Is Luther going to give me the coat or not?

DWIGHT: Come back for the coat, Bernette. It'll be here, waiting for you.

(*Bernette's face is suddenly very tight and very ugly.*)

BERNETTE: I wouldn't come back here for all the money in all the world. So let's be consistent, shall we? How about it?

(BERNETTE *reaches around to the back of her neck and wrestles with the clasp to her pearls. They come undone and slide down the front of her chest until she traps them with a slap, balls them up, and flings them at* DWIGHT. *They hit him in the chest and fall to the floor.*

Dwight's face works with rage as he bends to retrieve the pearls.

Bernette's hands go to her ears. She throws her diamond earrings at him, hard, one at a time.

Trying to contain himself, DWIGHT *holds the pearls tightly, one end in each hand. His knuckles are white.*

BERNETTE *starts tearing at the satin of her dress. With a final rip, the entire dress peels off in a large spiral and snakes down to the floor.*

BERNETTE *kicks the dress off of her leg and stands there defiantly in her sexy pink underclothes.*

There is absolutely nothing to do but stare. And everyone does. For a long, stunned moment.

Then, with a choked cry, BERNETTE *turns and runs from the room, brushing past* HARRY *on the way. After a brief moment, he follows her.*

No one knows what to say. JEAN *clears her throat.)*

JEAN: What a charming couple.

(Close on ANNIE, *watching* DWIGHT. *His wild eyes are glued to the door. Dissolve to:)*

INTERIOR: ANNIE'S APARTMENT. DAY.

The familiar strains of "None but the Lonely Heart" fill the small space.

ANNIE *stands in front of a mirror, smoking a cigarette and holding something to her cheek. Moving in, we see that it is Dwight's stolen handkerchief.*

ANNIE *(voice-over):* Six weeks passed and nothing happened. No word. No sign. (ANNIE *puts the handkerchief to her nose. She inhales.)* Was he back with her? Was he with somebody else? Was he alone? I couldn't stop thinking about it.

*(*ANNIE *moves to the telephone. Hesitates. Then dials a number. As she waits for someone to answer the line, she nervously pushes at her hair, and in the process singes it with the lit cigarette.)*

ANNIE: Hello, Dwight? . . .

INTERIOR: DRAWING ROOM. NIGHT.

ANNIE *(voice-over):* So back we went, for another glimpse at the real-life peepshow.

(As DWIGHT *crosses to greet them, he seems like a different man: lively steps; broad, easy smile; welcoming arms.)*

DWIGHT: Hello, hello!

*(*DWIGHT *vigorously shakes The Cipher's hand, kisses* JEAN *on the cheek.)*

DWIGHT: Annie, you look beautiful!

(*He gives* ANNIE *an affectionate kiss. She blushes.*)

ANNIE: Thank you.

(*Dissolve to:*)

INTERIOR: POWDER ROOM. NIGHT.

ANNIE *stands in front of the vanity mirror, happily putting on a fresh dose of lipstick.*

INTERIOR: HALLWAY. NIGHT.

ANNIE *walks down the hallway, toward the drawing room. Something catches her eye.*

It is a door, swung slightly open. Within, barely visible in the dim light, is a masculine bedroom.

Annie's eyes widen. She looks quickly toward the drawing room, then slips inside.

INTERIOR: DWIGHT'S BEDROOM. NIGHT.

ANNIE *pauses, taking in the room. Dwight's room.*

She moves to the bed and sits. Her hands move up and down the bedcover. ANNIE *slowly lies down on the bed. She takes a pillow and hugs it to her chest. Then she brings it to her face and smells it . . .*

Annie's expression changes. She smells a woman. ANNIE *abruptly gets up off the bed, taking another look around the room.*

Then she sees it: sticking out of a small trashcan at the foot of the bed is the toe of a woman's stocking. Annie's face falls.

INTERIOR: DRAWING ROOM. LATER THAT NIGHT.

DWIGHT, JEAN, *and* THE CIPHER *enjoy their after-dinner drinks.* ANNIE *stands far apart, trying to warm herself in front of the fireplace.*

ANNIE (*voice-over*): I tried, but I couldn't summon up the proper face. How do you put on a face when a ten-pound weight's been dropped on your head?

DWIGHT: Why don't you try tuning in to the Bowl concert, Luther?

(LUTHER *fiddles with the radio. Charlie Parker's music fills the room.*)

JEAN: If that's the Bowl concert, they've certainly picked up some bad habits.

DWIGHT: Luther, the open-air concert. At the Hollywood Bowl.

LUTHER: I can't seem to get it . . .

(ANNIE *pipes up from her perch by the window.*)

ANNIE: The concert was called off. One of the girls at the store had tickets.

DWIGHT: Called off? Why would they call it off?

(*Eye contact. The power of Dwight's gaze throws* ANNIE.)

ANNIE: On account of the rain.

DWIGHT: Is it raining?

ANNIE: It's drizzling.

DWIGHT: Oh.

(ANNIE *looks back out the window.*)

ANNIE (*voice-over*): I was wrong. It was a twenty-pound weight. And it was getting heavier all the time.

(DWIGHT *looks down at his watch. He shakes his wrist. Dissolve to:*)

INTERIOR: DRAWING ROOM/SITTING AREA. LATER.

ANNIE *still stands apart from the others.*

JEAN *and* DWIGHT *are watching* THE CIPHER *make a house of cards. He works with rapt attention, until he sneezes and the cards collapse. Expressionless,* THE CIPHER *begins building again.* JEAN *throws a tissue at him.*

JEAN: (*to* THE CIPHER): I told you to go on that antibiotic. (*To anybody listening:*) The doctor swore up and down that a little antibiotic would get rid of all his trouble. (DWIGHT *reacts.*) But does he listen? Of course not. He never listens to anybody.

(Suddenly, confident feminine footsteps rumble down the gallery. DWIGHT *looks at the clock.*

BERNETTE *appears in the doorway, unannounced, wearing her characteristic coat and pose. The pearls she threw at* DWIGHT *are prominently displayed around her neck.)*

ANNIE *(voice-over):* He'd made a few improvements on her. Her dress was a little higher at the neck now, and the phantom price tag had been taken off.

DWIGHT: Bernette. You remember Annie and Jean and Paul.

BERNETTE: Oh, yes, of course. How *are* you? (BERNETTE *takes off the mink and drapes it lavishly across the nearest chair.)* Sorry I'm so late. I stayed on to the very end of the concert.

DWIGHT *(tight):* Did you?

(JEAN and ANNIE *share a puzzled look.)*

BERNETTE: I simply couldn't tear myself away. You should have come with me, Billy. It was heavenly.

DWIGHT *(arch):* What did they play first?

*(BERNETTE *lights up a cigarette and inhales, relishing it.)*

BERNETTE: Shostakovich.

(JEAN and ANNIE *share a look of utter disbelief.* DWIGHT *looks down at the floor, his face quickly loosing color.*

BERNETTE *picks up the tension and grows uneasy.)*

BERNETTE: Didn't I pronounce it well?

DWIGHT: Too well.

*(BERNETTE *stands there, like a cornered animal, twisting her pearls around her finger.)*

ANNIE *(voice-over):* She couldn't figure out how, but she sensed that the jig was up. And it was a funny thing, but at that moment I felt kind of sorry for her.

BERNETTE: I have a headache.

JEAN: Shostakovich always gives me a headache, too.

(BERNETTE *shoots* JEAN *a hostile look as she picks up the mink coat.*)

BERNETTE: I think I'll go home. If you'll all excuse me . . .

DWIGHT (*jaw clenched*): There's nothing keeping you here, Bernette.

(BERNETTE *kisses* DWIGHT *and moves swiftly to the doorway.*)

BERNETTE: Well, then. Good night.

THE CIPHER: But you just arrived—

(JEAN *gives him a kick in the shin.*)

ANNIE (*voice-over*): The Cipher was evidently hoping that she was going to rip off her dress again.

(BERNETTE *proudly exits, her head held high. As she turns into the gallery, she leaves behind a large puff of smoke. Her footsteps retreat down the hall.*)

ANNIE (*voice-over*): Sometimes that's all the trace you leave behind in this world: a little cigarette smoke, quickly blown away.

There is a loud bang as the front door slams in the background.

INTERIOR: ANNIE'S BEDROOM. LATER THAT NIGHT.

Cigarette smoke curls up around Annie's reflection as she sits in front of her vanity mirror. She begins to slowly undo the buttons of her green dress.

Then a figure appears softly behind her. She watches as it approaches and bends to meet her reflection. It is DWIGHT.

DWIGHT *takes a double strand of pearls and lovingly drapes them around Annie's neck. She watches him as he clasps them at her nape.*

Then DWIGHT *reaches down and takes* ANNIE *by the shoulders, gently lifting her to a standing position and turning her to face him.*

DWIGHT *looks deeply into Annie's eyes. He slowly, slowly, pulls her closer, bending to kiss her. . . .*

ANNIE *closes her eyes . . . waiting for the kiss. Cut to:*

INTERIOR: ANNIE'S ROOM. NIGHT.

ANNIE *sits in front of her vanity mirror, eyes closed, hand at her neck. It has all been a fantasy. But from the look on Annie's face, it feels very real.*

ANNIE *opens her eyes and looks at herself.*

Then she makes a decision. She stands.

ANNIE *(voice-over):* I don't know where I got the courage to do what I did next. But before I could stop myself, I was already doing it.

EXTERIOR: BILLINGS HOUSE. NIGHT.

A taxi cab crunches to a stop on the gravel in front of the house. The lights are still on within. ANNIE *pays the driver and gets out. The cab drives off.*

ANNIE *moves to the front door. She rings the doorbell. Waits.*

ANNIE *pushes a stray hair from her forehead. The rain has done damage to her hairdo, and it's coming apart in soft ringlets around her face. She rings the doorbell again.*

DWIGHT *(off-screen):* Who is it?

ANNIE: Annie.

(There is a long beat. Then DWIGHT *opens the door a crack. He is dressed in a lounging robe.)*

ANNIE: Did I get you out of bed?

DWIGHT *(forced smile):* No. I was just getting ready, by easy stages.

*(*DWIGHT *makes no move to open the door further.)*

ANNIE: It's my key. I . . . I lost it. I can't get into my house. *(*DWIGHT *looks beyond her to the empty driveway.)* I didn't want to bother Jean and Paul with driving all the way back. I took a cab.

DWIGHT: It's not here. Your key's not here. I would have found it myself after you left.

ANNIE: Won't you let me come in a moment and look?

DWIGHT: But it's not here, Annie, I'm sure of it.

(He's obviously not going to move. Standoff.)

ANNIE: Oh. You're not alone. I'm sorry. I didn't mean to—

(DWIGHT *suddenly steps back, opening the door for her.*)

DWIGHT: You're mistaken. Come in.

(ANNIE *steps inside.*)

INTERIOR: BILLINGS ENTRY AND GALLERY. NIGHT.

ANNIE *follows* DWIGHT *down the long hallway.*

DWIGHT *(casually)*: Whatever gave you the idea that I wasn't alone? Even Luther's gone home for the night.

(*As they pass Dwight's bedroom,* ANNIE *pauses. The door is ajar, and dark within.*)

ANNIE: I think maybe I left the key here.

(DWIGHT *catches his breath slightly and firmly pulls the door shut.*)

DWIGHT: That's impossible. You weren't in my bedroom.

ANNIE: What if I was?

DWIGHT *(genuinely surprised)*: Then it would be a breach of manners on your part.

ANNIE: I could have wandered in there . . . by mistake.

(*Annie's eyeing the doorknob suggestively.* DWIGHT *moves behind* ANNIE *and ushers her toward the drawing room. Anything to get her away from that door.*)

DWIGHT: Come inside and we'll have a drink. Just you and me.

(*We hold on the closed door as they move down the hallway.*)

INTERIOR: DRAWING ROOM. NIGHT.

Dimly lit. Shadowy. ANNIE *sits down on the sofa, facing away from the door.*

DWIGHT *brings over two drinks. He sits in a chair opposite her.* ANNIE *pats the sofa.*

ANNIE: You don't have to sit in the next state, you know.

(DWIGHT *moves over next to* ANNIE. *She takes an unusually large gulp from her drink. Beat.*)

ANNIE: It was a pretty bad jolt.

DWIGHT: What was?

ANNIE: You don't have to pretend with me.

DWIGHT *(clearly pained):* Please. Let's not talk about it.

ANNIE: Does it hurt that much?

(He doesn't answer. ANNIE *leans toward him. As her hair falls down around her face, she looks more beautiful than we have seen her before. The obvious longing on her face only enhances this effect.)*

ANNIE: Why don't you put iodine on it?

DWIGHT *(bitter, ironic smile):* Is there iodine for such things?

ANNIE: Here's the bottle, right beside you . . . *(Leaning farther still.)* It stings for a minute, and then you heal. You heal clean. No festering. Won't you try . . . *(They are so close now that their breath is mingling. Annie's green eyes are dreamy-gray.)* . . . iodine? *(*DWIGHT *turns away. Just a little bit, but it sends a definite message.* ANNIE *regroups.)* Don't you understand me, Dwight? I'm making love to you. *(*DWIGHT *stares at her, astonished beyond words.)* Would it be that bad? Being married to me?

DWIGHT: Married?

ANNIE: You've just been proposed to, Dwight. That was the first proposal I've ever made. *(*DWIGHT *smiles uncomfortably, as if waiting to hear that it has all been a joke.)* You don't laugh when a lady proposes to you. You meet her on her own ground. You give her that much at least.

*(*DWIGHT *puts a hand on her knee, in apology, not affection.)*

DWIGHT: Annie—I'm not—cut out . . . It would be about the dirtiest trick I could play. You'd be sorry.

ANNIE: I want to be. Let me be sorry.

DWIGHT: It's you I'm thinking of. You don't want *me*.

ANNIE: You're getting your pronouns mixed. *(*DWIGHT *puts his arm around her in a comforting manner. He shouldn't have. She closes her eyes and leans her head against his shoulder. She whispers:)* Then on shorter terms. As short as you want. *(He tries to jerk his arm away. She catches it, holds it around herself.)* Even just—for tonight.

DWIGHT *(clearly pained):* My God!

> *(ANNIE lets go of his arm. He quickly pulls it back.)*

ANNIE: Seduction doesn't agree with you. *(She rises, tries to muster some dignity. He sits, watching her.)* You look positively harassed.

DWIGHT *(standing):* I'll see you out.

> *(ANNIE turns to the door.)*

ANNIE: Never mind.

> *(ANNIE stops in her tracks, because there, thrown on an ottoman to the left of the doorway, is Bernette's mink coat. ANNIE stares at the coat.)*

ANNIE *(voice-over):* A cold wind came from nowhere and knifed me where I stood.

> *(She looks back to DWIGHT. He meets her gaze. ANNIE turns and quickly walks from the room.)*

INTERIOR: HALLWAY. NIGHT.

> ANNIE *moves rapidly down the hallway.* DWIGHT *moves to the drawing-room doorway, still watching her.*

> ANNIE *stops in front of Dwight's bedroom.* DWIGHT *tenses at the end of the hallway, watching to see what she'll do.*

> ANNIE *defiantly reaches out toward the doorknob.*

DWIGHT *(utterly toneless):* Annie. There's the front door.

> *(ANNIE looks over to DWIGHT. He's standing in the doorway, waiting, like a cat about to spring.*

> *As ANNIE turns back again to the door, she accidentally kicks something with the toe of her shoe.*

> *It is a single pearl.* DWIGHT *and* ANNIE *both watch it roll slowly across the marble floor.*

> *Their eyes meet. It is a moment of silent and complete communication.* ANNIE *reaches out and deliberately puts her hand onto the doorknob. Squeezes it.*

> DWIGHT*'s eyes stare intensely, coldly. There is a long beat. Neither of them moves.)*

DWIGHT: Good night, Annie.

(ANNIE *drops her hand to her side, turns and walks rapidly to the front door.*

As ANNIE *moves through the front door, she sees* DWIGHT *reach out with one arm and support himself limply against the doorway.)*

ANNIE *(voice-over):* They tell you wrong when they tell you infatuation dies a sudden death.

(Then door is shut between them. Dissolve to:)

INTERIOR: ANNIE'S APARTMENT. AFTERNOON.

ANNIE, JEAN, *and* THE CIPHER *sit playing bridge, as before.*

ANNIE *(voice-over):* Infatuation dies a lingering, painful death. So I waited. I waited for an antibiotic for love.

JEAN: Your trick, honey. Your lead.

(ANNIE *reaches into her hand and throws out the Queen of Hearts. Dissolve to:)*

INTERIOR: ANNIE'S APARTMENT. EARLY MORNING.

The apartment is bright, open and airy. Windows up. Birds singing.

ANNIE *washes her hair in the kitchen sink.*

ANNIE *(voice-over):* Three weeks later I saw my last love again. By last, I don't mean latest, I mean my first and yet my final one.

(There is a small rap at the door. ANNIE *reacts with surprise. She hesitates for a beat.*

Another rap, louder this time. ANNIE *grabs a towel, gathers her robe to her chest, and moves to the door, wet hair and all. The effect is very sexy.)*

ANNIE *(through the door):* Who is it?

(Beat.)

DWIGHT *(off-screen):* It's Dwight.

ANNIE *(obviously shocked):* Dwight? . . .

(ANNIE *opens the peephole and looks through. Dwight's distorted image stares back at her from the other side of the door.* ANNIE *is speechless. She stands back, takes a breath, and then opens the door a crack. The chain remains latched.*)

DWIGHT: Did I get you out of bed?

ANNIE: No . . . uh, I was just getting ready. . . .

DWIGHT: By easy stages? (ANNIE *doesn't know what to say.* DWIGHT *picks up the ball.*) Uh, here's your newspaper . . . (*he hands her a newspaper through the small gap in the door*) and I picked up your mail downstairs . . .

ANNIE: Thanks . . .

(*He gives her her mail. There is an awkward beat.*)

DWIGHT: Listen, Annie. I've been thinking. About that night at my house—

ANNIE (*simultaneously/overlapping*): I don't want to know . . .

DWIGHT (*overlapping*): And I wanted you to know . . . I wanted you . . . I want you to . . . marry me. (ANNIE *just stares at him.*) Am I too late?

(ANNIE *is stunned silent.*)

DWIGHT: Let's get married, Annie . . . It's the first proposal I've ever made.

ANNIE: That's not funny.

DWIGHT: It's not meant to be funny. I want to marry you.

(DWIGHT *hands her a small parcel. She takes it from him and slowly opens it. Inside is a small jewelry box. Annie's eyes widen. She opens it, revealing—*

a delicate diamond engagement ring. In the center of it is a small pearl. ANNIE *looks down, at the ring, stunned.*)

DWIGHT: I could take care of you, Annie. I could protect you. (*He's staring at her meaningfully.*) And you could protect me. (ANNIE *swallows hard. Long, agonizing beat.*) Come on. Open up.

ANNIE (*voice-over*): Not exactly a fairy tale. But at least it had a happy ending. (ANNIE *looks to the small chain that separates them.*) Did I wonder about her? About that night? A little bit, but not for long. After all, the people you know never do things like that. The people you read about might, but never the people you know . . .

(Close on the latched chain as ANNIE *reaches toward it, and then hesitates. . . .*

Pull back as ANNIE *stands there, deciding, at the door.)*

The Quiet Room

Jonathan Craig

Detective Sergeant Carl Streeter's home on Ashland Avenue was modest. So were the dark gray suits he always wore, and the four-year-old Plymouth he drove. But in various lock boxes around the city he had accumulated nearly fifty thousand dollars.

He was thinking about the money now as he watched his daughter Jeannie clear away the dinner dishes. He never tired of watching her. She had just turned sixteen, but she was already beautiful, and lately she had begun to develop the infinitely feminine movements and mannerisms he had once found so irresistible in her mother.

The thought of his wife soured the moment, and he frowned. It had been wonderful, having Barbara away for a few weeks. But she'd be back from the seashore next Monday, and then the nagging and bickering and general unpleasantness would start up again. It didn't seem possible, he reminded himself for probably the ten thousandth time, that anyone who had once been almost as slim and lovely as Jeannie could have grown into two hundred pounds of shapeless, complaining blubber.

"More coffee, Dad?" Jeannie asked.

He pushed his chair back from the table and got up. "No," he said. "I guess I'd better get going if I want to get down to the precinct by seven."

"Seven? But I thought your shift didn't start till eight."

"It doesn't. There are a couple things I want to take care of down there, though."

"When will you be home?"

Depends. Not until three or four, anyhow. We're a little short-handed."

"You put in too many hours, Dad."

"Maybe," he said. He grinned at her and walked out to the front hall to get his hat. Just another few months, he thought. Six months at the outside, and I'll have enough to put Jeannie in a damned good college, ditch Barbara and her lard, and tell the Chief to go to hell.

Sally Creighton was waiting for him in the Inferno Bar. She pushed a folded piece of paper across the table as he sat down facing her.

"How's the Eighteenth Precinct's one and only policewoman?" Streeter asked.

Sally looked at him narrowly. "Never mind the amenities. Here's the list we got off that girl last night."

He put the list into his pocket without looking at it. "Did you check them?"

"Don't I always? Only two of them might be good for any money. I marked them. One's a dentist, and the other guy runs a bar and grill over on Summit." She lifted her beer and sipped at it, study-ing him over the rim of the glass. "There've been a few changes made, Carl." Her bony, angular face was set in hard lines.

"Like what?"

"From now on I'm getting fifty percent."

"We've been over that before."

"And this is the last time. Fifty percent, Carl. Starting as of now."

He laughed shortly. "I do the dirty work, and take the chances—and you come in for half, eh?"

"Either that, or I cut out." She put a quarter next to her glass and stood up. "Think it over, Sergeant. You aren't the only bruiser around the Eighteenth that can shake a guy down. Start making with the fifty percent, or I'll find another partner." She moved toward the door with a long, almost mannish stride.

Streeter spread his fingers flat against the table top, fighting back the anger that he knew would get him nowhere. For almost a full min-ute he stared at the broken, scarred knuckles of his hands. By God, he thought, if it's the last thing I ever do I'll knock about ten of that woman's yellow teeth down into her belly.

Hell, he'd taught her the racket in the first place. He'd shown her how to scare hell out of those under-age chippies until they thought they were going to spend the rest of their lives in jail if they didn't play ball. Why, he'd even had to educate Sally in the ways of keeping those girls away from the juvenile authorities until she'd had a chance to drain them.

He closed his right fist and clenched it until the knuckles stood up like serrated knobs of solid white bone. Damn that Sally, anyhow; she was getting too greedy. Fifty percent!

He got up slowly and moved toward the door.

Twenty minutes later, after he had checked in at the precinct and been assigned a cruiser, he pulled up in a No Parking zone and took out the list Sally had given him. His anger had subsided a little now. Actually, he realized, no cop had ever been in a better spot. His first real break with the Department had been when they had organized the Morals Squad and assigned him to it as a roving detective. The second break had occurred when Sally Creighton was transferred to the Eighteenth. He hadn't talked to her more than ten minutes that first day before he'd realized that he had found the right person to work into his ideas.

In three years, working alone every night as he did, he had loaded his safe deposit boxes with almost fifty thousand dollars.

He lit a cigarette and glanced at the list. Of the two names Sally had marked, the man who owned the bar and grill was the best bet. The other, the dentist, lived on the far side of town; and besides, Streeter had found it was always best to brace a man at his place of business. There was a tremendous psychological factor working on his side when he did that, and especially if the guy happened to be a professional man. He memorized the address of the bar and grill and eased the cruiser away from the curb.

It was too late for the short-order dinner crowd and too early for the beer drinkers, and Streeter had the long bar entirely to himself.

The bartender came up, a thin blond man in his middle thirties.

Streeter ordered beer, and when the blond man brought it to him he said, "I'm looking for Johnny Cabe."

The bartender smiled. "That's me. What can I do for you?"

"Quite a bit, maybe," Streeter said. "It all depends."

Some of the bartender's smile went away. "I don't follow you."

"You will," Streeter said. He took out his wallet and showed the other man his gold badge.

"What's the trouble?" Cabe asked.

"Well, now," Streeter said, "there really doesn't have to be any."
He took a swallow of beer and leaned a little closer to Cabe. "You had
quite a time for yourself last night, they tell me."

Cabe's eyes grew thoughtful. "Last night? You kidding? All I did
was have a few beers over at Ed Riley's place, and—"

"Yeah," Streeter said. "And then you picked up somebody."

"What if I did?"

"Then you took her over to your room."

"So what? They don't put guys in jail for—"

"The hell they don't," Streeter said. "Raping a girl can put you
away damned near forever, boy."

"Rape? You're crazy! Hell, she wanted to go. She suggested it."

"Next you're going to tell me she charged you for it."

"Sure, she did. Twenty bucks."

"That's a damn shame," Streeter said. "Because it's still rape, and
you're in one hell of a jam."

Cabe moved his lips as if to speak, but there was no sound.

"That girl you took home with you was only fifteen years old,"
Streeter said. "She—"

"Fifteen! She told me she was nineteen! She *looked* nineteen!"

"You should have looked twice. She's fifteen. That makes it statutory rape, and it doesn't make one damn bit of difference what you
thought, or whether she was willing, or if she charged you for it, or
anything else." He smiled. "It's statutory rape, brother, and that
means you've had it."

Cabe moistened his lips. "I can't believe it."

"Get your hat," Streeter said.

"You're arresting me?"

"I didn't come in here just for the beer. Hurry it up."

"God," the blond man said. "God, officer, I—"

"Kind of hard to get used to the idea, isn't it?" Streeter asked
softly.

Cabe's forehead glistened with sweat. "Listen, officer, I got a
wife. Best kid on earth, see. I don't know what came over me last
night. I just got tight, I guess, and . . . God, I—"

Streeter shook his head slowly. "Good thing you haven't got any
children," he said.

"But I have! Two of them. Seven and nine. And my wife, she's—
she's going to have another baby pretty soon. That's why—I mean

that's how come I was kind of anxious for a woman last night. I—" He broke off, biting at his lower lip.

"Tough," Streeter said. "Real tough. But it's that kind of world, friend. I've got a kid myself, so I know how it is. But—" he shrugged—"there isn't a hell of a lot I can do about it." He shook his head sadly. "When little guys—guys like you and me—get in a jam, it's just plain tough. But guys with dough . . . well, sometimes they can buy their way out."

Cabe looked at him a long moment. "How much dough?"

"Quite a bit," Streeter said. "More than you've got, Johnny. Better get your hat."

"Let's cut out this crap," Cabe said. "I asked you how much dough?"

"We got to think of your wife and kids," Streeter said. "So we'll have to go easy. Let's say a grand."

"I ain't got it."

"You can get it. A little at a time, maybe, but you can get it." He took another swallow of his beer. "How much you got in the cash register?"

"About three hundred. I got to pay the help tonight, or there wouldn't be that much."

"Too bad about the help," Streeter said. "Let's have the three hundred. In a couple weeks I'll be back. By that time you'll have the other seven hundred, eh, Johnny-boy?"

Cabe went to the cash register, took out the money, and came back. "Here," he said. Then, softly beneath his breath he added: "You bastard!"

Streeter put the money in his pocket and stood up. "Thanks, Johnny," he said. "Thanks a lot. You reckon I ought to give you a receipt? A little reminder to get up that other seven hundred bucks?"

"I'll remember," Cabe said.

"I'm afraid you might not," Streeter said, smiling. "So here's your receipt." He leaned across the bar and slammed his fist flush against the blond man's mouth.

Johnny Cabe crashed into the back-bar, blood trickling from the corners of his mouth.

"Thanks again, Johnny," Streeter said. "You serve a good glass of beer." He turned and went outside to the cruiser.

He spent the next four hours making routine check-ups and trying to think of improvements in the system he had worked out with

Sally Creighton. The system had been working nicely, but it was a long
way from foolproof. Most of the cops on the force were honest, and for
them Streeter had nothing but contempt. But there were a few like
himself, and those were the ones who worried him. He'd had reason
lately to suspect that a couple of them were getting on to him. If they
did, then his racket was over. They could politic around until they got
him busted off the Morals Squad. Then they'd take over themselves.
And, he reflected, they wouldn't even have to go that far. They could
simply cut themselves in on a good thing.

And that Sally . . . He'd have to start splitting down the middle
with her, he knew. Maybe she was even worth it. One thing was sure:
she'd learned how to terrify young girls better than anyone else he
could have teamed up with. He'd seen her work on just one girl, but it
had been enough to convince him. Sally had wrapped her arms around
a fourteen-year-old girl's throat in such a way that the girl was helpless.
Then, with a hand towel soaked with water, she had beaten the girl
across the stomach until she was almost dead. When the girl had recov-
ered slightly, she had been only too willing to tell Sally every man she'd
picked up during the last six months.

That particular list of names, Streeter recalled, had been worth a
little over ten thousand in shake-down money.

He came to a drug store and braked the cruiser at the curb.

In the phone booth, he dialed Sally's number, humming tune-
lessly to himself. He felt much better now, with Johnny Cabe's three
hundred dollars in his pocket.

When Sally answered, he said, "Streeter. Anything doing?"

"I got one in here now," Sally said. "A real tough baby. I picked
her up at Andy's trying to promote a drunk at the bar."

"She talking?" he asked.

"Not a damn word. I got her back in the Quiet room."

"What's her name?"

"Don't know. All she had in her bag was a lipstick and a few
bucks." She paused. "Like I said, she's tough. She won't even give us
the time of day."

"Listen," Streeter said. "Things are slow tonight. See if you can
get her talking. Maybe I can collect a bill here and there."

"That's an idea."

"You haven't lost your technique, have you?"

"No."

"All right. So turn it on. Give her that towel across the belly. That
ought to make her talkative."

For the first time he could remember, he heard Sally laugh.

"You know," she said, "I'm just in the mood for something like that. Maybe I will."

"Sure," Streeter said. "The sooner you get me some names, the sooner I get us some dough."

"Don't forget, Carl—it's fifty percent now."

"Sure."

He hung up and went back out to the cruiser.

After another slow hour of routine checks, he decided to see how Sally was making out with the tough pick-up. He stopped at a diner and called her.

"God," she said, as soon as he had identified himself, "we're really in it now, Carl." Her voice was ragged, and there was panic in it.

"What do you mean?"

"I mean I went too far. I was doing what you said, and—"

"For God's sake, Sally! What's happened."

"I—I think I broke her neck . . ."

"You think! Don't you know?"

There was a pause. "Yes. I broke her neck, Carl. I didn't mean to, but she was fighting, and all at once I heard something snap and . . ."

The thin film of perspiration along his back and shoulders was suddenly like a sheath of ice.

"When, Sally? When did it happen?"

"J-just now. Just a minute ago."

"You sure she's dead?"

"Dead or dying. There was a pulse a few seconds ago, but—"

"But her neck! You're positive it's broken? That it just isn't dislocated, or something?"

"It's broken. This is it, Carl. For both of us. God . . ."

"Listen, damn it!" he said. "Was she wearing stockings? Long ones?"

"Yes. What—"

"Take one of them off her and hang her up with it."

She seemed to have trouble breathing. "But I—I can't do that. I—"

"You've got to! Do you hear? It's the only way out. Tie one end of the stocking around her neck. Then put a chair beneath that steam pipe that runs across the ceiling. Haul her up on the chair with you and tie the other end around the pipe. Leave her hanging and kick the chair away, just like she'd done it herself."

He waited, breathing heavily.

"All right," Sally said. "I'll try."

"You'd better. And hurry. Get her up there and then leave the room for a few minutes. When you go back to see your prisoner, she's hanged herself. See? They'll give you hell for leaving her alone with stockings on, but that's all they can do. She panicked and hanged herself; that's all."

"But, Carl, I—"

"No buts! Get busy!"

He opened up the siren and kept it open all the way back to the Eighteenth. He ran up the station steps, through the corridors. He was breathing quickly. When he arrived at the second floor he was soaked with perspiration.

He forced himself to walk leisurely through the large room that housed the detective headquarters, back toward the short corridor that led to the Quiet room. The Quiet room was a small, soundproof detention cell where they sometimes put the screamers and howlers until they calmed down enough for questioning. It had been designed to provide some degree of quiet for the men out in the headquarters room, and not as a torture chamber.

But it had served Streeter and Sally Creighton well and often.

Streeter paused at the door to the corridor and drew a paper cup of water from the cooler. Where in hell was Sally? he wondered. She should be out here by now, killing time before she went back to discover that her prisoner had hanged herself.

He glanced about him. There were only two other detectives in the room, and both were busy with paper work. A man in a T-shirt and blue jeans sat dozing in a chair, one wrist handcuffed to a chair arm.

Then he heard footsteps behind him, and Sally's voice said, "Thank God you're here."

He turned to look at her. Her face was gray and her forehead was sheened with sweat.

"Where've you been?" he asked.

"To the john. I don't know . . . something about this made me sick in the stomach."

"Yeah. Well, let's go down there and get it over with."

He led the way down the corridor to the Quiet room and threw the heavy bolt. The goddamned little chippie, he thought. So she'd thought she was tough . . . Well, she'd asked for it, hadn't she? She'd asked for it, and she'd damn well got it.

He jerked the door open and looked up at the girl hanging from the steam pipe. Her body was moving, very slowly, a few inches to the right and then back again.

He stared at her while the floor seemed to tilt beneath his feet and something raw and sickening filled his stomach.

He took a faltering step forward, and then another, his eyes straining and misted. It was difficult for him to see clearly. Absently, he brushed at his eyes with his sleeve. The hanging figure before him sprang into sudden, terrifying focus.

The girl's body was as slim and graceful looking in death as it had been a few hours ago when he had watched her clearing away the dinner dishes. But not the face, not the horribly swollen face.

"Jeannie," he whispered. "Jeannie, Jeannie . . ."

The Quiet Room

Teleplay by

Howard A.

Rodman

Cast

Joe Mantegna	Carl Streeter
Bonnie Bedelia	Sally Creighton
Vinessa Shaw	Jeannie Streeter
J. E. Freeman	Johnny Cabe
Peter Gallagher	Morris Yorgrau
Kathy Kinney	Mrs. Sullivan
Patrick Breen	Doctor
Wayne Grace	Sergeant
Genia Michaela	Helen
Norman Large	Cop #1
Hank Stone	Cop #2

Executive Producer: Sydney Pollack
Producers: William Horberg, Lindsay Doran, Steve Golin
Co-Producer: David Wisnievitz
Directed by: Steven Soderbergh
Director of Photography: Emmanuel Lubezki
Production designed by: Armin Ganz
Costumes designed by: Shay Cunliffe
Casting by: Owens Hill and Rachel Abroms
Fallen Angels theme by: Elmer Bernstein
Music by: Peter Bernstein
Edited by: Stan Salfas
Story Editor: Geoffrey Stier

EXTERIOR: BRONSON AVENUE. DAY.

December 1951. A simple Hollywood bungalow, differing from its neighbors only in the color of its window trim.

A gray-on-gray 1947 Plymouth is parked in the driveway. We hear a voice: Let me tell you, sugar, what your *average* man would do . . .

INTERIOR: STREETER HOME. KITCHEN. DAY.

The voice belongs to CARL STREETER, *a solid, compact man in his mid-40s. He's wearing brown suspenders and a brown leather shoulder holster and when he raises his arms we can see the blued .38 Police Special.*

Carl's cooking breakfast for his sixteen-year-old daughter, JEANNIE. *She's wearing a white blouse, plaid skirt, and knee socks; her hands are folded in front of her: a masque of grooming and deportment.*

CARL *(continuing):* Your *average* man, he'd wait for the water to boil, one minute, two minutes, and then, when the water's boiling, he'd drop in the eggs. What happens? Sudden cold exposed to sudden heat—remember? Eggs crack. The white stuff just oozes out. *(JEANNIE makes a face.)* Exactly. Now the smart man—and someday, sweetheart, you can say your daddy, he taught you this—the smart man, puts the eggs in the water, *then* turns on the heat. Five minutes exactly. *(As if on cue, the wind-up kitchen timer rings loudly.* CARL *extracts the eggs with a slotted spoon.)* See? *(He runs the eggs under the tap. Counting on his fingers:)* Cold water, one, stops the cooking, two, cools 'em off. *(Now he places the eggs in ceramic holders of the cute variety: they look like rabbits.)* Makes 'em easy to handle. *(He puts one in front of* JEANNIE, *keeps the other for himself.)* Perfection. What do you say?

JEANNIE: Thank you.

(He eyes her sharply.)

CARL: In this house, there will be no sarcasm.

JEANNIE: I was not being sarcastic.

*(*JEANNIE *stares at him for a long time. He stares back. Finally:)*

CARL *(gesturing toward her eggcup):* Hey, pumpkin. Before it gets cold.

(He taps the egg with the side of his knife—gently, delicately, performing a tender surgery.)

JEANNIE: When will you be home?

CARL: Midnight. Well. 'Round holidays, we're always a little short-handed.

*(*JEANNIE *contemplates her egg.)*

JEANNIE: You work too hard.

CARL: If there's a chance for overtime, I grab it. You know how it is. *(Pausing:)* I want to *provide.*

(Jeannie's tone is slow, even, without affect.)

JEANNIE: It's not what you bring me. It's you. I just want you.

(Carl is about to say something about sarcasm—but he doesn't quite have enough evidence.)

EXTERIOR: STREETER HOME. DAY.

The gray Plymouth, in the driveway chugging away in neutral. JEANNIE, *holding a stack of books primly in front of her, stands motionless by the curb.*

A yellow school bus pulls in front of her. Stops. When it pulls away, she is not to be seen.

Only now does the Plymouth pull out of the driveway, heading off in the other direction.

INTERIOR: STATIONHOUSE. NIGHT.

About a half-dozen male cops—some in uniform, some in plain-clothes—lounge about the large bullpen drinking coffee, talking sports, typing up reports.

Now comes Patrolwoman SALLY CREIGHTON, *a hundred-ten pounds of trouble in a tight blue uniform. Her marcelled wave stays in place as she drags a very young woman in handcuffs (*HELEN*) through the bullpen.*

The young woman is wearing way too much makeup, and a dress that doesn't leave much to the imagination.

The patrolmen whistle and hoot.

COP #1: Sal's got one for the Quiet Room.

COP #2: Three since Monday? She's on a streak.

(Now CARL *calls out.)*

CARL *(gesturing to include* HELEN*)*: Hey, Sally. I see you've been hanging out with the elite.

SALLY: I don't recall seeing you in Ciro's last night.

CARL: Where you been working, Sal? Western Avenue again?

SALLY: You know how it is. I was visiting your mother and just happened to be in the neighborhood.

(The other patrolmen make "woo woo" noises. Carl's been hit.)

CARL *(playing to the crowd)*: You *can* tell them apart: one of 'em's got a badge. *(When the cops don't respond:)* She really got me with that last one. She really made me hurt. *(*SALLY *shoots him one last glance.)* Comedienne.

*(*SALLY *drags her charge through a door in the back.)*

INTERIOR: "QUIET ROOM." NIGHT.

A small, soundproof detention room in the back of the stationhouse. Cork walls, a bare light bulb, a sink, and exposed steam pipes running across the ceiling.

SALLY *and* HELEN, *the young woman, are seated at an old, scarred wooden table. The young woman looks to be no more than sixteen, with heavy lipstick and heavier mascara.*

SALLY *(gesturing towards the bullpen):* I don't want them taunting you. I don't want them looking at you. I don't want them thinking about you. *(*HELEN *begins to sob.)* I know how hard this is. I know. It is not fun out there. *(*HELEN *shakes her head: no.)* You look at me, you see a uniform, you say, "How could she possibly understand." *(Pausing:)* What's your name, sister?

HELEN: Helen.

SALLY: That's a beautiful name, Helen. A classic name. Helen of Troy, and so forth. *(Pausing:)* Helen what?

HELEN: My . . . my parents . . . *(Pausing:)* They would *kill* me.

*(*HELEN *breaks down in sobs.* SALLY *takes out a pack of cigarettes, and a steno pad.)*

SALLY: Listen to me. Helen. Look at me. This is not something your parents have to get involved in. *(Pausing:)* Need not be. *(Pausing:)* Would you like an Old Gold?

HELEN: Yes, please.

(As she talks, SALLY *is wetting a white cloth towel at the utility sink in the back of the room.)*

SALLY: Now what you need to do, Helen. Just relax. What you need to do, is just to talk to me. As simple as that. *(She is wringing the towel, coiling it tight.)* Let the words come. It's all right. The way to feel better, just to let it all out. *(*SALLY *walks back to the table.)* The man you were with tonight. Lift the burden. Don't keep the pain inside. You know his name? *(From the look on Helen's face, it's clear that she does.)* His name, Helen. That's all. I need to know his name.

*(*HELEN *worries her cigarette.)*

HELEN: Max. He said his name was Max.

SALLY: Believe him? (HELEN *shakes her head.*) Good. Because if you did, I would have to say you were stupid. I don't like stupid people. Now. He said his name was Max. But what *was* his name.

HELEN: And suppose I don't know.

(SALLY *whaps* HELEN *across the back with the wet towel. The cigarette goes flying.* HELEN *clutches at her side in pain—and in shock.*)

SALLY: Like I said. I don't *like* stupid people. Now. (*Pausing:*) Are you going to let me help you, or not? (*Another full whap to the kidneys. The chair clatters across the floor. Helen's eyes fill with tears.*) It's not something which requires much thought. (*She holds the towel. Quietly:*) What was his name?

INTERIOR: DENTIST'S OFFICE. DAY.

(Morris Yorgrau, D.D.S., *stencilled backwards on the inside of the ripple-glass door.* DR. YORGRAU *himself, a handsome man with a cheerful bow tie, is bending low over the dentist's chair, in which reclines, at the moment, the rather large* MRS. SULLIVAN.

Before YORGRAU *is a green enamel appliance containing spouts, valves, springs, tubing, several lights, and drills on spiderlike pantographic arms.*

We hear the high whine of the drill, lowering pitch as it hits bone.

A shadow now falls over Dr. Yorgrau's work. He looks up.

CARL STREETER, *framed in the doorway.*

YORGRAU *cuts the drill.*)

YORGRAU: There must be some mistake. (CARL *just stands there.*) Do you have an appointment? (CARL *lights a cigarette, taking his time about it.*) I'm booked today. If it's an emergency, I'd be happy to refer you to Dr. Fischbein. He's very good. If not, please see Dolores about an appointment.

(*He turns back to* MRS. SULLIVAN, *expecting* CARL *to disappear— which he doesn't. When* YORGRAU *finally turns back, there's* CARL, *lazily holding his badge.*)

CARL: I saw Dolores.

(YORGRAU, *drill in hand, looks terrified.*)

YORGRAU: What seems to be the trouble?

CARL *(smiling):* You had quite a time for yourself last night . . . *(On* MRS. SULLIVAN, *not quite knowing what to make of all this.)* Quite a time, they tell me.

YORGRAU *(to his patient):* Mrs. Sullivan. We will finish this up tomorrow. You may reschedule with Dolores on your way out. I regret, regret quite deeply, any inconvenience this may cause.

MRS. SULLIVAN: I don't understand.

(CARL watches.)

(On CARL, having the same trouble with SALLY that he has with his daughter: he can never quite tell when she's being sarcastic.)

CARL: What I'm saying— What I'm trying to say— Is maybe, in this room, it's the one place in the world, everything stays outside the door. Like no matter how bad it gets out there, in here, we still— You know what I mean?

SALLY: Yeah, I know. Bad world, great sex. *(She lights two Old Golds, hands him one.)* Carl. Don't tense up. But there's something we have to talk about. *(CARL says nothing.)* What we have to talk about, I need fifty. I need fifty percent.

CARL: I do the work—

SALLY: If you see it that way . . .

CARL: —I do the work, you come in for half?

SALLY: As of now, Carl. Starting as of now. *(SALLY reaches over to the nightstand, holds up a piece of steno paper—green, with wide lines, ripped at the top.)* Another john. A good one. *(Pausing:)* You want him? *(CARL moves to grab the paper from her hand, but she's just a little faster.)*

MRS. SULLIVAN: I have a hole in my tooth.

(YORGRAU sweeps away her apron, like a barber who's just finished with a shave.)

YORGRAU: Nothing that won't keep.

(She scurries out the door. We hear the door slam.)

YORGRAU: That was quite unnecessary. You might have waited.

CARL: It doesn't work like that. Let's go.

YORGRAU: Where?

CARL: Downtown.

YORGRAU *(unconvincingly)*: What for? *(Pausing:)* I had a beer at Ed Reilly's place. A beer or two.

CARL: A beer. Two beers. And then, on your way home, you picked up somebody.

YORGRAU: What if I did?

CARL: And you brought her back here—

YORGRAU: Where's the crime? *(Pausing:)* They don't put you in jail for—

CARL: The hell they don't. *(Pausing:)* The girl was fifteen years old.

(YORGRAU *takes a step back. Then another.*)

YORGRAU: *She said she was nineteen!*

CARL: It's not what she *said* that counts. *(He takes a breath.)* Doctor. You sat in this chair: here. You didn't take your shoes off. You loosened your trousers and let them slide and you spread your legs while she got down on her knees and performed a ten-dollar service, as you requested, in the French manner. Is this coming back to you? *(Pausing:)* Most men, they'd call it a night. Not you. You made her wait while you recuperated. And for ten dollars more—

YORGRAU: Shut up!

CARL: You're disgusting, you know that! You're not even human! You're subhuman! *(Taking him by the forearm:)* Downtown.

YORGRAU: I've got a wife. A kid. A *practice.*

CARL: Well there's not a hell of a lot I can do about that, is there?

YORGRAU *(as they approach the door)*: Officer? *(Pausing:)* Isn't there any way we can forget about this?

CARL *(smiling):* Guys who ain't Roosevelts, ain't Rockefellers . . . Little guys, guys like you and me . . . When we get in a jam, it's just plain tough. But guys with dough, well—sometimes they can—

YORGRAU: How much? How much dough?

(On CARL. Taking his own sweet time. Letting YORGRAU sweat.)

INTERIOR: FIRST CALIFORNIA BANK. BASEMENT. DAY.

Two men turn keys in the dual lock of a safe deposit box. One of them is a BANK GUARD. The other is CARL.

The GUARD disappears. CARL slides the box from its nest, and takes it to a small, private alcove.

INTERIOR: BANK VAULT. CLOSER.

His back shielding him from anyone's prying eyes, CARL pulls a large wad of money—mostly tens and twenties—from his jacket pocket. He counts, straightens, sorts.

Most of it goes into the box, adding to what is already a very substantial pile. A much smaller stack goes into a white business envelope, which CARL pockets.

Now CARL reaches up once more, replacing the box in its slot. It slides shut with a loud, metallic creak.

Otherwise, the room is dead silent.

EXTERIOR: ROOMING HOUSE. NIGHT.

A large, rambling rooming house, just west of downtown. Built in the 20s, when French Chateau moldings were all the rage. Now, a sign reads: Rooms. By the Day, the Week, the Month.

We hear Carl's voice:

CARL *(voice-over):* I don't know how you do it.

INTERIOR: ROOMING HOUSE. SMALL STUDIO APARTMENT. NIGHT.

One bed, one nightstand, one window, one door, one chair. CARL STREETER and SALLY CREIGHTON, naked, in bed.

CARL *(continuing):* Whatever it is—The work. The pressure. The goddamn holidays. But somehow, you find a way—to leave it all outside.

SALLY: Well, thanks, Carl.

CARL: What I'm saying is, in here, you're all woman.

SALLY: Carl? You're all man. I give you professionals. Men with means. *(Pausing:)* Fifty is fair, Carl. *(He says nothing.)* That's the way you do it with a partner.

> *(Finally, he puts out his hand. She gives him the piece of steno paper. He looks at it.)*

CARL: This "john." *(Pausing:)* What did he do, this "john"? *(He reaches over for her, lifts her up.)* What did he say? I need to know these things. What did he say to her, what did he want her to do? *(Now they are standing in the small room, without clothes, facing each other.)* Maybe you could describe it for me. *(As he puts his hands on her shoulders, grabbing hard:)* Maybe you could illustrate.

EXTERIOR: STREETER HOME. NIGHT.

> *(Almost dawn. CARL cuts the headlights, cuts the motor. Glides the remaining hundred feet into his driveway.*
>
> *He closes the car door with exquisite care. He opens the front door, silently silhouetted by the hallway light.)*

INTERIOR: STREETER HOME. JEANNIE'S BEDROOM. NIGHT.

> *(JEANNIE, in bed, quite awake, listening to the sounds of her father's arrival.*
>
> *Door. Footsteps.*
>
> *Kitchen sounds. Glass sounds. Ice-cube sounds.)*

INTERIOR: STREETER HOME. KITCHEN. NIGHT.

> JEANNIE, *in her bathrobe, rounds the doorway to find Carl, unshaven and rumpled, seated at the kitchen table. In front of him is a tumbler of Fleischmann's bonded rye.*

JEANNIE: Would you care for a cup of coffee? *(She speaks in a calm, cheerful tone, as if she were, say, the waitress at Streeter's Diner.)* Considering the time of day, it might be more appropriate. *(Filling the percolator):* I bought the good kind.

(As she talks, JEANNIE *places a cup and saucer in front of him—and takes away the tumbler of rye.*

He grabs it back. A bit violently.)

CARL: Don't you mother me now.

JEANNIE: I was trying to help. *(She turns and stares at him.)* You never come home anymore.

*(*CARL *can't quite look at her. He steps behind her chair, and puts his hands on her shoulders, kneading her back and neck.)*

CARL: You're the best daughter in the world and the best damn daughter a man could ask for. *(Pausing:)* With your mother gone, I have to be a mom and a dad. Well, sometimes, it's kind of a lot for one man to do. *(*JEANNIE *says nothing.)* And I go out there and work and get money so that you won't have to live the kind of life I've lived. *(He cups her chin.)* You got my looks, not hers. I mean, it's not like you're going to marry a Rockefeller. *(He stands.)* Maybe I work too hard. Maybe I do. But I do it because I want to provide. I want to provide because I love you. Do you understand?

(The coffee boils. Absently, JEANNIE *turns the flame down.)*

JEANNIE: I understand.

CARL *(glancing at his watch):* And you forgive me?

JEANNIE: You're going. You're going again.

CARL: Sugar, I promise. After the New Year. We'll take a vacation—

JEANNIE: Where *were* you last night?

CARL: —a long vacation. Just the two of us. Take that money I've been saving up, put it to good use.

(She pours the coffee.)

JEANNIE: You're not going to be any good to anyone if you don't get some sleep.

(He takes a gulp or two.)

CARL: Tonight. I'll be back tonight.

JEANNIE: When tonight?

CARL: Tonight, after dinner tonight.

JEANNIE: Nine o'clock? Ten o'clock? Ten-thirty o'clock?

(CARL *puts on his rumpled jacket.*)

CARL: At the latest. (*Taking inventory:*) Keys, wallet— You be good. Keys, wallet, hat, gun— There's a steak in the freezer. It's a porterhouse, the best kind. Whatever my faults—and I'm not without my faults, no man is—whatever my faults, you must know that I want only the best for you. (*Pausing:*) Porterhouse.

(*Patting himself down:*) Keys, wallet, hat, gun—handkerchief.

(*He's out the door, with only the smallest glance backward.*)

JEANNIE (*speaking to the door*): You ought to at least shower. You ought to at least change your shirt. (*Pausing:*) That's what your *average* man would do. (*Pausing:*) You *slept* in that shirt.

(*Several beats. The 60-cycle hum of the refrigerator.* JEANNIE, *at the table, frozen.*)

EXTERIOR: HOPE STREET. DAY.

A bright December Monday. Men in hats and generously cut jackets walk down Hope Street at a brisk, businesslike pace.

A department store Santa shakes his forlorn bell. It's in the low 90s, and he does not look very comfortable.

Parked in front of Delmonico's: An impressive dark maroon '51 Ford, well-polished, gleaming in the angular December light. In the driver's seat, SALLY CREIGHTON, *in uniform.*

Carl Streeter's four-year-old gray Plymouth pulls up from the opposite direction.

She hands him another piece of steno paper.

SALLY: Johnny Cabe. You'll find him every afternoon 'cept Mondays behind the bar at the Inferno. Married. Eleven kids, can you believe it? Clearly, his wife puts out. Clearly, that's not enough. I don't think Mr. Cabe knows how to keep it buttoned. Two nights ago he goes for a little sex. For fifteen bucks and a bottle of Seagram's—behind the counter, no less. Johnny Cabe, what he likes, what he likes is a certain practice involving a knotted rope.

CARL *(taking a long breath):* Got it.

SALLY: That little fact, I figure, is worth at least fifteen hundred. All that family, all those kids? A man with a business that's *all cash*? Fifteen hundred minimum. What do you say?

CARL: It's jake with me.

(CARL looks away.)

CARL: I may be going on leave. I'm a little tired.

SALLY *(smiling):* You look like shit, you know?

CARL: I get this from everyone. I don't need it from you.

SALLY: Tell you what. I'll see what I can do tonight. Bring in some little angels, put the squeeze on 'em, get some *names*—what do you say? You get rich and I get fifty-percent rich and everybody's happy.

CARL: Everybody's happy. That's what I like to hear.

SALLY: Well, that's what I said.

INTERIOR: INFERNO BAR. NIGHT.

The archetypal low-rent dive. The faces of the regulars grotesque, alluring in the neon underlight.

CARL *walks up to the bar.*

CARL: Rye and ginger. *(The bartender—heavy eyelids, big gut—pours without a single wasted motion. His name is* JOHNNY CABE. *Now* CARL *flashes his badge.)* I'd like a few words with you.

CABE *(polishing the glassware):* Everybody does.

CARL: Not philosophy. Not advice to the lovelorn. Listen to me. I am not a rumdum. I am not a lush wondering what to do with a liife that went wrong. *(Indicating the badge:)* I am a police officer and I'd like to speak with you on an official matter.

(CABE doesn't even look up.)

CABE: Shoot.

CARL: There was an incident last night concerning yourself and a young woman.

CABE: What is this, a shakedown?

(Cabe's tone is without affect—just this side of boredom.)

CARL *(taken aback, beginning again):* There was an incident last night—

CABE: Last night. Three nights ago. The night before that . . .

CARL: Do you know how *old* she was?

CABE: I do like 'em young, it's true.

CARL: Are you aware of the laws in this state—

(The phone rings, loudly. CABE takes his time about picking it up.)

CABE *(into phone):* Inferno. *(Pausing:)* Let me check. *(Now he speaks to the room—empty, of course, except for CARL and himself.)* Is there a Detective Carl Streeter?

(He holds out the phone and shrugs, as CARL takes it.)

CARL *(into phone):* What kind of trouble? *Oh my god.*

(He covers the phone and screams at CABE.)

CARL: *Can a man have a little privacy in this world?*

(Slowly, CABE *motions to the pay phone booth in the back.)*

INTERIOR: PHONE BOOTH. NIGHT.

In the background, we see CABE, *slicing limes, preparing the Collins mix.*

And although he's paying attention to his business, he seems very much to be enjoying the fact that CARL *is sweating.*

CARL: When? *(Pausing:)* Are you sure? *(Pausing:)* That it's broken? That it isn't just, you know, *dislocated? (Pausing:)* No wallet? No ID?

(He listens for a long time. Although we cannot quite make out the words, it's pretty clear that the person calling is SALLY. *And that she's in a blind panic.)*

CARL: Listen, dammit! Was she wearing stockings?

INTERIOR: STATIONHOUSE. NIGHT.

SALLY, *at her desk, speaking furtively into her telephone. Directly behind her is the closed door that leads to the Quiet Room.*

SALLY: Carl, I—I can't do that! *(Pausing:)* I just can't! *(Pausing:)* Dammit, Carl, she was fighting, and I didn't do anything! It wasn't even an accident! We were fighting and I just hear this *snap* . . .

INTERIOR: INFERNO. PHONE BOOTH. AS BEFORE.

CARL *(slowly and with authority):* This is it, Sal. This is the only way out. Listen to my voice. You take that stocking and you tie one end of it around her neck. Slipknot. Like a shoelace, you understand? The other end goes around the pipe. The chair is on the floor . . .

INTERIOR: STATIONHOUSE. AS BEFORE.

SALLY *is listening to the voice on the telephone. But her eyes are staring into the far distance, and, in most senses, she's not really here at all.*

INTERIOR: INFERNO. PHONE BOOTH. NIGHT. AS BEFORE.

CARL *(continuing):* Like she'd kicked the chair away, like she'd done it herself . . . Anything goes wrong, Sal, you didn't speak to me, okay? We'll play it like we always do—I'm just another cop, okay?

INTERIOR: STATIONHOUSE. AS BEFORE.

SALLY, *at her desk.*

The tinny voice on the other end of the phone, the sounds of the police station, now seem strange, echoic, distant . . .

INTERIOR: INFERNO. NIGHT. AS BEFORE.

CARL *hangs up the phone. He is drenched in sweat.*

As he heads for the door:

CABE: And Merry Christmas to you, too.

(Without breaking stride, CARL reaches across the bar, grabs Cabe's shirtfront, and slams him one to the jaw.)

CARL: Come on, hit me! Hit me! Hit the cop!

(CABE thinks about it. But doesn't move.)

CABE *(finally):* You're not welcome here anymore.

(Grinning wildly, CARL—*rumpled, sweaty, shaking—quits the bar.)*

INTERIOR: STATIONHOUSE. NIGHT.

CARL *walks through the doors. He takes three steps when he's stopped by a middle-aged, red-faced* SERGEANT.

SERGEANT: Bad news, Carl. *(*CARL *swallows.)* Sally. She lost one.

CARL: Jesus.

SERGEANT: In the Quiet Room. Sally went to get some coffee. When she came back—*(Pausing:)* With a stocking.

CARL: Christ.

SERGEANT: It happens. Hey, I lost a couple in my time. It happens.

*(*CARL *fights to keep the relief off his face. And wins.)*

CARL: Anything we can do? *(Pausing:)* You send her home?

SERGEANT: You might try the morgue.

INTERIOR: MORGUE. NIGHT.

A small room with three rows of sliding aluminum cabinets. It looks very much like the rows of safe deposit boxes we saw in the basement of First California.

In the flickering greenish light, CARL *and* SALLY *embrace.*

SALLY: I don't ever want to do this again.

CARL: It's going to be all right.

SALLY: I just feel so—sick.

CARL: Everything's going to be all right.

SALLY: Just hold me.

CARL: We made it, Sal. It's all downhill from here.

(Footsteps in the hallway. CARL *and* SALLY *jump apart.*

Now a DOCTOR *in a white coat, holding a clipboard, stands in the doorway.)*

DOCTOR: Officer Creighton? *(SALLY nods.)* We need you to look, and sign.

(SALLY nods again. Although she seems to be keeping her composure, there is something strange, something very off, about the look in her eyes.

Behind the Doctor's back, SALLY holds Carl's hand.)

SALLY *(whispering to CARL):* I don't know. It sounds funny to hear myself say it— *(The DOCTOR slides open drawer #3. There is a body, covered by a thick black rubber sheet.)* —but maybe, somehow, this is a *good* thing. I know that sounds terrible. What I mean is— *(The DOCTOR pulls back the sheet.)* —that maybe, good may *come* of it.

(Now SALLY takes a perfunctory look. Nods. The DOCTOR holds out his clipboard and SALLY scribbles a signature.

The DOCTOR is about to slide the drawer shut. But something that CARL sees out of the corner of his eye . . .

On the bruised, swollen face of the body beneath the rubber sheet.

When he speaks it's with tenderness, with a strange curiosity more than anything else.)

CARL: *Jeannie? Jeannie?*

(He falls to his knees. SALLY and the DOCTOR exchange a brief glance; they don't understand what's going on here.

Now CARL buries his face against the rubber sheet.)

CARL *(whispering):* *Jeannie?*

(Very close now, as the sightless eyes of his daughter stare back at him. CARL rises and turns to face SALLY.

A moment ago, she was his friend, colleague, lover; now she's his daughter's murderer.

Dead calm, he reaches into his jacket and draws his .38. His voice is flat now, drained of all emotion.)

CARL: You killed her. *(He takes slow aim, pointing the gun at the middle of her chest.)* You killed her.

SALLY: Carl? Carl?

DOCTOR *(backing away):* Now, officer . . . Now, officer . . .

SALLY *(overlapping):* Carl? It doesn't have to be this way. We can get through this, Carl. We can get through this together.

CARL *(flatly):* You killed Jeannie. You killed my daughter Jeannie.

SALLY: I know how hard this is, Carl. I know how hard. You're looking at me now and you're saying, how could she possibly understand—

(Carl's hand begins to tremble. Tears are streaming down Sally's face.)

SALLY: Carl—*(pausing)* I love you, Carl. *(Pausing:)* And maybe you love me.

(Clearly, not the right thing to say because: BLAM!

The shot echoes in the small, metal-lined room. SALLY *crumples backwards. Dead.)*

CARL *(softly):* Comedienne.

DOCTOR: Put down the gun, sir. Just put down that gun. We don't want anyone else to get hurt here—

*(*CARL *takes a step or two forward. The* DOCTOR *recoils in fear.*

Carl's gun is pointed at the DOCTOR—*but his eyes are very far away.)*

CARL: *Jeannie . . .*

(Slowly, CARL *bends to the floor. He's in the corner now, slumped, listless. But he still has not let go of the gun.)*

DOCTOR: Let's talk about it . . . Can't we talk?

(Carl's point of view:

SALLY, *dead, against the far wall.*

JEANNIE, *cold, white, serene.*

We hear a siren and, closer by, the sound of footsteps rushing down the corridor.)

DOCTOR: Can't we talk?

(CARL *holds the gun; not pointing it anymore, just cradling it absently in his hand—something to hold on to.*)

Since I Don't Have You

You

James Ellroy

During the post-war years I served two masters—running interference and hauling dirty laundry for the two men who defined LA at that time better than anyone else. To Howard Hughes I was security boss at his aircraft plant, pimp, and troubleshooter for RKO Pictures—the ex-cop who could kibosh blackmail squeezes, fix drunk drivings, and arrange abortions and dope cures. To Mickey Cohen—rackets overlord and would-be nightclub shtickster—I was a bagman to the LAPD, the former Narco detective who skimmed junk off niggertown dope rousts, allowing his Southside boys to sell it back to the hordes of Schwartzes eager to fly White Powder Airlines. Big Howard: always in the news for crashing an airplane someplacc inappropriate, stubbing his face on the control panel in some hicktown beanfield, then showing up at Romanoff's bandaged like the Mummy with Ava Gardner on his arm; Mickey C.: also a pussy hound par excellence, pub crawling with an entourage of psychopathic killers, press agents, gag writers, and his bulldog Mickey Cohen, Jr.,—a flatulent beast with a schlong so large that the Mick's stooges strapped it to a roller skate so it wouldn't drag on the ground.

Howard Hughes. Mickey Cohen. And me—Turner "Buzz" Meeks, Lizard Ridge, Oklahoma, armadillo poacher; strikebreaker goon; cop; fixer; and keeper of the secret key to his masters' psyches:

they were both cowards mano a mano; airplanes and lunatic factotums their go-betweens—while I would go anywhere, anyplace—gun or billy club first, courting a front-page death to avenge my second-banana life. And the two of them courted me because I put their lack of balls in perspective: it was irrational, meshugah, bad business—a Forest Lawn crypt years before my time. But I got the last laugh there: I always knew that when faced with the grave I'd pull a smart segue to keep kicking—and I write this memoir as an old, old man—while Howard and Mickey stuff caskets, bullshit biographies their only legacy.

Howard. Mickey. Me.

Sooner or later, my work for the two of them had to produce what the yuppie lawyer kids today call "conflict of interest." Of course, it was over a woman—and, of course, being a suicidal Okie shit-kicker, forty-one years old and getting tired, I decided to play both ends against the middle. A thought just hit me: that I'm writing this story because I miss Howard and Mickey, and telling it gives me a chance to be with them again. Keep that in mind—that I loved them—even though they were both world-class shitheels.

January 15, 1949.

It was cold and clear in Los Angeles, and the papers were playing up the two-year anniversary of the Black Dahlia murder case—still unsolved, still speculated on. Mickey was still mourning Hooky Rothman's death—he French-kissed a sawed-off shotgun held by an unknown perpetrator—and Howard was still pissed at me over the Bob Mitchum reefer roust: he figured that my connections with Narco Division were still so solid that I should have seen it coming. I'd been shuttling back and forth between Howard and Mickey since New Year's. The Mick's signature fruit baskets stuffed with C-notes had to be distributed to cops, judges, and City Council members he wanted to grease, and the pilot/mogul had me out bird-dogging quiff; prowling bus depots and train stations for buxom young girls who'd fall prey to RKO contracts in exchange for frequent nighttime visits. I'd been having a good run: a half dozen midwestern farm maidens were now ensconced in Howard's fuck pads—strategically located apartments tucked all over LA. And I was deep in hock to a darktown bookie named Leotis Dineen, a six-foot-six jungle bunny who hated people of the Oklahoma persuasion worse than poison. I was sitting in my quonset hut office at Hughes Aircraft when the phone rang.

"That you, Howard?"

Howard Hughes sighed. "What happened to 'Security, may I help you'?"

"You're the only one calls this early, Boss."

"And you're alone?"

"Right. Per your instructions to call you Mr. Hughes in the presence of others. What's up?"

"Breakfast is up. Meet me at the corner of Melrose and La Brea in half an hour."

"Right, Boss."

"Two or three, Buzz? I'm hungry and having four."

Howard was on his all-chili-dog diet; Pink's Dogs at Melrose and La Brea was his current in-spot. I knew for a fact that their chili was made from horsemeat air freighted up daily from Tijuana. "One kraut, no chili."

"Heathen. Pink's chili is better than Chasen's."

"I had a pony when I was a boy."

"So? I had a governess. You think I wouldn't eat—"

I said, "Half an hour," and hung up. I figured if I got there five minutes late I wouldn't have to watch the fourth richest man in America eat.

Howard was picking strands of sauerkraut off his chin when I climbed in the backseat of his limousine. He said, "You didn't really want it, did you?"

I pressed the button that sent up the screen that shielded us from the driver. "No, coffee and doughnuts are more my style."

Howard gave me a long, slow eyeballing—a bit ill at ease because sitting down we were the same height, while standing I came up to his shoulders. "Do you need money, Buzz?"

I thought of Leotis Dineen. "Can niggers dance?"

"They certainly can. But call them colored, you never know when one might be listening."

Larry the chauffeur was Chinese; Howard's comment made me wonder if his last plane crash had dented his cabeza. I tried my standard opening line. "Getting any, Boss?"

Hughes smiled and burped; horse grease wafted through the backseat. He dug into a pile of papers beside him—blueprints, graphs, and scraps covered with airplane doodles—pulling out a snapshot of a blonde girl naked from the waist up. He handed it to me and said,

"Gretchen Rae Shoftel, age nineteen. Born in Prairie du Chien, Wisconsin, July 26, 1929. She was staying at the place on South Lucerne—the screening house. This is the woman, Buzz. I think I want to marry her. And she's gone—she flew the coop on the contract, me, all of it."

I examined the picture. Gretchen Rae Shoftel was prodigiously lunged—no surprise—with a blonde pageboy and smarts in her eyes, like she knew Mr. Hughes's two-second screen test was strictly an audition for the sack and an occasional one-liner in some RKO turkey. "Who found her for you, Boss? It wasn't me—I'd have remembered."

Howard belched again—my hijacked sauerkraut this time. "I got the picture in the mail at the studio, along with an offer—a thousand dollars cash to a P.O. box in exchange for the girl's address. I did it, and met Gretchen Rae at her hotel downtown. She told me she posed for some dirty old man back in Milwaukee, that he must have pulled the routine for the thousand. Gretchen Rae and I got to be friends, and, well . . ."

"And you'll give me a bonus to find her?"

"A thousand, Buzz. Cash, off the payroll."

My debt to Leotis Dineen was eight hundred and change; I could get clean and get even on minor league baseball—the San Diego Seals were starting their pre-season games next week. "It's a deal. What else have you got on the girl?"

"She was carhopping at Scrivner's Drive-In. I know that."

"Friends, known associates, relatives here in LA?"

"Not to my knowledge."

I took a deep breath to let Howard know a tricky question was coming. "Boss, you think maybe this girl is working an angle on you? I mean, the picture out of nowhere, the thousand to a P.O. box?"

Howard Hughes harrumphed. "It had to be that piece in *Confidential,* the one that alleged my talent scouts take topless photographs and that I like my women endowed."

"*Alleged,* Boss?"

"I'm practicing coming off as irate in case I sue *Confidential* somewhere down the line. You'll get on this right away?"

"Rapidamente."

"Outstanding. And don't forget Sid Weinberg's party tomorrow night. He's got a new horror picture coming out from the studio, and I need you there to keep the autograph hounds from going crazy. Eight, Sid's house."

"I'll be there."

"Find Gretchen Rae, Buzz. She's special."

Howard's one saving grace with females is that he keeps falling in love with them—albeit only after viewing Brownie snaps of their lungs. It more or less keeps him busy between crashing airplanes and designing airplanes that don't fly.

"Right, Boss."

The limousine's phone rang. Howard picked it up, listened and murmured, "Yes. Yes, I'll tell him." Hanging up, he said, "The switchboard at the plant. Mickey Cohen wants to see you. Make it brief, you're on my time now."

"Yes, sir."

It was Howard who introduced me to Mickey, right before I got wounded in a dope shoot-out and took my LAPD pension. I still give him a hand with his drug dealings—unofficial liaison to Narcotics Division, point man for the Narco dicks who skim x number of grams off every ounce of junk confiscated. The LAPD has got an unofficial heroin policy: it is to be sold only to coloreds, only east of Alvarado and south of Jefferson. I don't think it should be sold anywhere, but as long as it is, I want the five percent. I test the shit with a chem kit I stole from the crime lab—no poor hophead is going to croak from a Mickey Cohen bindle bootjacked by Turner "Buzz" Meeks. Dubious morality: I sleep well ninety percent of the time and lay my bet action off with shine bookies, the old exploiter washing the hand that feeds him. Money was right at the top of my brain as I drove to Mickey's haberdashery on the Strip. I always need cash, and the Mick never calls unless it is in the offing.

I found the man in his back room, surrounded by sycophants and muscle: Johnny Stompanato, guinea spit curl dangling over his handsome face—he of the long-term crush on Lana Turner; Davey Goldman, Mickey's chief yes-man and the author of his nightclub shticks; and a diffident-looking little guy I recognized as Morris Hornbeck—an accountant and former trigger for Jerry Katzenbach's mob in Milwaukee. Shaking hands and pulling up a chair, I got ready to make my pitch: You pay me now; I do my job after I run a hot little errand for Howard. I opened my mouth to speak, but Mickey beat me to it. "I want you to find a woman for me."

I was about to say "What a coincidence," when Johnny Stomp

handed me a snapshot. "Nice gash. Not Lana Turner quality, but USDA choice tail nonetheless."

Of course, you see it coming. The photo was a nightspot job: compliments of Preston Sturges' Players Club, Gretchen Rae Shoftel blinking against flashbulb glare, dairy-state pulchritude in a tight black dress. Mickey Cohen was draping an arm around her shoulders, aglow with love. I swallowed to keep my voice steady. "Where was the wife, Mick? Off on one of her Hadassah junkets?"

Mickey grunted. " 'Israel, the New Homeland.' Ten-day tour with her mah-jongg club. While the cat is away, the mice will play. Va-va-va-voom. Find her, Buzzchik. A grand."

I got obstreperous, my usual reaction to being scared. "Two grand, or go take a flying fuck at a rolling doughnut."

Mickey scowled and went into a slow burn; I watched Johnny Stomp savor my bravado, Davey Goldman write down the line for his boss's shticks, and Morris Hornbeck do queasy double takes like he wasn't copacetic with the play. When the Mick's burn stretched to close to a minute, I said, "Silence implies consent. Tell me all you know about the girl, and I'll take it from there."

Mickey Cohen smiled at me—his coming-from-hunger minion. "Goyische shitheel. For a twosky I want satisfaction guaranteed within forty-eight hours."

I already had the money laid off on baseball, the fights, and three horse parlays. "Forty-seven and change. Go."

Mickey eyed his boys as he spoke—probably because he was pissed at me and needed a quick intimidation fix. Davey and Johnny Stomp looked away; Morris Hornbeck just twitched, like he was trying to quash a bad case of the heebie-jeebies. "Gretchen Rae Shoftel. I met her at Scrivner's Drive-In two weeks ago. She told me she's fresh out of the Minnesota sticks, someplace like that. She—"

I interrupted. "She said 'Minnesota' specifically, Mick?"

"Right. Moosebreath, Dogturd, some boonies town—but definitely Minnesota."

Morris Hornbeck was sweating now; I had myself a hot lead. "Keep going, Mick."

"Well, we hit it off; I convince Lavonne to see Israel before them dune coons take it back; Gretchen Rae and I get together; we va-va-va-voom; it's terrific. She plays cagey with me, won't tell me where she's staying, and she keeps taking off—says she's looking for a man—some friend of her father's back in Antelope Ass or wherever the fuck she comes from. Once she's gassed on vodka collinses and gets misty about some hideaway she says she's got. That—"

I said, "Wrap it up."

Mickey slammed his knees so hard that Mickey Cohen, Jr., asleep in the doorway twenty feet away, woke up and tried to stand on all fours—until the roller skate attached to his wang pulled him back down. "I'll fucking wrap you up if you don't find her for me! That's it! I want her! Find her for me! *Do it now!*"

I got to my feet wondering how I was going to pull this one off—with the doorman gig at Sid Weinberg's party thrown smack in the middle of it. I said, "Forty-seven, fifty-five and rolling," and winked at Morris Hornbeck—who just happened to hail from Milwaukee, where Howard told me Gretchen Rae Shoftel told him a dirty old man had snapped her lung shots. Hornbeck tried to wink back; it looked like his eyeball was having a grand mal seizure. Mickey said, "Find her for me. And you gonna be at Sid's tomorrow night?"

"Keeping autograph hounds at bay. You?"

"Yeah, I've got points in Sid's new picture. I want hot dope by then, Buzzchik. *Hot.*"

I said, "Scalding," and took off, almost tripping over Mickey Cohen, Jr.'s appendage as I went out the door.

A potential three grand in my kick; Morris Hornbeck's hinkyness doing a slow simmer in my gourd; an instinct that Gretchen Rae Shoftel's "hideaway" was Howard Hughes's fuck pad on South Lucerne— the place where he kept the stash of specially cantilevered bras he designed to spotlight his favorite starlet's tits, cleavage gowns for his one-night inamoratas, and the stag film collection he showed to visiting defense contractors—some of them rumored to co-star Mickey Cohen, Jr., and a bimbo made up to resemble Howard's personal heroine: Amelia Earhart. But first there was Scrivner's Drive-In and a routine questioning of Gretchen Rae's recent co-workers. Fear adrenaline was scorching my soul as I drove there—maybe I'd played my shtick too tight to come out intact.

Scrivner's was on Sunset three blocks east of Hollywood High School, an eat-in-your-car joint featuring a rocket ship motif—chromium scoops, dips, and portholes abounding—Jules Verne as seen by a fag set designer scraping the stars on marijuana. The carhops—all zoftig numbers—wore tight space-cadet outfits; the fry cooks wore

plastic rocket helmets with clear face shields to protect them from spattering grease. Questioning a half dozen of them was like enjoying the
DT's without benefit of booze. After an hour of talk and chump-
change handouts, I knew the following:

That Gretchen Rae Shoftel carhopped there for a month, was
often tardy, and during mid-afternoon lulls tended to abandon her
shift. This was tolerated because she was an atom-powered magnet
that attracted men by the shitload. She could tote up tabs in her head,
deftly computing sales tax—but had a marked tendency toward spilling
milkshakes and french fries. When the banana-split-loving Mickey
Cohen started snouting around after her, the manager gave her the go
by, no doubt leery of attracting the criminal elements who had made
careers out of killing innocent bystanders while trying to kill the Mick.
Aside from that I glommed one hard lead plus suppositions to hang it
on: Gretchen Rae had persistently questioned the Scrivner's crew
about a recent regular customer—a man with a long German surname
who'd been eating at the counter, doing arithmetic tricks with meal
tabs and astounding the locals with five-minute killings of the *LA
Times* crossword. He was an old geez with a European accent—and he
stopped chowing at Scrivner's right before Gretchen Rae Shoftel hired
on. Mickey told me the quail had spoken of looking for a friend of her
father's; Howard had said she was from Wisconsin; German accents
pointed to the dairy state in a big way. And Morris Hornbeck, Mr.
Shakes just a few hours before, had been a Milwaukee mob trigger and
money man. And—the lovely Gretchen Rae had continued carhopping
after becoming the consort of two of the richest, most powerful men in
Los Angeles—an eye-opener if ever there was one.

I drove to a pay phone and made some calls, straight and collect. An
old LAPD pal gave me the lowdown on Morris Hornbeck—he had
two California convictions for felony statch rape, both complainants
thirteen-year-old girls. A guy on the Milwaukee force that I'd worked
liaison with supplied midwestern skinny: Little Mo was a glorified
bookkeeper for Jerry Katzenbach's mob, run out of town by his boss in
'47, when he was given excess gambling skim to invest as he saw best
and opened a call house specializing in underaged poon dressed up as
movie stars—greenhorn girls coiffed, cosmeticed, and gowned to resemble Rita Hayworth, Ann Sheridan, Veronica Lake, and the like.

The operation was a success, but Jerry Katzenbach, Knights-of-Columbus family man, considered it bum PR. Adios, Morris—who obviously found an amenable home in LA.

On Gretchen Rae Shoftel, I got bubbkis; ditto on the geezer with the arithmetic tricks similar to the carhop/vamp. The girl had no criminal record in either California or Wisconsin—but I was willing to bet she'd learned her seduction techniques at Mo Hornbeck's whorehouse.

I drove to Howard Hughes's South Lucerne Street fuck pad and let myself in with a key from my fourteen-pound Hughes Enterprises key ring. The house was furnished with leftovers from the RKO prop department, complete with appropriate female accoutrements for each of the six bedrooms. The Moroccan Room featured hammocks and settees from *Casbah Nocturne* and a rainbow array of low-cut silk lounging pajamas; the *Billy the Kid* room—where Howard brought his Jane Russell look-alikes—was four walls of mock-saloon bars with halter-top cowgirl getups and a mattress covered by a Navajo blanket. My favorite was the Zoo Room: taxidermied cougar, bison, moose, and bobcats—shot by Ernest Hemingway—mounted with their eyes leering down on a narrow strip of sheet-covered floor. Big Ernie told me he decimated the critter population of two Montana counties in order to achieve the effect. There was a kitchen stocked with plenty of fresh milk, peanut butter, and jelly to sate teenage tastebuds, a room to screen stag movies, and the master bedroom—my bet for where Howard installed Gretchen Rae Shoftel.

I took the back staircase up, walked down the hall, and pushed the door open, expecting the room's usual state: big white bed and plain white walls—the ironic accompaniment to snatched virginity. I was wrong; what I saw was some sort of testament to squarejohn American homelife.

Mixmasters, cookie sheets, toasters, and matched cutlery sets rested on the bed; the walls were festooned with Currier & Ives calendars and framed *Saturday Evening Post* covers drawn by Norman Rockwell. A menagerie of stuffed animals was admiring the artwork—pandas and tigers and Disney characters placed against the bed, heads tilted upward. There was a bentwood rocker in a corner next to the room's one window. The seat held a stack of catalogs. I leafed through them: Motorola radios, Hamilton Beach kitchen goodies, bed quilts from a mail-order place in New Hampshire. In all of them the less expensive items were checkmarked. Strange, since Howard let his master bedroom poon have anything they wanted—top-of-the-line charge accounts, the magilla.

I checked the closet. It held the standard Hughes wardrobe—low-cut gowns and tight cashmere sweaters, plus a half-dozen Scrivner's carhop outfits, replete with built-in uplift breastplates, which Gretchen Rae Shoftel didn't need. Seeing a row of empty hangers, I checked for more catalogs and found a Bullocks Wilshire job under the bed. Flipping through it, I saw tweedy skirts and suits, flannel blazers, and prim and proper wool dresses circled; Howard's charge account number was scribbled at the top of the back page. Gretchen Rae Shoftel, math whiz, searching for another math whiz, was contemplating making herself over as Miss Upper-Middle-Class Rectitude.

I checked out the rest of the fuck pad—quick eyeball prowls of the other bedrooms, a toss of the downstairs closets. Empty Bullocks boxes were everywhere—Gretchen Rae had accomplished her transformation. Howard liked to keep his girls cash-strapped to insure their obedience, but I was willing to guess he stretched the rules for this one. Impersonating a police officer, I called the dispatcher's office at the Yellow and Beacon cab companies. Paydirt at Beacon: three days ago at 3:10 P.M., a cab was dispatched to 436 South Lucerne; its destination: 2281 South Mariposa.

Big paydirt.

2281 South Mariposa was a Mickey Cohen hideout, an armed fortress where the Mick's triggers holed up during their many skirmishes with the Jack Dragna gang. It was steel-reinforced concrete; shitloads of canned goods in the bomb shelter/basement; racks of Tommys and pump shotguns behind fake walls covered by cheesecake pics. Only Mickey's boys knew about the place—making it conclusive proof that Morris Hornbeck was connected to Gretchen Rae Shoftel. I drove to Jefferson and Mariposa—quicksville.

It was a block of wood frame houses, small, neatly tended, mostly owned by Japs sprung from the relocation camps, anxious to stick together and assert their independence in new territory. 2281 was as innocuous and sanitary as any pad on the block: Mickey had the best Jap gardener in the area. No cars were in the driveway; the cars parked curbside looked harmless enough, and the nearest local taking the sun was a guy sitting on a porch swing four houses down. I walked up to the front door, punched in a window, reached around to the latch, and let myself in.

The living room—furnished by Mickey's wife, Lavonne, with sofas and chairs from the Hadassah thrift shop—was tidy and totally silent. I was half expecting a killer hound to pounce on me before I snapped that Lavonne had forbid the Mick to get a dog because it might whiz on the carpeting. Then I caught the smell.

Decomposition hits you in the tear ducts and gut about simultaneously. I tied my handkerchief over my mouth and nose, grabbed a lamp for a weapon, and walked toward the stink. It was in the right front bedroom, and it was a doozie.

There were two stiffs—a dead man on the floor and another on the bed. The floor man was lying face down, with a white nightgown still pinned with a Bullocks price tag knotted around his neck. Congealed beef stew covered his face, the flesh cracked and red from scalding. A saucepan was upended a few feet away, holding the caked remains of the goo. Somebody was cooking when the altercation came down.

I laid down the lamp and gave the floor stiff a detailed eyeing. He was fortyish, blond, and fat; whoever killed him had tried to burn off his fingerprints—the tips on both hands were scorched black, which meant that the killer was an amateur: the only way to eliminate prints is to do some chopping. A hot plate was tossed in a corner near the bed; I checked it out and saw seared skin stuck to the coils. The bed stiff was right there, so I took a deep breath, tightened my mask and examined him. He was an old guy, skinny, dressed in clothes too heavy for winter LA. There was not one mark of any kind on him; his singed-fingered hands had been folded neatly on his chest, rest in peace, like a mortician had done the job. I checked his coat and trouser pockets—goose egg—and gave him a few probes for broken bones. Double gooser. Just then a maggot crawled out of his gaping mouth, doing a spastic little lindy hop on the tip of his tongue.

I walked back into the living room, picked up the phone and called a man who owes me a big, big favor pertaining to his wife's association with a Negro nun and a junior congressman from Whittier. The man is a crime-scene technician with the Sheriff's Department; a med school dropout adept at spot-checking cadavers and guessing causes of death. He promised to be at 2281 South Mariposa within the hour in an unmarked car—ten minutes of forensic expertise in exchange for my erasure of his debt.

I went back to the bedroom, carrying a pot of Lavonne Cohen's geraniums to help kill the stink. The floor stiff's pockets had been picked clean; the bed stiff had no bruises on his head, and there were now two maggots doing a tango across his nose. Morris Hornbeck, a pro, probably packed a silencered heater like most Mickey muscle—he looked too scrawny to be a hand-to-hand killer. I was starting to make Gretchen Rae Shoftel for the snuffs—and I was starting to like her.

Lieutenant Kirby Falwell showed up a few minutes later, tap-tap-tap on the window I broke. I let him in, and he lugged his evidence kit into the bedroom, pinching his nose. I left him there to be scientific, staying in the living room so as not to bruise his ego with my inside scoop on his wife. After half an hour he came out and greeted me:

"We're even, Meeks. The clown on the floor was hit on the head with a flat, blunt object, maybe a frying pan. It probably knocked him silly. Then somebody threw their dinner in his face and gave him second-degree burns. Then they strangled him with that negligee. I'll give you asphyxiation as cause of death. On Pops, I'd say heart attack—natural causes. I mighta said poison, but his liver isn't distended. Heart attack, fifty-fifty odds. Both dead about two days. I picked the scabs off both sets of fingers and rolled their prints. I suppose you want a forty-eight-state teletype on them?"

I shook my head. "California and Wisconsin—but quick."

"Inside four hours. We're even, Meeks."

"Take the nightgown home to the wife, Kirby. She'll find a use for it."

"Fuck you, Meeks."

"Adios, Lieutenant."

I settled in, the lights off, figuring if Mo Hornbeck and Gretchen Rae were some kind of partners, he would be by to dump the stiffs, or she would be, or someone would drop in to say hello. I sat in a chair by the front door, the lamp in my hand ready to swing if it came to that kind of play. Danger juice was keeping me edgy; my brain fluids were roiling, trying to figure a way out of the parlay—my two benefactors hiring me to glom one woman for their exclusive use, two corpses thrown in. As hard as I brainstormed, I couldn't think up squat. With half an hour to kill before I called Kirby Falwell, I gave up and tried the Other Guy Routine.

The Other Guy Routine dates back to my days as a youth in Oklahoma, when my old man would beat the shit out of my old lady, and I'd haul a mattress out into the scrub woods so I wouldn't have to listen. I'd set my armadillo traps down, and every once in a while I'd hear a snap-squeak as some stupid 'dillo ate my bait and got his spine crunched for his trouble. When I finally fell asleep, I'd usually wake up to screeches—men hurting women—always just wind playing havoc with the scrub pines. I'd start thinking then: ways to get the old man off the old lady's back without consulting my brother Fud—in the Texas Pen for armed robbery and grievous aggravated assault. I knew I didn't have the guts to confront Pop myself, so I started thinking about other people just to get him off my mind. And that always let me develop a play: some church woman conned into dropping off a pie and religious tracts to calm the old man down; steering some local slick who thought Mom was a beauty in her direction, knowing Pop was a coward with other men and would love up the old girl for weeks and weeks just to keep her. That last play stood all of us good at the end—it was right before the old lady caught typhus. She took to bed with a fever, and the old man got in with her to keep her warm. He caught it himself—and died—sixteen days after she did. Under the circumstances, you have to believe there was nothing but love between them—right up to curtains.

So the Other Guy Routine gets you out of the hole and makes some other poor fuck feel good in the process. I worked it in niggertown as a cop: let some pathetic grasshopper slide, send him a Mickey fruit basket at Christmas, get him to snitch a horse pusher, and skim five percent full of yuletide cheer. The only trouble with it this time is that I was locked on the horns of a jumbo dilemma: Mickey, Howard—two patrons, only one woman. And claiming failure with either man was against my religion.

I gave up thinking and called Kirby Falwell at the Sheriff's Bureau. His two-state teletype yielded heat:

The floor stiff was Fritz Steinkamp, Chicago-Milwaukee gunsel, one conviction for attempted murder, currently on parole and believed to be a Jerry Katzenbach torpedo. Mr. Heart Attack was Voyteck Kirnipaski, three-time loser, also a known Katzenbach associate, his falls for extortion and grand larceny—specifically stock swindles. The pic-

ture getting a little less hazy, I called Howard Hughes at his flop at the
Bel Air Hotel. Two rings, hang up, three rings—so he'd know it's not
some gossip columnist.

"Yes?"

"Howard, you been in Milwaukee the past few years?"

"I was in Milwaukee in the spring of '47. Why?"

"Any chance you went to a whorehouse that specialized in girls
made up like movie stars?"

Howard sighed. "Buzz, you know my alleged propensity in that
department. Is this about Gretchen Rae?"

"Yeah. Did you?"

"Yes. I was entertaining some colleagues from the Pentagon. We
had a party with several young women. My date looked just like Jean
Arthur, only a bit more . . . endowed. Jean broke my heart, Buzz. You
know that."

"Yeah. Did the high brass get looped and start talking shop
around the girls?"

"Yes, I suppose so. What does this—"

"Howard, what did you and Gretchen Rae talk about—besides
your sex fantasies?"

"Well, Gretchy seemed to be interested in business—stock mergers, the little companies I've been buying up, that sort of thing. Also
politics. My Pentagon chums have told me about Korea heating up,
implying lots of aircraft business. Gretchy seemed interested in that,
too. A smart girl always interests herself in her lovers' endeavors, Buzz.
You know that. Have you got leads on her?"

"I surely have. Boss, how have you managed to stay alive and rich
so long?"

"I trust the right people, Buzz. Do you believe that?"

"I surely do."

I gave my sitting-in-the-dark stakeout another three hours, then raided
the icebox for energy and took the Other Guy Routine on the road, a
mitzvah for Mickey in case I had to play an angle to shoot Gretchen
Rae to Howard—his very own teenage murderess. First I wrapped up
Fritz Steinkamp in three windows' worth of chintz curtains and hauled
him out to my car; next I mummified Voyteck Kirnipaski in a bedspread and wedged him into the trunk between Fritz and my spare tire.
Then it was a routine wipe of my own possible prints, lights off, and a

drive out to Topanga Canyon, to the chemical debris dump operated by the Hughes Tool Company—a reservoir bubbling with caustic agents adjacent to a day camp for underprivileged kids: a Howard tax dodge. I dumped Fritz and Voyteck into the cauldron and listened to them snap, crackle, and pop like Kellogg's Rice Krispies. Then, just after midnight, I drove to the Strip to look for Mickey and his minions.

They weren't at the Trocadero, the Mocambo, or the La Rue; they weren't at Sherry's or Dave's Blue Room. I called the DMV night information line, played cop, and got a read on Mo Hornbeck's wheels—1946 tan Dodge Coupe, CAL–4986–J, 896¼ Moonglow Vista, South Pasadena—then took the Arroyo Seco over the hill to the address, a block of bungalow courts.

At the left-side tail end of a stucco streamline job was 896¼—rounded handrails and oblong louvers fronting tiny windows strictly for show. No lights were burning; Hornbeck's Dodge was not in the carport at the rear. Maybe Gretchen Rae was inside, armed with stuffed animals, negligee garrotes, stew pots, and frying pans—and that suddenly made me not give a fuck whether the world laid, prayed, stayed, or strayed. I kicked the door in, flipped on a wall light, and got knocked flat on my ass by a big furry mother with big, shiny razor-white teeth.

It was a Doberman, sleek black muscle out for blood—mine. The dog snapped at my shoulder and got a snootful of Hart, Schaffner & Marx worsted; he snapped at my face and got an awkwardly thrown Meeks right jab that caused him to flinch momentarily. I dug in my pocket for my Arkansas toad stabber, popped the button, and flailed with it; I grazed the beast's paws and snout—and he still kept snapping and snarling.

Giving the fucker a stationary target was the only way. I put my left arm over my eyes and tried to stay prone; Rex the Wonder Dog went for my big, fat, juicy elbow. I hooked my shiv up at his gut, jammed it in and yanked forward. Entrails dropped all over me; Rex vomited blood in my face and died with a snap-gurgle.

I kicked the day's third corpse off of me, stumbled to the bathroom, rummaged through the medicine cabinet, and found witch hazel. I doused my elbow bite and the blood-oozing teeth marks on my knuckles. Deep breathing, I splashed sink water on my face, looked in the mirror, and saw a middle-aged fat man, terrified and pissed to his drawers, in deep, deep shit without a depth gauge. I held the gaze, thinking it wasn't me for long seconds. Then I smashed the image with the witch hazel bottle and eyeballed the rest of the bungalow.

The larger of the two bedrooms had to be Gretchen Rae's. It was all girlish gewgaws: pandas and arcade Kewpie dolls, pinups of matinee idols and college pennants on the walls. Kitchen appliances still in their boxes were stacked on the dresser; publicity glossies of RKO pretty boys littered the bedspread.

The other bedroom reeked of Vapo Rub and liniment and sweat and flatulence—bare walls, the floor space almost completely taken up by a sagging Murphy Bed. There was a medicine bottle on the night-stand—Dr. Revelle prescribing Demerol for Mr. Jamelka—and check-ing under the pillow got me a .38 police special. I flipped the cylinder, extracted four of the shells and stuck the gun in my waistband, then went back to the living room and picked up the dog, gingerly, so as not to drench myself in his gore. I noticed that it was a female; that a tag on its collar read "Janet." That hit me as the funniest thing since vaude-ville, and I started laughing wildly, shock coming on. I spotted an Abercrombie & Fitch dog bed in the corner, dumped Janet in it, doused the lights in the room, found a couch, and collapsed. I was heading into some sort of weird heebie-jeebie haze when wood creak-ing, a choked "Oh, my god!" and hot yellow glare jolted me to my feet.

"Oh Janet no!"

Mo Hornbeck beelined for the dead dog, not even noticing me. I stuck out my leg and tripped him; he hit the floor almost snout to snout with Janet. And I was right there, gun at his head, snarling like the psycho Okie killer I could have been. "Boy, you're gonna blab on you, Gretchen Rae, and them bodies on Mariposa. You're gonna spill on her and Howard Hughes, and I mean *now.*"

Hornbeck found some balls quicksville, averting his eyes from the dog, latching them onto me. "Fuck you, Meeks."

"Fuck you" was acceptable from a ranking sheriff's dick in my debt, but not from a statch raper hoodlum. I opened the .38's cylinder and showed Hornbeck the two rounds, then spun it, and put the muz-zle to his head. "Talk. *Now.*"

Hornbeck said, "Fuck you, Meeks"; I pulled the trigger; he gasped and looked at the dog, turning purple at the temples, red at the cheeks. Seeing myself in a cell next to Fud, the Meeks boys playing pinochle sideways through the bars, I popped off another shot, the hammer clicking on an empty chamber. Hornbeck bit at the carpet to staunch his tremors, going deep purple, then subsiding into shades of crimson, pink, death's-head white. Finally he spat dust and dog hair and gasped, "The pills by my bed and the bottle in the cupboard."

I obeyed, and the two of us sat on the porch like good buddies and killed the remains of the jug—Old Overholt Bonded. Hornbeck blasted Demerol pills along with the juice, flew to cloud nine, and told me the saddest goddamn story I'd ever heard.

Gretchen Rae Shoftel was his daughter. Mom hit the road shortly after she was born, hightailing it to parts unknown with a Schlitz Brewery driver rumored to be double-digit hung, like the human equivalent of Mickey Cohen, Jr. Mo raised Gretch as best he could, nursing a bad case of the hots for her, ashamed of it until he picked up scads of unrelated skinny that his wife was servicing the entire Schlitz night shift during the time his little girl was conceived. On general principles he stayed hands off, taking his lust out on girls from the greenhorn hooker camps up in Green Bay and Saint Paul.

Gretchy grew up strange, ashamed of her old man—a gang stooge and occasional killer. She took her old lady's maiden name and buried her head in books, loving arithmetic tricks, figures, calculations—stuff that proved she was smart. She also took up with a rough South Milwaukee crowd. One crazy Polack boyfriend beat her silly every night for a week straight when she was fifteen. Mo found out, put the kid in cement skates, and dumped him in Lake Michigan. Father and daughter were happily reunited by the revenge.

Mo moved up in Jerry Katzenbach's organization; Gretch got a bundle together tricking the hotel bars in Chicago. Mo installed Gretchen Rae as sixteen-year-old pit boss of a swank whorehouse: movie-star surrogates, the rooms bugged to pick up gangland and political skinny that might prove valuable to Jerry K. Gretch got friendly with stock swindler Voyteck Kirnipaski; she just happened to be listening through a vent one night when Howard Hughes and a cadre of army three-stars were cavorting with Jean Arthur, Lupe Velez, and Carole Lombard, greenhorn versions. Gretch picked up lots of juicy Wall Street gossip, and realized that this could be the start of something big. Mo contracted stomach cancer about that time and got the word: half a decade tops—enjoy life while you can. Cash skimmed off Jerry Katzenbach's books provided class A treatment. Mo held his own against the big C. Jerry K. got bum press for his whorehouse, kiboshed it, and banished Mo to the Coast, where Mickey Cohen welcomed him with open arms, using his juice to get Mo's two statch-rape indiscretions plea-bargained to bubbkis.

Back in Milwaukee, Gretchen Rae audited business classes at Marquette, and hauled Voyteck Kirnipaski's ashes for free when she learned he was working for Jerry K. and was dissatisfied with the pay. Then Mo had a relapse and came back to Milwaukee on a visit; Voyteck Kirnipaski skipped town with a bundle of Katzenbach's money so he could bankroll stock swindles in LA; Gretchen Rae, always reading the papers with an eye toward political repercussions, put her overhead dope from Howard and the high brass together with whispers on the Korea situation and decided to get more info from the man himself. Mo took some lung shots of his little girl and mailed them to Big How; he bit. Gretchy glommed leads that the on-the-lam and hotly pursued Voyteck was hanging out at Scrivner's Drive-In, and, wanting to enlist his aid in possible squeeze plays, got a job there. Mickey Cohen's crush on her put a monkey wrench into things—but she thought, somehow, that the little big man could be tapped for juice. She became his consort concurrent with Howard, father and daughter pretending to be strangers at Mickey's nightclub get-togethers. Then, at a Santa Monica motel, she located Voyteck, terrified that Katzenbach triggers were right behind him. Mo gave her the key to Mickey's Mariposa Street hideout; she ensconced Voyteck there, moving back and forth between Howard's fuck pad, pumping information subtly and pumping Kirnipaski blatantly—attempting to lure him into her web of schemes. She was making progress when Fritz Steinkamp made the scene. And damned if Gretchy didn't rise to the occasion and throttle, scald, and frying pan him to death. She attempted to soothe the terrified Voyteck afterward, but he went into cardiac arrest: the volatile combo of a murder attempt, a murder, and a murderess tongue. Gretchen Rae panicked and took off with Voyteck's pilfered cash—and was currently trying to unload "secret insider" prospectuses on Hughes stock to a list of potential customers Kirnipaski had compiled. The girl was holed up someplace—Mo didn't know where—and tomorrow she would be calling at the homes and offices of her last wave of potential "clients."

Somewhere in the course of the story I started liking Mo almost as much as I liked Gretchen Rae. I still couldn't see any way out of the mess, but I was curious about one thing: the girly gewgaws, the appliances, all the squarejohn homey stuff Gretchy had glommed. When Mo finished his tale, I said, "What's with all the clothes and gadgets and stuffed animals?"

Morris Hornbeck, worm bait inside six months, just sighed. "Lost time, Meeks. The father-and-daughter act someplace safe, the shtick we shoulda played years ago. But that's tap city, now."

I pointed to the dead dog, its paws starting to curl with rigor mortis like it was going to be begging biscuits for eternity. "Maybe not. You sure ain't gonna have a trusty mascot, but you might get a little taste of the rest."

Morris went to his bedroom and passed out. I laid down on the homey dreambed, holding a stuffed panda, the lights off to insure some good brainwork. Straight manipulation of Mickey and Howard fell by the wayside quick, so I shifted to the Other Guy Routine and made a snag.

Sid Weinberg.

RKO Line Producer.

Filthy rich purveyor of monster cheapies, drive-in circuit turkeys that raked in the cash.

A valuable RKO mainstay—his pictures never flopped. Howard kissed his ass, worshipped his dollars-and-cents approach to movie making and gave him carte blanche at the studio.

"I'd rather lose my you know what than lose Sid Weinberg."

Mickey Cohen was indebted to Sid Weinberg, the owner of the Blue Lagoon Saloon, where Mickey was allowed to perform his atrocious comedy routines without cops hanging around—Sid had LAPD connections.

The Mick: "I'd be without a pot to piss in without Sid. I'd have to buy my own nightclub, and that's no fun—it's like buying your own baseball team so you can play yourself."

Sid Weinberg was a widower, a man with two grown daughters who patronized him as a buffoon. He often spoke of his desire to find himself a live-in housekeeper to do light dusting and toss him a little on the side. About fifteen years ago, he was known to be in love with a dazzling blonde starlet named Glenda Jensen, who hotfooted it off into the sunset one day, never to be seen again. I'd seen pictures of Glenda; she looked suspiciously like my favorite teenage killer. At eight tomorrow night Sid Weinberg was throwing a party to ballyhoo *Bride of the Surf Monster*. I was to provide security. Mickey Cohen and Howard Hughes would be guests.

I fell asleep on the thought, and dreamed that benevolent dead dogs were riding me up to heaven, my pockets full of other guys' money.

* * *

In the morning we took off after the prodigal daughter. I drove, Mo Hornbeck gave directions—where he figured Gretchen Rae would be, based on their last conversation—a panicky talk two days ago; the girl afraid of phone taps; Mo saying he would let the evidence chill, then dispose of it.

Which, of course, he didn't. According to Mo, Gretch told him Voyteck Kirnipaski had given her a list of financial district sharks who might be interested in her Hughes Enterprises graphs: when to buy and sell shares in Toolco, Hughes Aircraft and its myriad subsidiaries— based on her new knowledge of upcoming defense contracts and her assessment of probable stock price fluctuations. Mo stressed that that was why Gretchy raped the Bullocks catalog—she wanted to look like a businesswoman, not a seductress/killer.

So we slow-lane trawled downtown, circuiting the Spring Street financial district, hoping to catch a streetside glimpse of Gretchen Rae as she made her office calls. I'd won Mo partially over with kind words and a promise to plant Janet in a ritzy West LA pet cemetery, but I could still tell he didn't trust me—I was too close to Mickey for too long. He gave me a steady sidelong fisheye and only acknowledged my attempts at conversation with grunts.

The morning came and went; the afternoon followed. Mo had no leads on Gretchen Rae's home calls, so we kept circling Spring Street— Third to Sixth and back again—over and over, taking piss stops at the Pig & Whistle on Fourth and Broadway every two hours. Dusk came on, and I started getting scared: my Other Guy Routine would work to perfection only if I brought Gretchy to Sid Weinberg's party right on time.

6:00.

6:30.

7:00.

7:09. I was turning the corner onto Sixth Street when Mo grabbed my arm and pointed out the window at a sharkskin clad secretary type perusing papers by the newsstand. "There. That's my baby."

I pulled over; Mo stuck his head out the door and waved, then shouted, "No! Gretchen!"

I was setting the hand brake when I saw the girl—Gretch with her hair in a bun—notice a man on the street and start running. Mo piled out of the car and headed toward the guy; he pulled a monster hand-cannon, aimed, and fired twice. Mo fell dead on the sidewalk, half his face blown off; the man pursued Gretchen Rae; I pursued him.

The girl ran inside an office building, the gunman close behind. I caught up, peered in, and saw him at the top of the second-floor landing. I slammed the door and stepped back; the act coaxed two wasted shots out of the killer, glass and wood exploding all around me. Four rounds gone, two to go.

Screams on the street; two sets of footsteps scurrying upstairs; sirens in the distance. I ran to the landing and shouted, "Police!" The word drew two ricocheting bang-bangs. I hauled my fat ass up to floor three like a flabby dervish.

The gunman was fumbling with a pocketful of loose shells; he saw me just as he flicked his piece's cylinder open. I was within three stairs of him. Not having time to load and fire, he kicked. I grabbed his ankle and pulled him down the stairs; we fell together in a tangle of arms and legs, hitting the landing next to an open window.

We swung at each other, two octopuses, blows and gouges that never really connected. Finally he got a choke hold on my neck; I reached up through his arms and jammed my thumbs hard in his eyes. The bastard let go just long enough for me to knee his balls, squirm away, and grab him by the scalp. Blinded now, he flailed for me. I yanked him out the window head first, pushing his feet after him. He hit the pavement spread-eagled, and even from three stories up I could hear his skull crack like a giant eggshell.

I got some more breath, hauled up to the roof, and pushed the door open. Gretchen Rae Shoftel was sitting on a roll of tar paper, smoking a cigarette, two long single tears rolling down her cheeks. She said, "Did you come to take me back to Milwaukee?"

All I could think of to say was, "No."

Gretchen reached behind the tar paper and picked up a brief-case—brand-new, Bullocks Wilshire quality. The sirens downstairs were dying out; two bodies gave lots of cops lots to do. I said, "Mickey or Howard, Miss Shoftel? You got a choice."

Gretch stubbed out her cigarette. "They both stink." She hooked a thumb over the roof in the direction of the dead gunman. "I'll take my chances with Jerry Katzenbach and his friends. Daddy went down tough. So will I."

I said, "You're not that stupid."

Gretchen Rae said, "You play the market?"

I said, "Want to meet a nice rich man who needs a friend?"

Gretchen Rae pointed to a ladder that connected the roof to the fire escape of the adjoining building. "If it's now, I'll take it."

In the cab to Beverly Hills I filled Gretchy in on the play, promising all kinds of bonuses I couldn't deliver, like the Morris Hornbeck scholarship for impoverished Marquette University Business School students. Pulling up to Sid Weinberg's tudor mansion, the girl had her hair down, make-up on, and was ready to do the save-my-ass tango.

At 8:03 the manse was lit up like a Christmas tree—extras in green rubber monster costumes handing out drinks on the front lawn and loudspeakers on the roof blasting the love theme from a previous Weinberg tuna, *Attack of the Atomic Gargoyles*. Mickey and Howard always arrived at parties late in order not to appear too eager, so I figured there was time to set things up.

I led Gretchen Rae inside, into an incredible scene: Hollywood's great, near-great, and non-great boogie-woogieing with scads of chorus boys and chorus girls dressed like surf monsters, atomic gargoyles, and giant rodents from Mars; bartenders sucking punch out of punchbowls with ray-gun like siphons; tables of cold cuts dyed surf-monster green—passed up by the guests en masse in favor of good old booze—the line for which stood twenty deep. Beautiful gash was abounding, but Gretchen Rae, hair down like Sid Weinberg's old love Glenda Jensen, was getting the lion's share of the wolf stares. I stood with her by the open front door, and when Howard Hughes's limousine pulled up, I whispered, *"Now."*

Gretchen slinked back to Sid Weinberg's glass-fronted private office in slow, slow motion; Howard, tall and handsome in a tailored tux, walked in the door, nodding to me, his loyal underling. I said, "Good evening, Mr. Hughes," out loud; under my breath, "You owe me a grand."

I pointed to Sid's office; Howard followed. We got there just as Gretchen Rae Shoftel/Glenda Jensen and Sid Weinberg went into a big open-mouthed clinch. I said, "I'll lean on Sid, Boss. Kosher is kosher. He'll listen to reason. Trust me."

Inside of six seconds I saw the fourth richest man in America go from heartsick puppy dog to hardcase robber baron and back at least a dozen times. Finally he jammed his hands in his pockets, fished out a wad of C-notes, and handed them to me. He said, "Find me another one just like her," and walked back to his limo.

I worked the door for the next few hours, chasing crashers and autograph hounds away, watching Gretchen/Glenda and Sid Weinberg work the crowd, instant velvet for the girl, youth recaptured for the sad old man. Gretchy laughed, and I could tell she did it to hold back tears; when she squeezed Sid's hand I knew she didn't know who it belonged to. I kept wishing I could be there when her tears broke for real, when she became a real little girl for a while, before going back to being a stock maven and a whore. Mickey showed up just as the movie was starting. Davey Goldman told me he was pissed: Mo Hornbeck got himself bumped off by a Kraut trigger from Milwaukee who later nosedived out a window; the Mariposa Street hideout had been burglarized, and Lavonne Cohen was back from Israel three days early and henpecking the shit out of the Mick. I barely heard the words. Gretchy and Sid were cooing at each other by the cold cut table—and Mickey was headed straight toward them.

I couldn't hear their words, but I could read the three faces. Mickey was taken aback, but paid gracious respect to his beaming host; Gretch was twitching with the aftershocks of her old man's death. LA's #1 hoodlum bowed away, walked up to me, and flicked my necktie in my face. "All you get is a grand, you hump. You shoulda found her quicker."

So it worked out. Nobody made me for snuffing the Milwaukee shooter; Gretchy walked on the Steinkamp killing and her complicity in Voyteck Kirnipaski's demise—the chemical-sizzled stiffs, of course, were never discovered. Mo Hornbeck got a plot at Mount Sinai Cemetery, and Davey Goldman and I stuffed Janet into the casket with him at the mortuary—I gave the rabbi a hot tip on the trotters, and he left the room to call his bookie. I paid off Leotis Dineen and promptly went back into hock with him; Mickey took up with a stripper named Audrey Anders; Howard made a bundle off airplane parts for the Korean War and cavorted with the dozen or so Gretchen Rae Shoftel look-alikes I found him. Gretchy and Sid Weinberg fell in love, which just about broke the poor pilot-mogul's heart.

Gretchen Rae and Sid.

She did her light dusting—and must have thrown him a lot on the side. She also became Sid's personal investment banker and made him a giant bundle, of which she took a substantial percentage cut, invested it in slum property, and watched it grow, grow, grow. Slumlord

Gretch also starred in the only Sid Weinberg vehicle ever to lose money, a tear jerker called *Glenda* about a movie producer who falls in love with a starlet who disappears off the face of the earth. The critical consensus was that Gretchen Rae Shoftel was a lousy actress, but had great lungs. Howard Hughes was rumored to have seen the movie over a hundred times.

In 1950 I got involved in a grand jury investigation that went bad in an enormous way, and I ended up taking it on the road permanently, Mr. Anonymous in a thousand small towns. Mickey Cohen did a couple of fed jolts for income-tax evasion, got paroled as an old man, and settled back into LA as a much-appreciated local character, a reminder of the colorful old days. Howard Hughes ultimately went squirrelshit with drugs and religion, and a biography that I read said that he carried a torch for a blonde whore straight off into the deep end. He'd spend hours at the Bel Air Hotel looking at her picture, playing a torchy rendition of "Since I Don't Have You" over and over. I know better: It was probably scads of different pictures, lung shots all, the music a lament for a time when love came cheap. Gretchy was special to him, though. I still believe that.

I miss Howard and Mickey, and writing this story about them has only made it worse. It's tough being a dangerous old man by yourself—you've got nothing but memories and no one with the balls to understand them.

Since I Don't Have You

You

Teleplay by

Steven Katz

Cast

James Woods	Mickey Cohen
Gary Busey	Buzz Meeks
Tim Matheson	Howard Hughes
Aimee Graham	Gretchen Rae Shoftel
Ken Lerner	Sid Weinberg
Dick Miller	Morris Hornbeck
Robert L. Minor	Leotis
Dino Anello	Johnny Stompanato
Gary Grossman	Tailor
Cindy Ambuehl	Blonde #2
Elaine Hendrix	Blonde #1
Simone Wright	Blonde #3
Bruce Meade	Corpse
Michael Milgrom	Milwaukee Trigger
George Rodriguez	Man with Photos

Executive Producer: Sydney Pollack
Producers: William Horberg, Lindsay Doran, Steve Golin
Co-Producer: David Wisnievitz
Directed by: Jonathan Kaplan
Director of Photography: Declan Quinn
Production designed by: Armin Ganz
Costumes designed by: Shay Cunliffe
Casting by: Owens Hill and Rachel Abroms
Fallen Angels theme by: Elmer Bernstein
Music by: Peter Bernstein
Edited by: Stan Salfas
Story Editor: Geoffrey Stier

INTERIOR: SOUNDSTAGE. DAY.

Close on BLONDE #1 *screaming. She is gorgeous in a tight dress and a Veronica Lake hairdo. Over her screams, we begin to hear the voice of Turner "Buzz" Meeks.*

MEEKS *(voice-over; Oklahoma twang):* For half a score years after the end of the war, I lived in the city of Los Angeles, California, and served two masters. I guess you could say them two fellas defined that town at that time just about better'n anyone else.

As the camera pulls away from BLONDE #1, *we realize that we're watching an audition in a Hollywood soundstage.* BLONDE #1 *returns her script, exits, and is soon replaced by* BLONDE #2. *As we continue to pull away, we watch, from a distance, as* BLONDE #2 *picks up the script and starts screaming:*

BLONDE #2: No! No! It's alive!! Arghhhhhh!

(Off to one side of the soundstage, we find MEEKS, *forty-one, tired, balding, and overweight. He's wearing an old linen suit with a bolo tie cinched at his throat and cowboy boots stretched out on a crate in front of him. Right now he's watching the audition and shoveling chewing tobacco into his craw.)*

MEEKS *(voice-over):* That sorry-looking son-of-a-bitch is me, Turner Meeks, originally outta Lizard Ridge, Oklahoma. You can call me "Buzz." I've been an armadilla poacher and a strikebreaker, a cop and a fixer. And sooner or later my work for them two fellas I was talking about had to produce what lawyers nowadays would call a "conflict a' interest." Of course, it was over a woman.

(Casting agents dismiss BLONDE #2 *and* BLONDE #3 *takes her place. One of the men,* SID WEINBERG, *strolls over to a glass-fronted office and dejectedly sits down at his desk. On the wall behind him we see a big 1940s-style monster movie poster.)*

MEEKS *(voice-over):* June 1948. I was killing time watching Sid Weinberg audition blondes for one a' his schlockola horror pictures. Matter of fact, that's Sid right over there.

*(*SID WEINBERG—*a bald, middle-aged Jewish guy—still in his office. He looks at the movie poster, crying like a baby.)*

MEEKS *(voice-over):* For the past fifteen years, Sid's been carrying a torch for a starlet named Glenda Jensen who hot-footed it off into the sunset one day never to be seen again. From that day to this, Sid's been holding the world's longest continuous casting session. That's Glenda there, up on the wall.

Poster: The Mummy's Daughter

A beautiful blonde, in a cunningly torn dress, being menaced by a monster which vaguely resembles those of The Mummy *ilk.*

MEEKS *(voice-over):* Sid ain't one of the fellas I work for or nothing. Just pointing him out as a matter of historical interest, is all.

INTERIOR: SOUNDSTAGE. DAY.

One of the casting agents comes over to MEEKS *and hands him an envelope.* MEEKS *opens it:*

Close on envelope filled with casting agent's photos of beautiful starlets.

MEEKS *and* AGENT, *as before: The* CASTING AGENT *winks at* MEEKS *and walks away.* MEEKS *heads for the door.*

INTERIOR/EXTERIOR: STREET. DAY.

As MEEKS *walks toward his parked car, he notices a menacing black man in a zoot suit waiting for him.*

MEEKS: Now, say there fella, what're you doing in these parts? The management hereabouts can take a pretty heavy hand with fellas of the colored persuasion. Not that it matters to me, you understand.

(Suddenly, a very tall black man, also in a zoot suit, appears. The other man takes up a position beside him.)

LEOTIS: You're a real friend to the colored people, Mister Meeks.

MEEKS: Oh, hey there, Leotis. Don't tell me now: I do believe I am deep in hock to you.

LEOTIS: Two thousand and change.

MEEKS: I'm tapped out now, Leotis. (LEOTIS *pops the switchblade and displays it to* MEEKS.) Listen, I just need a little more time.

LEOTIS: I'll tell you what, Mr. Meeks. I'll give you 'til tomorrow night. You gonna be at Sid Weinberg's party?

MEEKS *(surprised)*: Are you?

LEOTIS: I've got an investment in his new picture. So I'll being seeing you and your two thousand at, let's say, midnight tomorrow.

(Suddenly LEOTIS *grabs* MEEKS *hard by the bolo tie, pulling him up onto tiptoes.)*

LEOTIS: Don't you fuck with me, boy. *(Drops choking* MEEKS.) You know my feelings toward people of the Oklahoma persuasion.

*(*LEOTIS *puts on his fedora and turns away with his goon.)*

EXTERIOR: HUGHES AIRCRAFT HANGAR. DAY.

(An old prop plane. Thick black smoke spews from its engine. A pilot emerges from the cockpit, face obscured by helmet and goggles. Heads toward us.)

MEEKS *(voice-over)*: The fella walking this way is my principal employer. Howard Hughes. Pilot, designer, movie mogul, fourth richest man in America.

(HOWARD HUGHES takes off his helmet and goggles. He's tall and lanky, with a Clark Gable mustache and a Texas accent. MEEKS leans against his car—a beat-up four-door with running boards.)

MEEKS: Howdy, boss. *(Points to plane.)* What's with the bug-smasher?

HUGHES: Department of War contract. Cost plus. You ever hear of a country called Korea, Buzz?

MEEKS: Nope.

HUGHES: Howzabout a country called Mammon?

MEEKS: Mammon?

HUGHES: Money, Buzz. I'm asking if you need any money.

MEEKS: Does Doans make little pills?

HUGHES: They surely do.

MEEKS *hands* HUGHES *the envelope full of starlet photos that we saw earlier.* HUGHES *looks at the pictures without interest as he strolls inside the hangar.* MEEKS *follows.*

INTERIOR: HUGHES AIRCRAFT HANGAR. DAY.

HUGHES *sits at a cluttered, paper-covered desk just inside the huge doors of the empty hangar. He tosses the envelope onto the desk and picks up the phone.*

HUGHES: This is Howard Hughes. Please route my calls to this telephone.

(HUGHES hangs up and begins digging around in the papers. After a few seconds, he withdraws a photo from the mess and looks at it longingly. He hands it to MEEKS.

Close on a photo of a blonde, naked from the waist up, with beautiful breasts.

MEEKS *and* HUGHES, *as before.)*

MEEKS: Nice set a' lungs.

HUGHES: Her name's Gretchen Rae Shoftel. She's nineteen years old. Born in Prairie du Chien, Wisconsin, on July 26, 1929. This is the woman, Buzz. This is the woman I'm going to marry.

MEEKS: Is that a fact?

HUGHES: I want you to find her for me.

MEEKS: What do you mean? She's done gone?

HUGHES: Flew the coop.

MEEKS *(pocketing the picture):* Who found her for you in the first place, boss? It wasn't me.

HUGHES: I got the picture in the mail at the studio. The deal was a thousand dollars cash to a P.O. box in exchange for the girl's address. I did it, and met Gretchen Rae at a hotel downtown. She said she posed for some dirty old man back in Milwaukee. He must've been the mug who sent the picture. Anyway, I stashed her at the place on South Lucerne, she and I got to be . . . friends, and, well . . .

MEEKS: And you'll give me five C-notes to find her?

HUGHES: A thousand, Buzz. Cash. Off the payroll.

MEEKS *(plenty happy):* Okie-dokie, it's a deal.

HUGHES: By tomorrow night.

MEEKS *(thunderstruck):* Whoa now! That kid could be clear back to Wisconsin by now.

HUGHES: I've got complete faith in your abilities, Buzz.

BUZZ: Well, help me out here, boss. What else you got on her?

HUGHES: I've told you everything I know.

MEEKS *(panicking):* Listen to me, Howard. With that kind of skinny I couldn't find my butt in the bathtub by tomorrow night.

HUGHES: Midnight tomorrow, as a matter of fact. Sid Weinberg's party.

MEEKS: Oh boy . . .

(The phone rings. HUGHES picks it up.)

HUGHES *(into the phone):* Howard Hughes. *(He listens for a few seconds and then hangs up.)* That was the switchboard at the plant. Mickey Cohen wants to see you. Make it brief, you're on my time now.

MEEKS: Yessir.

INTERIOR: HABERDASHERY. NIGHT.

From the balcony inside we watch MEEKS *enter a swank deco haberdashery.*

MEEKS *(voice-over):* Two masters. To Howard Hughes I was security boss at his aircraft plant, pimp, and trouble-shooter for RKO pictures. But to Mickey Cohen, rackets overlord and L.A.'s number one hoodlum, I was a bagman to the LAPD.

*(*MICKEY COHEN, *tough and trim, is being fitted by a tailor. A couple of thugs lounge around watching him, including* MORRIS HORN-BECK, *sixty, a small, sickly looking accountant with rimless glasses; and* JOHNNY STOMPANATO, *thirty-five, wise-guy bodyguard to* COHEN.*)*

COHEN: Buzzie boy! You still making your bets with the schwartzes?

MEEKS: They don't like it when you call them that, Mick.

COHEN: Why don't you do yourself a favor and get a nice Jewish bookie?

TAILOR *(on his knees):* You want cuffs, Mr. Cohen?

COHEN: No, no cuffs. *(To a thug:)* Johnny, make a note: "no cuffs." *(To* MEEKS:*)* Buzz, you know my muscle Johnny Stompanato? And this is Morris Hornbeck. Mo use to run a cat house for the Jerry Katzenbach mob, but now he's doing my accounting. Costs me a fortune, but the guy can juggle books like fucking W. C. Fields.

MEEKS *(in a hurry):* Okay, okay, so what's the poop, Mickey? You got a fruit basket stuffed with C-notes you want delivered to some city councilman?

COHEN: What's with you? You got ants in your pants or something? *(To* JOHNNY:*)* Johnny, give Buzz the pic. *(To* MEEKS:*)* Buzzchick, I want you to find a dame for me.

MEEKS *(voice-over):* Well, I guess y'all could see it coming a mile off.

*(*JOHNNY *hands* MEEKS *a "Player's Club" folder.* MEEKS *opens it.)*

(Close on photo of GRETCHEN RAE SHOFTEL *in a booth in a night-club with her arm around* MICKEY COHEN.*)*

MEEKS *(voice-over):* The photo was a nightspot job, compliments of Preston Sturges's Player's Club. Gretchen Rae Shoftel, blinking against the flash, her dairy-state pulchritude poured into a tight black number.

(Haberdashery, as before.)

MEEKS *(closing the picture):* So where's the wife, Mick?

COHEN: Hadassah junket. Ten-day tour to the Holy Land with her mah-jongg club. While the cat's away, the mice will va-va-va-voom. Find her, Buzzchick. There's a G in it for you.

MEEKS: Make it two Gs, Cochise. Or take a flying fuck at a rolling doughnut.

*(*COHEN *goes into a slow burn.)*

TAILOR *(holding Cohen's jacket):* You want vents, Mr. Cohen?

*(*COHEN *goes berserk. He wildly strips off his jacket and trousers, whips out a gun, and starts parading around in his boxer shorts.)*

COHEN *(screaming):* Yeah vents! Vents but no cuffs! Vents but no cuffs! Johnny, make a note: vents but no cuffs. Now get this schvantz outta my sight! (*JOHNNY *ushers the* TAILOR *upstairs.* COHEN *calms down and starts looking at ties. Looking at* MEEKS *in the mirror:)* You Okie crumbum . . .

MEEKS: So tell me Mick: what do you know about this girl?

COHEN: Gretchen Rae Shoftel. I met her a coupla weeks ago at the counter of Schwab's Drug Store. Just like Lana Turner, eh Johnny? She was having a shake. I was having a banana split. She's fresh out of the sticks, Buzzchick. Minnesota.

MEEKS: Minnesota? She said Minnesota?

COHEN: Yeah, something like that. Minnesota, Moosebreath, Dog-turd, some boonies town.

MEEKS *(to* MORRIS HORNBECK*):* You're from Milwaukee, aren't you Mo?

MORRIS *(getting very nervous):* What of it?

MEEKS: Jerry Katzenbach's mob is based in Milwaukee.

COHEN: What's your point, putz?

MEEKS: No point. Just a Nosy Parker, is all.

COHEN: You better find her for me, Buzzchick. For a twosky I want satisfaction guaranteed by tomorrow night.

MEEKS *(sick feeling):* Tomorrow night?

COHEN: Twelve midnight. At Sid Weinberg's. Bring the broad, then make yourself scarce. Now take a powder, you goyishe shitheel.

(MEEKS *leaves.*)

EXTERIOR: HUGHES'S BUNGALOW. DAY.

Meeks's car is parked in the driveway of a small bungalow.

MEEKS *(voice-over):* My first stop the next day was the bungalow on South Lucerne. The one where Howard kept Gretchen Rae.

(MEEKS *climbs the steps, unlocks the door and enters.*)

INTERIOR: HUGHES'S BUNGALOW. DAY.

The bungalow reeks of 1940s sex appeal: Swedish modern furniture, a conspicuously well-stocked bar, hunting trophies, and luscious color photos of bathing beauties. As MEEKS *prowls around:*

MEEKS *(voice-over):* My primary job for Howard Hughes was bird-dogging bus depots and train stations for buxom young girls. Howard would sign them to RKO contracts in exchange for frequent nighttime visits, and then have me ensconce them in fuck pads like this one all over L.A. I ain't proud of it, but there it is.

(*As he's about to go into the kitchen . . .*)

MEEKS *(gagging):* Oh Christ!

(*He holds a handkerchief over his mouth and nose, and opens a door.*

Staircase: There's a body on the stairs—upside-down, with a face full of beef stroganoff. He arranges the corpse into a sitting position, and then lifts one of the man's hands.

Close on hands: the fingertips are singed.)

MEEKS *(as before. To himself):* Amateur.

(MEEKS *frisks the man. He doesn't find anything, but he does notice that the corpse is wearing an underarm holster.*)

MEEKS *(to corpse):* Well, I'll say this much: it's hard to make you through congealing beef stroganoff, Cochise. What do y'all have to say for yourself?

(*The corpse has no comment. Inside the lapel of the man's jacket,* MEEKS *finds a label that reads:* Mayron's of Milwaukee, Affordable Men's Suits.

MEEKS *picks up a frying pan lying beside the body.*)

MEEKS *(to the corpse):* Looks to me like the kinda weapon a woman would use, don't it? I'm starting to develop a real fondness for Gretchen Rae Shoftel. I suppose you don't share my high opinion of the little lady.

(MEEKS *leaves the room. Offscreen we hear the sound of silverware falling and glass breaking, and when he returns* MEEKS *is carrying a tablecloth. He checks his watch, then starts rolling the body up. He looks particularly put out.*)

INTERIOR/EXTERIOR: HUGHES AIRCRAFT HANGAR. DAY.

Through the huge open doors of the hangar, we see Meeks's car pull up. MEEKS *gets out, opens the trunk, pulls out the tablecloth-wrapped corpse and drags it off.*

MEEKS *(voice-over):* I just didn't have the time or the inclination to be disposing of incriminating evidence, but a body's a body. I high-tailed it to the aircraft plant and dumped the stiff into an old chrome-plating reservoir bubbling with acid. The body disappeared like a soggy Rice Krispie: snap, crackle, and pop . . .

(*Still from inside the hangar we see* MEEKS *reappear without the body. He walks into the hangar, sits down at the desk, and picks up the phone.*)

MEEKS: Yeah, gimme the Yellow Cab Company. Yellow Cab? This is . . . (MEEKS *picks up a newspaper from the desk. Close on newspaper: an* L.A. Times *with the headline* GEN MACARTHUR WARNS OF RED CHINESE THREAT*)* MacArthur, LAPD. Check your dispatch records. Any cabs sent to 436 South Lucerne in the last week? Yeah, I'll wait.

(MEEKS *cradles the phone against his shoulder, pulls out a bag of chewing tobacco, and begins filling his craw.* HOWARD HUGHES *drives up in the distance, exits his car, and removes something that looks like a woman's torso from the back seat.*)

MEEKS *(into phone):* Oh yeah? When? Three days ago? What was its destination? *(Writing:)* 2281 South Mariposa. Thanks. *(To himself:)* Pay dirt.

(*Enter* HUGHES, *carrying a mannequin torso sporting a woman's cantilevered brassiere.*)

HUGHES: Buzz! Have you given much serious thought to the ladies' brassiere?

MEEKS: Same as the next man.

HUGHES *(considers this):* Hmmm.

MEEKS: Howard, you been in Milwaukee lately?

HUGHES: Spring of '47. Why?

MEEKS: Any chance you went to a whorehouse there?

HUGHES: Buzz, you know my propensities in that department. Say, take a look at this. (HUGHES *produces a little velvet box and opens it. Inside is a diamond ring of epic proportions.*) Picture this riding on the fourth finger of Gretchen Rae's pretty hand.

MEEKS: Did you or didn't you, boss?

HUGHES: Did I or didn't I what?

MEEKS: The whorehouse.

HUGHES: Yes I did. I remember the girl looked like Jean Arthur. Jean broke my heart, Buzz, you know that.

MEEKS: Yeah. Were you alone?

HUGHES: No, I was entertaining some colleagues from the Pentagon.

MEEKS: Howard, what did you and Gretchen Rae talk about together? You know what I'm saying? Your pillow talk.

HUGHES: Well, Gretchy seemed to be interested in business—stock mergers, acquisitions, that sort of thing. Also politics. Lately my

Pentagon chums have been talking a blue streak about this burg Korea heating up. There's going to be a lot of new aircraft business if we go toe-to-toe with the reds. Gretchy seemed interested in that too. A smart girl's always interested in her lover's endeavors, Buzz. You oughta know that. Why do you ask? Now don't tell me you think that Gretchy . . .

(MEEKS *heads for the door.*) HUGHES *follows him.*)

MEEKS *(at the door):* Boss, let me ask you one more question: How have you managed to stay alive and rich so long?

HUGHES: Why, I trust the right people, Buzz. Do you believe that?

MEEKS: I surely do.

INTERIOR: 2281 SOUTH MARIPOSA. DAY.

There's a sound of breaking glass, and then we watch as MEEKS *opens a window and climbs in.*

MEEKS *(voice-over):* 2281 South Mariposa was a Mickey Cohen hideout, an armed fortress where the Mick's triggers holed up during their skirmishes with the Jack Dragna gang.

(Suddenly MEEKS *hears a key turning in the front door. He quickly sneaky-petes behind the door just as it opens and* MORRIS HORNBECK, *arms full of groceries, enters.)*

MORRIS *(calling):* Gretchen Rae! I'm home, honey!

(He slams the door. MEEKS *sticks out a foot, tripping him up in a mess of spilled groceries. Suddenly a gun appears at Morris's temple.* MORRIS *freezes and grabs his heart just as* MEEKS *flips him over onto his back, and points the gun at Morris's nose.)*

MEEKS: Mo Hornbeck! Well whadda ya know about that? Okie-dokie, Mo, where's the quail?

MORRIS: Fuck you, Meeks.

(MEEKS opens the cylinder, empties all of the bullets save one, snaps it back in, spins it, and puts the gun to Morris's head.)

MEEKS: Looky here, Cochise, I got a date with a lady at the witching hour. I ain't got time for you to play the tough guy.

MORRIS *(gasping for breath):* Fuck you.

(MEEKS *pulls the trigger. Click. He spins the cylinder again.*)

MEEKS: That's it! Talk right now, you hinky son-of-a-bitch or prepare
to meet your maker.

(MORRIS *starts to have a coronary. He grabs his heart and starts
wheezing.*)

MORRIS: Pills . . .

MEEKS: What?

MORRIS: In the bathroom. Little yellow pills . . .

INTERIOR: 2281 SOUTH MARIPOSA. NIGHT.

MORRIS *is slumped in an easy chair, an open bottle of little yellow
pills on the coffee table.* MEEKS *prowls the living room checking out the
assorted books, magazines, and knick-knacks. Logs crackle in the fireplace, bathing the room in amber light.*

MORRIS: Meeks, I'm gonna tell you the saddest goddamn story you
ever heard . . . *(Drinks from flask.)* Gretchen Rae Shoftel is my
daughter. When she was sixteen, I put her to work in the cat
house I looked after for Jerry Katzenbach.

*(The camera pans a coffee table covered in 1940s movie magazines
and across their airbrushed covers featuring glamorous depictions of female stars: Rita Hayworth, Gene Tierney, etc.)*

MORRIS: And it was some deal: it specialized in young girls dressed up
as movie stars. Rita Hayworth, Veronica Lake, Lupe Valez, you
name it. My Gretchen—the kid's got her mother's looks and my
head for numbers. Before I know it, she's picking up lots of juicy
Wall Street gossip doing her star turns for Howard Hughes and
his Pentagon pals.

MEEKS: So it was you who sent Hughes that picture of Gretchen Rae.

MORRIS: He bit, she glommed onto him. The deal was, she was going
to use the inside info to make a fortune in the stock market on the
Korea situation.

MEEKS: Where was her investment money coming from?

(MEEKS notices a thick volume next to a pile of textbooks: What You
Need to Know About the Stock Market, *etc.)*

MORRIS: Me. After Gretchen Rae hooked up with Hughes, I skipped town with a bundle of Katzenbach's money to finance the deal. I was Katzenbach's accountant so I figured he'd never miss it.

MEEKS: You figured wrong, Mo.

MORRIS: You can say that again. This town's crawling with Katzenbach triggers.

MEEKS: Like the iced stiff in Hughes's bungalow on South Lucerne. You know him?

MORRIS: Fritz Steinkamp. A Katzenbach torpedo. Gretchen Rae killed him.

MEEKS: I thought as much. So where's Mickey Cohen fit into all of this?

MORRIS: Kismet, Meeks. Rotten luck. Cohen's crush on Gretchen Rae put a monkey wrench into the works, but Gretchy figured she could play the Mick for more money once she got the deals set up.

(MORRIS *reaches behind the easy chair and picks up a framed baby picture of Gretchen Rae. He looks at it sadly.*)

MORRIS: Money to play the father-daughter shtick we shoulda done years ago. But that's tap city now. (*He throws the picture down on the ground in disgust.*) Lost time, pal.

MEEKS: Maybe not. So, tell me Mo: where's my favorite teenage killer now?

MORRIS: I think I know where we can find her.

INTERIOR: MEEKS'S CAR. NIGHT.

MEEKS *is driving with* MORRIS.

MEEKS (*voice-over*): Mo figured Gretchen Rae was in the financial district, trying to land an after-hours stock shark. The deal had gotten some urgency now that Katzenbach's muscle was on their tail.

EXTERIOR: 4TH AND MAIN STREETS. NIGHT.

MEEKS *and* MORRIS *are sitting in the car, parked in front of an office building.* MEEKS *looks at his watch.*

MEEKS: It's the eleventh hour, Mo. In sixty minutes I'm gonna be so deep in shit . . .

(Suddenly a woman in a business suit comes out the front door carrying a briefcase.)

MORRIS *(perking up):* There, Meeks. That's her. That's my baby. *(MORRIS gets out of the car, followed by MEEKS. At the same time, MORRIS spots a man reading a newspaper near the door.)* No! Gretchen!

(The man drops the paper, pulls a gun, and shoots MORRIS. MEEKS shoots and kills the man, grabs the stunned GRETCHEN RAE, and throws her into the back seat. In the background, we hear a police siren as GRETCHEN RAE presses her tear-stained face against the window and MEEKS starts the car.)

GRETCHEN: Is Daddy dead?

MEEKS *(breathing hard):* Yeah, Daddy's dead.

(The car takes off leaving MORRIS face down in a pool of blood.)

INTERIOR: CAR. NIGHT.

GRETCHEN RAE *sits in the back seat and nervously lights a cigarette.*

GRETCHEN RAE: Are you here to take me back. To Milwaukee? *(MEEKS shakes his head.)* It wouldn't matter if you did. All our plans are shot to hell now. I was going to get married. To a nice man. A banker. Like Fredric March in *The Best Years of Our Lives.*

MEEKS: Gretchen Rae . . .

GRETCHEN RAE: And I would be Myrna Loy. And Daddy would be . . . Daddy. In a room above the garage. Teaching his grandkiddies how to fish.

(MEEKS checks his watch.)

MEEKS: Look . . . Mickey or Howard?

GRETCHEN RAE: What?

MEEKS: It's your choice. Mickey or Howard.

GRETCHEN RAE *(the tough side returning):* Some choice. The millionaire and the meshuggener. Between the two of 'em they ain't got the nuts to feed a friggin' guinea pig. *(Snuffing out her cigarette:)* They both stink.

(As she furiously pounds at the cigarette stub, a lock of hair falls over one eye, Veronica Lake-style. MEEKS gets an idea.)

MEEKS *(looking at her admiringly):* Gretchen . . . you want to meet a nice man who needs a friend?

(She smiles pathetically under running mascara.)

EXTERIOR: HUGHES'S BUNGALOW. NIGHT.

Meeks's car is at the curb.

INTERIOR: HUGHES'S BUNGALOW. UPSTAIRS. NIGHT.

While GRETCHEN RAE *crosses from the bathroom to the bedroom, changing into a slinky evening gown,* MEEKS *sits on the steps below chewing tobacco and sneaking peeks at her reflection in the full-length mirror in the bedroom.*

MEEKS *(voice-over):* We were just shy a' midnight. So whiles Gretchen Rae got ready, I laid it out for her. *(Out loud:)* Mickey and Howard. If we're gonna play one side off the other and both sides off the middle, it's gotta be one helluva middle man. And there's only one fella in L.A. who can face down both Mickey and Howard mano a mano. Besides me, a' course. Sid Weinberg.

(We see SID WEINBERG *as he was in his office, crying his eyes out.)*

MEEKS *(voice-over):* Sid Weinberg, RKO Line Producer, filthy rich purveyor of monster cheapies and drive-in circuit turkeys. Sid Weinberg was the only real friend Howard Hughes had in this world who didn't love him for his money and Howard had a soft spot for Sid on account of it.

EXTERIOR: HUGHES AIRCRAFT HANGAR. DAY.

HUGHES *as we saw him before—standing outside the hangar.*

HUGHES: I'd rather lose my you-know-whats than lose Sid Weinberg.

INTERIOR: HUGHES'S BUNGALOW. AS BEFORE.

MEEKS: Mickey Cohen is indebted to Sid Weinberg, too. As it happens, Sid did the honors when the Mick's kid had his circumcision.

INTERIOR: HABADASHERY. NIGHT.

COHEN *getting fitted with the world's ugliest blazer.*

COHEN: He's just like family, that schmuck Sid.

INTERIOR: HUGHES'S BUNGALOW. AS BEFORE.

MEEKS: Sid's a widower with two grown-up daughters who despise him. But, before the war, Sid was known to be in love with a blonde bombshell named Glenda Jensen who threw him over in a big way and broke his heart.

(GRETCHEN RAE, *applying lipstick, catches* MEEKS *watching her in the mirror. She smiles at him warmly.*)

GRETCHEN RAE: How do I look?

(*Close on* GLENDA JENSEN *as seen earlier on the movie poster. She looks identical to* GRETCHEN RAE SHOFTEL.

The camera pulls away and we realize that we're:)

INTERIOR: SOUNDSTAGE. NIGHT.

Right now a big Hollywood bash is going on. The stage is done up like a cemetery, complete with gravestones, grass, and ground fog. Waiters in zombie costumes circulate with trays of champagne. Reveal MEEKS *with* GRETCHEN RAE.

MEEKS *(voice-over):* It was a party to ballyhoo Sid's latest: *It Came From the Crypt.* Hollywood's great, near-great, and non-great hobnobbed with bar girls and chorus boys. But Gretchen Rae, dazzlingly got out like Glenda Jensen, was getting the lion's share of the wolf stares.

(MEEKS *and* GRETCHEN RAE *are standing in the center of the party when* HOWARD HUGHES *appears at the front door. At the same moment they see* MICKEY COHEN *and* JOHNNY STOMPANATO *coming in from the opposite direction.*

Both men are converging on MEEKS *and* GRETCHEN RAE.)

GRETCHEN RAE *(panicking):* I can't go through with it. I have to get out of here.

MEEKS *(reassuringly):* Come on now, sister. This is Mickey Mouse stuff compared to killing a man with a frying pan full of beef stroganoff. *(MEEKS calmly points toward Sid's glass-fronted office. SID WEINBERG sits inside.)* Okay, baby, shake your stuff.

(She slinks into the office . . . and drapes herself over Sid Weinberg's desk. He looks up with an expression of utter astonishment.

MICKEY COHEN is stomping on the camera of some hapless shutter-bug who flashed the Mick's pic without permission . . . giving HOWARD HUGHES, in a tux, the first shot at MEEKS.)

MEEKS: Howdy, boss. Y'all owe me a grand.

(MEEKS cocks a thumb in the direction of the office. From their point of view, we see GRETCHEN RAE, on the desk with her evening gown hiked up, making sloppy love to SID WEINBERG.)

MEEKS: You want me to lean on Sid for you, boss?

(HUGHES crosses the emotional spectrum from jealousy to anger to heartbreak to resignation. Finally, he fishes around in his pocket, pulls out a money clip, and hands ten $100 bills to MEEKS.)

HUGHES: Find me another one. Just like her.

(He exits the party. MICKEY COHEN and JOHNNY stride up to MEEKS.)

COHEN: Are you and the test pilot done kibbitzing here?

MEEKS: Howdy, Mick. How y'all doing?

COHEN: How am I doing? I'm pissed off major league, Buzzy boy. Mo Hornbeck got himself bumped off tonight by a Milwaukee trigger outside of an office building downtown.

MEEKS: You don't say.

COHEN: I do say, you dumb Okie.

JOHNNY: And the wife's back . . .

COHEN: And—oy gevalt—my wife's back three days early from the Holy Land and henpecking the shit outta me already. So cut the crap, cowboy, and gimme what you got.

(MEEKS indicates Sid's office. SID and GRETCHEN are really at it by now. COHEN sees them, blanches, and then nods like a man taking it all in stride. He turns back to MEEKS and flips his necktie in his face like the Three Stooges.)

COHEN: Johnny, pay this hump his money. A grand is all you're getting, you redneck piece a' shit. You shoulda found her quicker.

(COHEN storms back out the way he came in. JOHNNY hands over the money and then walks away. MEEKS, smiling, begins counting his money. He turns toward the door—only to find LEOTIS standing there. LEOTIS snatches the money out of Meeks's hands. He quickly counts it.)

MEEKS: You don't have to count it, Leotis. Two thousand and not one penny more. Believe me.

LEOTIS: Thank you, Mister Meeks. Always a pleasure.

(Exit LEOTIS. MEEKS looks toward Sid's office:)

(Entangled in Sid's limbs, GRETCHEN RAE looks up to give MEEKS a final grateful—but sad—look.)

MEEKS *(voice-over):* Well . . . nothing lost, nothing gained. As it turned out, nobody made me for snuffing the Milwaukee shooter and Gretchy walked on the other trigger's killing. I paid off Leotis and then promptly went back into debt with him.

(MEEKS, as before. Resigned, he shrugs his shoulders and heads for the bar. The camera begins to slowly pull away from the party.)

MEEKS *(voice-over):* That's it. End of story, 'cept for a few facts of a historical nature you might find interesting. Mickey Cohen did a couple of fed jolts for income tax evasion . . . got paroled as an old man, and settled back into L.A. as a much-appreciated local character . . .

INTERIOR: SOUNDSTAGE. A FEW YEARS LATER. DAY.

We watch MEEKS walking alone through the huge space.

MEEKS *(voice-over):* As for me, in '55 I got involved in a grand jury investigation that went as bad as it could go, and I ended up taking it on the road permanently. Mr. Anonymous. *(From a distance, we watch as MEEKS opens a door in the back of the soundstage and disappears through it.)* Gretchen Rae Shoftel became Sid Weinberg's personal investment banker, made him a giant bundle in slum property, and even starred in one of Sid's cheapie horror flicks.

INTERIOR: SCREENING ROOM. NIGHT.

All we see is the flickering black-and-white image of GRETCHEN RAE *in out-takes from a scene in one of Sid's horror cheapies. Take after take, the same action over and over: she looks up—straight into the lens, and starts to recoil slowly as the camera stalks her into the shadows.*

MEEKS *(voice-over):* Howard Hughes was rumored to have seen this mind-numbing piece of crap one hundred times.

(Suddenly a bony hand with long, Fu Manchu fingernails appears, silhouetted against the screen.)

HOWARD HUGHES *(voice-over; old and decrepit):* Run it again, please. From the beginning.

PROJECTIONIST *(thru intercom):* Whatever you say, Mr. Hughes.

MEEKS *(voice-over):* Howard ultimately went squirrelshit with drugs and religion and, from what I heard, carried a torch for an unknown blonde straight off into the deep end.

(The hand disappears. Cigarette smoke curls in front of the flickering image of GRETCHEN RAE. *In the background, a torchy rendition of "Since I Don't Have You" begins.)*

MEEKS *(voice-over):* A thought just hit me: that I'm telling this story because I miss those fellas. Telling this story's been my way of being with them again. I guess I loved them both, in my way. (Pausing:) Even though they were both world-class shitheels.

(The music swells as we fade to black—end of "Since I Don't Have You.")

List of Photographs and Credits

I'll Be Waiting

Bruno Kirby
Tom Hanks
Bruno Kirby and Jon Polito
Marg Helgenberger
Director Tom Hanks and Bruno Kirby

Photographed by Gusmano Cesaretti, represented by The Gallery of Contemporary Photography, Santa Monica.

The Quiet Room

Bonnie Bedelia
Steven Soderbergh and Joe Mantegna (upper left)
Genia Michaela (upper right)
Joe Mantegna and Bonnie Bedelia (lower left)
Vinessa Shaw (lower right)

Photographed by: Frank W. Ockenfels 3, represented by The Gallery of Contemporary Photography, Santa Monica.

Dead-End for Delia

Gary Oldman and Director Phil Joanou
Gary Oldman
Gary Oldman on the set

Photographed by: Michael Tighe, represented by Outline, New York and Los Angeles.

Murder, Obliquely

Alan Rickman and Laura Dern

Photographed by: Max Aquilera Hellweg, represented by The Gallery of Contemporary Photography, Santa Monica.

The Frightening Frammis

Director Tom Cruise
Isabella Rossellini
Peter Gallagher
Nancy Travis

Photographed by: Antonin Kratochvil, represented by The Gallery of Contemporary Photography, Santa Monica.

Since I Don't Have You

Tim Matheson
Aimee Graham
Gary Busey

Tim Matheson and Aimee Graham photographed by: James Fee, represented by The Gallery of Contemporary Photography, Santa Monica.

Gary Busey photographed by: Richard Foreman, represented by Onyx, Los Angeles.